D0782578

I'm from Bouctouche, Me

Footprints Series
JANE ERRINGTON, Editor

The life stories of individual women and men who were participants
in interesting events help nuance larger historical narratives, at times
reinforcing those narratives, at other times contradicting them. The
Footprints series introduces extraordinary Canadians, past and present,
who have led fascinating and important lives at home and throughout
the world.

The series includes primarily original manuscripts but may consider the
English-language translation of works that have already appeared in an-
other language. The editor of the series welcomes inquiries from authors.
If you are in the process of completing a manuscript that you think might
fit into the series, please contact her, care of McGill-Queen's University
Press, 3430 McTavish Street, Montreal, QC H3A 1X9.

I'm from Bouctouche, Me

Roots Matter

Donald J. Savoie

McGILL-QUEEN'S UNIVERSITY PRESS

Montreal & Kingston · London · Ithaca

© McGill-Queen's University Press 2009
ISBN 978-0-7735-3575-6

Legal deposit third quarter 2009
Bibliothèque nationale du Québec

Printed in Canada on acid-free paper that is 100% ancient forest free
(100% post-consumer recycled), processed chlorine free

This book has been published with the help of a grant from the Université de Moncton.

McGill-Queen's University Press acknowledges the support of the Canada Council for
the Arts for our publishing program. We also acknowledge the financial support of the
Government of Canada through the Book Publishing Industry Development Program
(BPIDP) for our publishing activities.

Library and Archives Canada Cataloguing in Publication

Savoie, Donald J., 1947–
I'm from Bouctouche, me : Roots matter / Donald J. Savoie.

(Footprints series 11)
Includes index.
ISBN 978-0-7735-3575-6

1. Savoie, Donald J., 1947–. 2. Acadians–New Brunswick–Biography.
3. New Brunswick–Politics and government–1952–1970.
I. Title. II. Series: Footprints series 11

FC2475.1.S38A3 2009   971.5'104092   C2009-900530-1

This book was designed and typeset by studio oneonone in Sabon 10.4/14

This book is dedicated to

Margaux, Julien, and Linda – they know why
My parents, for making it possible
My ancestors, for never giving up
and
Louis J. Robichaud, for giving Acadians all the tools
they needed

Contents

Preface

My mother often said that I was born under a lucky star. Indeed, I was fortunate to see first-hand how a people came of age, how they shed their "backward" image, built new institutions and businesses, and forged a new relationship with the English-speaking majority that surrounded them.

This is the story of the struggle of Acadians to take their rightful place in Canadian society. I am one of them, so it is also my story. It begins in a small hamlet where people looked to the Roman Catholic Church for hope and to farming, fishing, and construction for a living. In a generation, the Acadian world was transformed, turned upside down. It is a story worth telling, not only for the benefit of Acadians but for other minority groups and indeed all Canadians. The story speaks to Canada's tolerance, openness, and willingness to embrace diverse groups, respecting the rights of all. In a world in which these values seem to be in short supply, this story celebrates Canada and the opportunities it affords all its people.

My hope is that the reader will gain insight into the experience of the Acadian community and its struggle for survival as a minority group in the twentieth century. There are sharp differences in how the majority and minorities view society and their roles within it. The majority takes many things for granted that minorities do not – not least, their survival. We Acadians have been in a struggle to survive from one generation to the next, attempting to preserve our language, culture, and sense of community in the face of fragmentation, dislocation, and globalization. This explains our deep attachment to our roots: they are the symbol of our survival and the anchor of our ongoing struggle. As I was writing this preface, my daughter Margaux and son-in-law Matthew were attending a public meeting in Saint John to pressure the provincial government to establish a French-language elementary school in Quispamsis so that our first grandchild could be educated in French. Margaux was profoundly impressed by the turnout, which included two Canadians of Asian descent, who were there to argue that learning French would improve the education of their children, and two anglophone New Brunswickers, who made every effort to speak French in order to impress on government officials the importance of creating opportunities for all Canadians to learn both official languages. We have, indeed, come a long way.

I have many to thank for making this book possible. Joan Harcourt, as always, helped me polish the text. She made numerous editorial suggestions, and the book is greatly improved as a result. Two anonymous reviewers made important suggestions for improving it. I also owe a special thank you to Carlotta Lemieux who, with a keen eye and a competent pencil, copyedited the manuscript. I have always enjoyed the full support of administrators and colleagues at the Université de Moncton. They have given me every opportunity to pursue my research (keeping to a strict minimum meetings in which I am obliged to participate). All of this support has meant and continues to mean a great deal to me.

DONALD J. SAVOIE
Canada Research Chair in
Public Administration and Governance

I'm from Bouctouche, Me

Introduction

I am an Acadian, born in a small hamlet just outside a small community, Bouctouche, in eastern New Brunswick. Being born Acadian meant that one was Roman Catholic, probably a supporter of the Liberal Party and almost certainly of the Montreal Canadiens. Being a Maritimer meant that one was also very likely to be a supporter of the Boston Red Sox. I was all of that and to this day have remained loyal to the Montreal Canadiens and the Boston Red Sox.

Growing up Acadian meant a number of other things. Most of Acadian society in the 1950s was poor, rural, uneducated, isolated, insecure, and dominated by the Roman Catholic clergy. Bouctouche lies in the very middle of Kent County, which was classified in the 1950s and 1960s as the poorest county in Canada. We owned precious few businesses, and for generations, Acadians earned a living as best they could from the land and sea. We went to church every Sunday morning, come what may and whether we wanted to or not. It was a mortal sin not to attend mass, and we quickly learned to stay away from mortal sins. They were a one-way ticket to hell. I remember looking at the frescoes on our church walls depicting hell, and I resolved not to go there.

Priests often reminded parishioners that it was easier for a camel to go through the eye of a needle than for a rich man to go to heaven. Businesses belonged to the English Protestants, and we somehow convinced ourselves that they would eventually pay a heavy price for this. Growing up, I often tried to imagine how English Protestants could possibly squeeze through the eye of a needle to get to where we, on the other hand, were sure to go.

For the most part, we fished, farmed, or worked in the woods as loggers or in the construction industry as labourers and carpenters. Many in Kent County packed their bags and went off to Waltham or to other communities in Massachusetts to work in the construction industry or in factories. A precious few went to university, and those who did usually became priests or medical doctors, dentists or lawyers. If one wants to have a fairly accurate picture of the level of poverty in many Acadian communities in the 1950s, one could look at some Aboriginal communities today.

But things took a drastic turn for the better during the next decade. In 1960 one of our own, Louis J. Robichaud, became the first Acadian to be elected premier in the history of New Brunswick. And in 1968 Pierre Trudeau, a Québécois who actually believed that French Canada meant something more than just Quebec, became prime minister of Canada. Robichaud's "Programme of Equal Opportunity" sent shock waves to every corner of the province. In the process he was accused by some of the English language media, of "robbing Peter to pay Pierre." The highly controversial program was designed to provide a uniform level of services and opportunities throughout the province in education, social services, and health – hence the term "equal opportunities for all." Robichaud also gave us our very own university in 1963, the Université de Moncton, and both he and Trudeau enacted into law official languages acts, one for New Brunswick and the other for Canada.

The national media, preoccupied as always with Ontario and Quebec, hardly noticed but we, too, were having a revolution, one that was more daring, more dislocating, and more disquieting than Quebec's Quiet Revolution. I was very fortunate in having a front-row seat at that time to see a once backward community begin to take its rightful place in society.

This, then, is my story. I have published several books, but this one, obviously, is special. I have long wanted to tell my story – not, I want to assure the reader, because of any desire to report on my own contributions. Indeed, my academic story is not very different from that of some of my peers, nor have I run for elected office or built a business from scratch. Rather, I decided to write my story to show Canada to Canadians through the eyes of an Acadian who was a witness to his community's coming of age as part of the larger Canadian family. And since I was not a bystander, this book also details some of my activities and the relationships with the people I collaborated with over the years.

I write my story in the hope that Canadians will gain from it a deeper appreciation of their country, its values, and the reasons for our linguistic and regional tensions. Few observers have looked at Canada from an Acadian perspective. This is not only because there are few of us but also because it is only relatively recently that we have learned to write, let alone write books.

I greatly enjoyed working on this book. For the first time, I had less need to produce, review, check, and recheck literally thousands of references and endnotes as has been the case with all my previous books. There is also an added bonus – my own family, my sisters, and a number of my friends will find the book much more accessible and of greater interest to them than all of my previous publications combined. In his review of one of my books, *The Politics of Public Spending in Canada*, historian Michael Bliss had some very positive things to say about my work, but he added, "It is not easy reading."[1] If my academic work is not an easy read for Bliss, then one can only imagine what it must be like for those with only a passing interest in public policy and public administration.

There is even a good chance that my family and friends will actually read this book. This point was brought home to me by Ginette Benoit, my assistant for the past twenty-six years. She has, over the years, organized my work, helped me find things, planned my stays abroad, and typed all of my manuscripts – always with good cheer, a high degree of loyalty, and an extraordinary level of competence. She is highly respected by everyone at the Université de Moncton and by those who have been in contact with her, a reputation that is well deserved. She has often had the unenviable task of explaining why I would not attend a meeting or conference or accept a speaking engagement. But that is not all. She has a well-honed capacity to call a spade a spade. Several pages into typing this manuscript, she said, "This book is very different from all your previous books. This one will be very interesting." I hope others will agree with her, up to a point!

I have been told that one can only claim to be an Acadian if at least one line of ancestors was present during the Grand Dérangement – our term to describe the great upheaval. Accordingly, I can claim to be an Acadian twice over because my ancestors on both my father's and my mother's side were forceably removed from their land and possessions in present-day Nova Scotia during the Acadian expulsion of 1755–62.

As I understand it, my ancestors were able to avoid being put on boats and deported to the eastern seaboard of the United States, or to France or other faraway places, by escaping through the woods. They made their way north to coastal communities along what is today the New Brunswick coastline and eventually came to Bouctouche, now a beautiful seaside community on the Northumberland Strait. There, my parents told me, our ancestors settled on virgin land to fish, farm, and cut wood. Some, I was informed, did not bother to register their land, probably not knowing how, or perhaps for fear of being discovered by the English. I later found that the Savoie side of my ancestors had indeed registered their Bouctouche land. In 1794 Jean Savoie had petitioned New Brunswick's lieutenant governor for 1,400 acres of land and 50 acres of marshland near Bouctouche.[2] They cultivated the land and built very modest houses.

Years later, the English came to Bouctouche and claimed the cultivated land that had not been registered, and once again some Acadian families were on the move. As I understand it, the non-Savoie side of my ancestors decided on Saint-Maurice, a hamlet named after my great-grandfather, Maurice Arsenault, the first to settle in Saint-Maurice. Some descendants of Jean Savoie also decided to move to Saint-Maurice. The hamlet is inland and some six kilometres away from "all civilization," meaning Bouctouche. There, they started all over again, cutting trees, cultivating the land, and building modest houses. This time, however, they made sure to register their land with the government. The British settlers, meanwhile, gradually left Bouctouche and moved on in search of new economic opportunities elsewhere. Many Acadians then returned to Bouctouche, and all made a point of registering their land with the local land registry office. All of this, I hasten to add, is based on oral history. The stories may well have been embellished as they flowed from one generation to the next. What we do know for certain is that, today, Acadians make up well over 90 percent of the Bouctouche population.

Being Acadian means one can never divorce oneself from one's ancestors. To this day, in Saint-Maurice or Bouctouche I am not Donald Savoie. Rather, I am Donald à Adelin (my father), à François (my paternal grandfather), à Aimé (my great-grandfather). So if you were to go to Bouctouche and ask, "Do you know Donald Savoie?" you might well be asked, "Do you mean Donald à Adelin?" But even that might not be enough. Reuben Cohen, a well-known Moncton-based financier and a good friend, loves to tell the following story around Moncton. He reports that he met a young receptionist in a medical clinic in Moncton and asked where she was from. She said that he would not know her village because it was much too small but that it was very near Bouctouche. He insisted on knowing which village. She finally relented and said, "Saint-Maurice."

"Oh," Reuben said, "I know Saint-Maurice. You have a famous son who comes from there. He has published about forty books."

"Who?" she asked.

"Donald Savoie – do you know him?"

"Nope!" she said. " I have never heard of him."

I consulted a number of Acadians in search of an explanation of why Acadians have always felt the need to string the names of their ancestors after their first name. Some report that it became necessary because we were a small community with plenty of Savoies, LeBlancs, Thériaults, Cormiers, and a few others, so it was important to nail down one's identity through parents and grandparents. Others, based on the notion that the apple never falls far from the tree, point out that it was simply a matter of "know the parents, know the child." Maurice Basque, a historian here at the Université de Moncton, offers probably the most plausible explanation. "Acadians," he points out, "were for a very long time illiterate. We had no choice but to turn to oral history to establish who we were and where we came from, so that Donald à Adelin, à François, à Aimé revealed to everyone in your community everything they needed to know about you."

Throughout my career I have repeated, time and again, the line "I'm from Bouctouche, me," as friends, colleagues, and even casual acquaintances will attest. "I'm from Bouctouche, me" has at times been my way of asking someone to clarify a point that he or she has just made but which I did not quite understand. Yet it is much more than that. I know that I say it much too often for some people's liking. Indeed, I know full well that it has annoyed more than a few friends and colleagues from away. I recall Jocelyne Bourgon, former clerk of the privy council and secretary to the cabinet during the Chrétien years, responding to "I'm from Bouctouche, me" by saying, "I'm from Papineauville, so what's your point?" Jim Travers, a columnist with the *Toronto Star*, probably after hearing me repeat the line more often than he cared to hear it, said, "Savoie, after you published *Governing from the Centre*, that line really does not work anymore for you." I may also have annoyed some New Brunswickers. Frank McKenna once said to me during a golf game, "I don't know why you keep saying 'I'm from Bouctouche.' I could say that I am from Apohaqui, which is smaller than Bouctouche, but I don't."

In 2004 I served as the Simon Reisman Fellow with the Canadian government in Ottawa where I was asked to assist the Treasury Board Secretariat to come up with responses to the sponsorship scandal that had taken place during the Chrétien years. As a result, I met frequently with Reg Alcock, the Treasury Board president. Alcock is a giant of a man, not only exceptionally tall but at the time weighing over 130 kilograms. He had the ability to generate a new idea every hour – or more often, if he thought it necessary. Some of his ideas had merit, but I felt that many were off the wall, with no practical value. To these I would say, "Minister, I'm from Bouctouche, me, and I can tell you that that would not fly with the folks at Tim Horton's in Bouctouche." After I said this a few times, he would anticipate it with, "Yeah! Yeah! I know that will not fly at Tim Horton's in Bouctouche!"

In the spring of 2005 the federal Liberal caucus met in Halifax. Alcock's next engagement was in Fredericton, a five-hour drive from Halifax. While driving through Moncton, Alcock asked the driver to detour 40 kilometres north, to Bouctouche. Accompanied by an assistant, with camera in hand, Alcock went to the local Tim Horton's. He wanted a photo taken to show me that he, too, had been to Bouctouche and he, too, had talked with the folks there. The young woman at the counter didn't know what to make of this English-speaking giant from away, wearing a leather jacket with a rather large Canada crest on it, while his assistant clicked away on her camera. The waitress decided that caution was in order and went to the back of the store to get the manager.

The manager went up to Alcock, cocked his head back so that he could look up at him, and asked, "Can I help you with anything?"

Alcock looked down and replied, "You do not know me, but I am a big man in Ottawa."

The manager, staring back at this giant, said without hesitation, "Well, you are a big man in Bouctouche too."

Alcock explained that he meant that he was the president of the Treasury Board in Ottawa and thus a minister in the Paul Martin cabinet, and also the reason he was there. They all had a big laugh, and the big man together with his assistant left Bouctouche with photos in hand.

There are several reasons for my tendency to say, "I'm from Bouctouche, me," despite the fact that I left the area at a very young age. It is because of my Acadian roots. It has often been said that Acadians have a greater commitment to their community than most other people do. If the defining historical moment of a people is being forcibly removed from their homes and having their villages burned to the ground, one can easily appreciate the very close attachment to any new-found community. It is no coincidence, for example, that Antonine Maillet, the first author outside France to win the Prix Goncourt, won it for her novel *Pélagie-la-Charrette*, the story of Acadians making their way back to their roots.

The Bouctouche remark also speaks to our past reliance on oral history. Identifying the Acadian village you are from automatically reveals many things about you. Until recently, l'Acadie consisted of nothing more than a string of small villages that dotted the coastline of New Brunswick, Nova Scotia, and Prince Edward Island. I always, for example, ask my Acadian students at the Université de Moncton, when I first meet them at the beginning of term, for their name and the community they are from. Once, one responded with pride, "My name is Marc Comeau and I'm from Comeauville," a small community in Nova Scotia.

"I'm from Bouctouche" has also been my way of speaking up for my ancestors. I have often imagined what it must have been like to be forced to abandon all your belongings, not once but at least twice, and to move to unsettled land to begin anew with nothing but courage, a deep religious belief, and the hope that somehow and for some reason tomorrow will be better than today. This, too, explains our sense of community.

That said, I acknowledge that "I'm from Bouctouche, me" means very little to non-Acadians and also perhaps now to some Acadians, particularly the younger generation who have moved to urban areas such as Moncton and Halifax. Why should it? But it means everything to me. It defines who I am; it speaks to the hardships of my ancestors, to our rich history, and to my roots. Roots matter a great deal to Acadians because for a long, long time we had little else of value. It was the only thing we owned and, in the immediate aftermath of the Grand Dérangement, the only thing we were allowed to own. Moreover, until quite recently, we had no literature, no written history, no business, and virtually no presence in government. But we had a profound sense of place and belonging that we could call home. In brief, we have always had roots.

I love Bouctouche. It is truly a magical place. It is neatly nestled between the Northumberland Strait, a beautiful river, a picturesque small harbour, and sand dunes that have been described as "one of the last remaining great sand dunes on the northeastern coast of North America."[3] It is home to Le Pays de la Sagouine – a replica of an Acadian village inspired by one of Antonine Maillet's novels – and of the Irving Eco-Centre, which serves to protect and increase the public's understanding of the local sand dunes.

The reader need not take my word about Bouctouche's beauty. Its merits are widely recognized today. Bouctouche was selected in February 2008 as "the only Canadian finalist" for the top prize in the destination award category for the Tourism for Tomorrow competition held by the World Travel and Tourism Council.[4] By this measurement, Bouctouche is now a world-class community. Moreover, the town and its adjacent communities are home to a number of distinguished Canadians. Antonine Maillet is from Bouctouche, and more will be said about her in later chapters. K.C. Irving, one of Canada's leading entrepreneurs and industrialists of the twentieth century, also was from Bouctouche. He launched his business career there, kept the old homestead, and returned every summer. He is reported to have said many times, "Bouctouche is the only place in the world where I truly feel at home." He and his three sons have endowed Bouctouche with several first-class facilities and attractions. Louis J. Robichaud, who brought New Brunswick kicking and screaming into the modern era and is the single most important architect of the Acadian renaissance, was born and raised in Saint-Antoine, only a short drive from Bouctouche.

My story begins in Saint-Maurice. I was the youngest of seven children. By today's standards, seven children is a large family.

But in Acadian communities at the time, this was a typical family. Since Saint-Maurice is several kilometres away from the coast, fishing was not an option, and it was soon discovered that the land was not very good for farming. The best one could hope for was to grow a garden to feed one's family. There was only one job for the early settlers – working in the woods – and that is what many did. Those who did not had to relocate elsewhere temporarily to find work.[5]

I went to a one-room school with no running water or electricity, where the teacher taught grades 1 to 6. After grade 6, my family moved to Moncton, which has been my home base ever since. I cannot imagine a better, happier, more fulfilling, and more satisfying life than mine. As I was growing up, the youngest of seven children, my mother often said (at times probably to the annoyance of my sisters and brothers) that I was born under a lucky star. "Everything you try or touch," she said, "for some reason always turns out fine." Looking back, I understand what she meant. I truly believe that I could not have had a more charmed life.

I am in debt to my ancestors, my parents, my brothers and sisters, my wife, who made it all possible with a level of patience that even Job could never match, my children, who tolerated my obsession with my work, my university, my province, my region, my country, and last but certainly not least, Louis J. Robichaud. Together, they made everything possible by giving me all the opportunities that I could ever have asked for. I can think of no better life than having a ringside seat watching a people coming out of their shell, gaining confidence, and taking their rightful place under the sun.

This story, then, is a happy story. I was a witness to a people pushing aside a difficult history to carve themselves a place in society. The reader may well conclude that there is a bit of a Pollyanna in me. I do not write about enemies, nor do I try to settle old scores. While I may have had enemies, I paid no attention to them, so I have very few old scores to settle. I concluded a long time ago that dealing with enemies or disagreeable people requires time and effort. It is never good for the soul. I have always had the ability to disconnect completely from any individual with whom I did not want to be associated. Admittedly, I have had the good fortune of being in a line of work that allows me to do this.

I have always had an aversion to meetings, except for those where you are there to get things done. Similarly, I avoid conferences and academic gatherings except when I have no choice. The truth is that, for me, time spent away from writing or researching is time lost. John L. Manion, former associate clerk of the privy council and a good friend over the years, was aware of this. He once told a deputy minister, "There is something you need to know about Savoie; he will never sacrifice his writing for anything."

At times, I have become a kind of medieval monk beavering away on a book, oblivious to everything around me. There has been a moment in each of them when I have had to concentrate all my energy on defining the "hook," or central theme, the one idea on which everything in the book hangs. That "moment" can last up to six weeks, during which I become very insular and need only five or six hours' sleep a night. In each case, both my wife Linda and my assistant Ginette have recognized early on when I was in the thick of things, searching for the hook. Ginette became familiar with the signs when she helped me with the very first book she worked on. She became adept at screening telephone calls and turning down invitations to attend meetings and conferences, sometimes without even discussing the matter with me.

Looking back, I can see that I have not always been the most enjoyable guest at social gatherings. I get lost in my own thoughts and I am reminded of the song in *Midnight Cowboy*: "Everybody's talking at me, I don't hear a word they're saying." I have done eccentric things when searching for the hook. Once, Yvon Fontaine, our president here at the Université de Moncton and also one of my former students, invited me for coffee early one morning. When I walked into his office, he looked at me and said, "I know it's cold outside, but did you put your sweater on like that on purpose?" I looked down to discover that the V in my V-neck sweater was on my back rather than in front. There are mornings when I have left home before Linda has had a chance to ensure that everything is on right and the colours match.

I write the above so that my friends and sisters will now understand what Linda, Ginette, and I hope my children understood all along. Some may conclude that I have walked through life in a detached, cold-hearted way. If I have hurt or offended family and friends, I am sorry. I write all of the above so that they will know why I have appeared to be abstracted and distant, and if there were any slights, I want to assure them that they were never intended.

Ginette Benoit is right, of course, that this book is vastly different from anything else I have written. It is personal – my story and my take on the "Acadian reconnaissance." There is a great risk for an academic to go down this road. Success in one genre hardly assures success in another. Here, I think back to Stephen Leacock, English Canada's iconic writer of humorous fiction. What some people may not know is that he was also a professor of political economy at McGill University. He once published a book on monetary policy, and in its review the *Economist* wrote that it was by far Leacock's funniest book. Not the review that Leacock was hoping for perhaps, but at least he could appreciate the irony.

I have consistently refused to have a book launch for any of my previous books. I saw no need to say yes. This time, I actually asked for the opportunity, on the understanding that the launch would be held in Bouctouche at Le Pays de la Sagouine. My hope is that the reader will enjoy the book as much as I have enjoyed working on it.

The Hon. Reg Alcock in Bouctouche, New Brunswick (courtesy Hon. Reg Alcock)

Participants to a conference that I organized in Bouctouche in 1999 to honour Louis J. Robichaud. *First row, left to right*: Henry Irwin (minister in the Robichaud cabinet), Donald J. Savoie, Wendell M. Meldrum (minister in the Robichaud cabinet), Michel Cormier (journalist), Louis J. Robichaud, Ginette Benoit, Norbert Thériault (minister in the Robichaud cabinet), and Georges Cyr; *second row, left to right*: Joseph Yvon Thériault, Bernard A. Jean (minister in the Robichaud cabinet), B. Fernand Nadeau (minister in the Robichaud cabinet), Jacqueline Robichaud, Chedly Belkhodja, Roger Ouellette, Maurice Beaudin, Tony Barry (administrative assistant to Premier Robichaud), Robert Pichette, Wendell Fulton (adviser to Premier Robichaud), and Robert A. Young. Absent from the photo: Alcide Godin, Pier Bouchard, and Sylvain Vézina (courtesy of the Vieux Presbytère, Bouctouche)

The Université de Moncton campus with a statue of the Rev. Clément Cormier, its founder (courtesy Université de Moncton)

Le Pays de la Sagouine, Bouctouche, New Brunswick (courtesy Le Pays de la Sagouine)

The author in Oxford. In the background, the University Church of St Mary the Virgin, All Souls College, and Queen's College (with the cupola) (photo by Linda J. Savoie)

1

L'Acadie: How It All Began

A brief history of l'Acadie is in order. While many Acadians know their history, particularly as it relates to the Grand Dérangement, those from away need to have some background, however preliminary, of l'Acadie's beginnings and early years in order to understand my story. It takes only a moment's reflection, however, to appreciate that I can hardly do justice to the rich and colourful history of l'Acadie and Acadians. This chapter is, by definition, incomplete, but if I am able to whet the reader's appetite about Acadians and their history, then it's all to the good. There are now available some excellent and recently produced historical studies of l'Acadie, from its early years to today.[1]

It all began in 1604 when eighty men set sail from western France in search of a base for a continual presence in North America. As is well known, Europeans had been roaming the eastern shores of North America for a century in search of fish and furs. Guided by Samuel de Champlain, the explorers dropped anchor in a secluded harbour which they christened Port-Royal, today's Annapolis Royal in Nova Scotia. From there, they moved north to an island at the mouth of the St Croix River, which today separates New Brunswick from the state of Maine. They made camp for the winter, but as is also well known, it was a particularly harsh winter. Thirty-six men died of scurvy and malnutrition. The following spring, the remaining men moved back to Port-Royal, which in 1605 thus became the first permanent French establishment of Europeans in North America – and not, as some have claimed, Quebec City, which dates back to 1608.[2] There, they were welcomed by hundreds of Mi'kmaq and allowed to establish a "fort and habitation."[3] Historians report that the French and the Mi'kmaq forged a close bond that day, a bond that lasted more than a hundred years, or until the Grand Dérangement. Indeed, it is unlikely that l'Acadie could have survived without the settlers' faithful friends. This friendship was further strengthened by the intermarriage of native daughters with some French settlers.

Relations between the Mi'kmaq and the French settlers soured up to a point when the native community was hard hit by diseases previously unknown to them – syphilis, gonorrhoea, measles, smallpox, and cholera. But they had to weigh the impact of these dreaded diseases and the problem of alcohol addiction against the advantages of trade with the French. Trade brought all manner of new tools and benefits. The Mi'kmaq hunters quickly learned to concentrate their efforts on pelts with high commercial value, such as beaver, moose, and deer. In exchange, they received hatchets, copper kettles, knives, and needles.

Life in the New World was not for the faint of heart. Everything about it was hard, from crossing the Atlantic to dealing with the harsh winter months. Survival depended on the arrival of the annual supply ship from France and continued support from the home country. At one point, the French went back home in search of new financial support after the revenue from the furs sent to France the previous year had not been sufficient to pay for the cost of maintaining an outpost at Port-Royal.[4]

The French returned in 1610 with new settlers, new supplies, and new financial support. This time, they brought a priest along to convert the Natives to Catholicism. The Mi'kmaq again welcomed them with open arms. But new problems surfaced. Internal conflicts, raids by English settlers from the American colonies, and lack of support from France, including from the French state itself, made life no less difficult than it had been in 1605.

Another persistent problem was that the wars in Europe between England and France were invariably felt in l'Acadie. The years between 1604 and 1632 were particularly difficult, and the Acadian colony barely survived. The recurrent raids, the difficulty of attracting new settlers from France, and political uncertainty in Europe made life in the colony both uncertain and challenging. For example, in 1613 Samuel Argall, a Welsh privateer working under the direction of Governor Thomas Dale of Jamestown, entered Port-Royal basin, found that all the villagers were away, either fishing or working in the fields at "the great meadow" up-river, and had his men load the ships "with everything they could carry" and then destroy the village.[5]

James I of England (who was also James VI of Scotland) rewarded one of his courtiers, William Alexander, with a royal mandate to develop the lands "lying between our colonies in New England and Newfoundland, to be known as New Scotland," or Nova Scotia.[6] The Scottish colony eventually failed and England and France signed a peace treaty in 1632, the Treaty of Saint-Germain-en-Laye, which restored l'Acadie to the control of France.[7] My ancestor François Savoie, the first Savoie to come to l'Acadie, arrived in Port-Royal in 1643 from Loudun, a community in western France about halfway between Paris and Bordeaux.[8]

Things were progressing well and an Acadian community, with its own identity forged in the New World, began to emerge. But the new community required a degree of political stability to take root and survive. This was never certain, though France ruled l'Acadie for most of the seventeenth century. There were some exceptions, including the years 1654–67 when it was under English rule. This period posed a special problem for Acadians, as would all future conflicts between England and France. Still, some accommodation was made, and the seven hundred or so Acadians were offered the choice of returning to France or remaining "unmolested" with "liberty of conscience allowed to religion." They decided to stay and agreed to take an oath not to bear arms against the English.[9] This laid the seed for a special arrangement that would guide relations between England and l'Acadie – a qualified oath of allegiance – until the Grand Dérangement. France regained the colony in 1667 with the signing of the Treaty of Breda. This did not, however, stop raids from New England, which French troops had to address.

Political jurisdiction over l'Acadie was settled once and for all – at least, in the eyes of some – in 1713 when the English gained control of it through the Treaty of Utrecht. This represented the last change of imperial authority for the colony.[10] However, the impact on l'Acadie was not at first nearly as negative as one might imagine. Naomi Griffiths, arguably Canada's leading authority on Acadian history, writes that between 1713 and 1755, the Acadian community expanded considerably and took its own distinctive form. She writes about the infusion of Mi'kmaq influence, the role of the Roman Catholic Church in the colony, the forging of strong family ties, and the building of dykes, a task that called for a community-wide effort. The language was French, which was a blend of the language spoken in a number of regions in France and a vocabulary adapted to the new conditions and circumstances in the colony. She, along with other historians, have labelled this period the Golden Age of Acadian Life.[11]

The Acadians settled along the coast in the lowlands (*les terres basses*) on the salt marshes. They needed to reclaim some of the land for agricultural purposes, and Yale historian John Mack Faragher writes that they came up with "one of the most remarkable developments of seventeenth-century North American colonization," a highly sophisticated system of dykes (*les aboiteaux*).[12] The dykes eventually created more productive land than the highlands (*les terres hautes*), and this enabled the Acadians to farm without infringing on Mi'kmaq land. Griffiths argues that "the building of dykes, a task that demanded much cooperation among the inhabitants, also worked to produce closely knit communities."[13]

This period, she says, was the Golden Age of Acadian Life because the majority of Acadian settlements "knew neither warfare, nor epidemics, neither famine nor persecution."[14] The economy, based on the fisheries, agriculture, the fur trade, lumber, and general commerce, flourished. Trade with New England was increasing, and the region, thanks to the dykes, had become self-sufficient in basic foodstuffs as early as the 1680s.

But new political tensions were brewing in faraway Europe, and they were felt in l'Acadie however much its inhabitants tried to ignore them. The English began to demand an oath of allegiance on the heels of the 1713 Treaty of Utrecht, which had given Britain full jurisdiction over what is today Nova Scotia, except for Cape Breton. This demand for an oath of allegiance was not unusual at the time in Europe, but the Acadian response was unusual. Naomi Griffiths explains that it was neither a rejection nor an acceptance, but something in between – a made-in-Acadie solution.

The Acadians had had enough of the impact of European wars on their lives. As their sense of self-identity took form, they increasingly became detached from the mother country and less interested in the old conflicts between England and France. They were not prepared to give an unconditional promise of allegiance to the British authorities, but they were ready to promise to remain neutral in any future English-French conflicts. Thus, Acadians attached an important caveat to the oath, namely, that they would "take up arms neither against his Britannic Majesty, nor against France, nor against any of their subjects or allies."[15] The British finally agreed to this in 1730, and from that moment on Acadians were known in London, Paris, Boston, and Quebec as neutrals.[16]

Although the Acadians wanted no part in future conflicts and were unwilling to take sides, the Treaty of Utrecht was hardly the final word on European wars and English-French tensions. British military officials soon began to question the wisdom of agreeing to Acadian neutrality. As Griffiths explains, "like so many border people when their more powerful neighbours declared war on each other, the Acadians found their neutrality questioned."[17] Both English and French military personnel saw important strategic advantages in Acadian lands, and some believed that if ever they were pushed into taking sides, the Acadians would go with France.

To make matters worse, conflicts between England and France flared up every few years after Britain's agreement with the Acadians. In 1742, for example, war broke out again. But the Acadians remained steadfastly neutral. It seemed, at least to them, that the made-in-Acadie solution to European conflicts was working.

By the late 1740s and early 1750s, England and France were again at war, but this time both sides made deliberate attempts to strengthen their position in North America. During this period, the French pushed aside the concept of neutrality and encouraged Acadians to leave their communities in Port-Royal and elsewhere and relocate in Cape Breton Island (Île Royale), which was under French control. Some did, but the great majority said no. The Mi'kmaq, long viewed as key allies of the Acadians, were invited to relocate in Île Royale, but they were even less enthusiastic.[18] Acadians and Mi'kmaq were intimately interconnected and became, in the words of John Faragher, "kindred peoples, actors in the same history."[19]

The British had yet another force to control in the region – New England settlers. Raids and counter-raids involving New Englanders, Aboriginals, and Acadians had obvious implications for all. Even trade between New England and Acadians became much more difficult in the years leading up to the Grand Dérangement. The New Englanders looked with envy at the rich agricultural land that the Acadians had been able to recapture with their dykes. Military officials in the American colonies were upset when in 1749 British authorities returned the fortress of Louisbourg to French control after New England troops, with some support from the British navy, had captured it only four years earlier.

William Shirley, the governor of Massachusetts, for one, believed that the Acadians constituted a threat to Massachusetts and other American colonies. Rumours swirled in New England and in English communities in Nova Scotia that France and French privateers, together with Mi'kmaq warriors, were poised to attack them. Still, Shirley was uncertain what to do about the Acadians, for he recognized that they enjoyed the right to be neutral, given that their position had the official sanction of the British government.[20]

It is unclear to what extent others accepted the right of Acadians to neutrality. There seems to be no question that Colonel Richard Philipps, as governor of Nova Scotia, did give his word to Acadians in 1730 that they could enjoy a neutral status in further conflicts. He did not, however, commit his decision to paper, nor did he forward a written confirmation to London. Philipps concluded that a conditional oath was better than no oath and felt he had pushed the issue as far as he could. What was key for the Acadians was that they would not take up arms against France, the Mi'kmaq, or *le Roy d'angleterre ni contre son gouvernement* (the King of England or his government).[21] The French foreign minister subsequently poked fun at the Acadians for their naïveté in failing to insist that Philipps provide them with a written commitment.

Neutrality was a relatively new concept in the New World, and it would not have been easy to make it work even in the best of times. Eighteenth-century Europe and the politics of New England, New France, and l'Acadie did not provide the best of times. For one thing, the British had every reason to be concerned about the role of the Roman Catholic Church in l'Acadie. Priests were appointed by the Bishop of Quebec and remunerated by the French crown. They arrived in l'Acadie with a limited sense of Acadian history and little appreciation of the importance that Acadians attached to the principle of neutrality. There were numerous incidents in which priests tried to agitate Acadians against the British forces.

New England Puritans, meanwhile, had a distinct dislike of Catholicism, and they too were pushing the authorities to deal with the Acadian problem. When Louisbourg was first captured in 1745, the victory was celebrated in Boston, and some New Englanders believed that it was the first step towards a "British Protestant empire" from the "River of Canada to the ends of America." The Reverend Thomas Prince of Boston declared that in winning

Louisbourg, God "had triumphed over his and our antichristian enemies."[22] Governor Shirley of Massachusettes believed that one solution to the Acadian problem would be to encourage the migration of French Protestants to the region and to take steps to transform the next generation of Acadians into English speakers.

By 1750 the Acadians were being surrounded by forces that could only spell trouble. The British decided to develop Halifax which, as is well known, is one of the best natural harbours found anywhere. Halifax thus became an important new home for the British navy, and the community was soon able to attract a population of five thousand. As a matter of policy, it was populated by Protestants. New England settlers applauded the British decision to establish Halifax, and some of them decided to move there. The implications of all this were not lost on the Acadians. They would no longer dominate l'Acadie and have to deal only with relatively isolated British garrisons adjacent to some communities. Halifax, in short order, developed an important political, economic, and military presence in the region. A number of Acadians realized that things would never be the same, and fearing a turn for the worse, decided to move to Île Royale, Île Saint-Jean (now Prince Edward Island), and the area north of the Chignecto Isthmus, all under French control.

France, meanwhile, did not sit idly by. Soon after Britain returned Louisbourg to the French, France decided to strengthen its position on Île Royale. It also decided to strengthen its claim to the territory north of the Chignecto Isthmus, the land bridge that today separates New Brunswick from Nova Scotia. In response, the British built a fort in 1750 to stake their position in the area, whereupon the French followed by building Fort Beauséjour, a short distance away, in 1751.

Charles Lawrence, a career soldier, was appointed lieutenant-governor in the region in 1754. History now tells us that Lawrence saw all things from a military perspective. He continually pressed his superiors in London to force Acadians to take an unqualified oath of allegiance and, failing that, to have them deported. To be sure, military concerns dominated the 1750s on both sides of the

Atlantic. Events were building up to the Seven Years War (1756–63) that pitted England and its allies, Prussia and Hanover, against France, Austria, Saxony, and Russia. Hostilities between the two empires had in fact surfaced as early as 1754 in the American colonies, which made the concept of Acadian neutrality more difficult to sustain, at least in the eyes of Lawrence and the American colonies.

The above suggests that the British authorities recognized the legitimacy of the conditional oath given to Governor Philipps in 1730. We also know that the Acadians resisted, time and again, changes to what they had agreed with Philipps, insisting that military conflicts outside their communities were of no interest to them. They wanted above all to remain *neutre* (neutral), to practise their Roman Catholic faith, and not take up arms against anyone, particularly their Mi'kmaq friends.

In 1749 British forces were attacked in Nova Scotia by the Mi'kmaq, Abenaki, and Maliseet. The British later discovered that some Acadians were involved, forced into action by the Mi'kmaq "on pain of death."[23] Lawrence was in no mood to hear Acadians blame the Mi'kmaq for their involvement. There were also flare-ups along the Chignecto Isthmus, where priests had pressed Acadians to take up arms against British forces. Fearing trouble ahead, more Acadians decided to move to lands under French control.

By the mid-1750s, the situation in l'Acadie had become untenable, at least from Lawrence's perspective. The New England colonies were encouraging him to deal with the Acadian problem swiftly, and events in Europe were pointing to another war between the English and French. The scene was set for Lawrence to resolve what he had always considered an unwise decision by Governor Philipps, placing Britain in an impossible position. With the support of William Shirley, he decided to join forces and attack Fort Beauséjour. Within a few days, the French surrendered.

Lawrence saw the Acadians as a liability, pure and simple, and could not imagine that they could ever be of any value to Nova Scotia. He gave them one last chance to take an unconditional oath of allegiance to the British crown, albeit without clearly spelling out the consequences if they did not. The Acadians responded, "We and our fathers having taken an oath of Fidelity which was approved many times, in the name of the British King … and under the privileges of which we remained faithful and subject to His British Majesty … will never commit the inconstancy of taking an oath which changes so much the conditions and privileges in which our Sovereign and our fathers placed us in the past." They added that they had no intention of ever fighting against the British, insisting once more that they wanted to remain *neutre*. Lawrence labelled their letter an act of "treason" and declared that Acadians could no longer be regarded as British subjects. He never tried to persuade them, however, that taking an unqualified oath would guarantee them peaceful possession of their lands.

Shirley, in Massachusetts, agreed with Lawrence, and both saw expulsion as the only viable solution. London, however, continued to argue against such action. It had two concerns: the first was that a sudden depopulation of Nova Scotia would have far-reaching economic consequences; the second was the damage the deportation would have on Britain's image with its allies. Whitehall, already recognized as the centre of the British government by the eighteenth century, never agreed to expulsion and even sent a letter on 13 August 1755 to reiterate the point. The letter was in response to one sent by Lawrence on 28 June, in which he had raised the possibility of deporting Acadians. However, the government's letter did not arrive in Halifax until late October 1755, too late to have an effect.[24] The deportation of the Acadians was by then essentially a *fait accompli*.

Through all the conflicts between England and France, the Acadians had been able to forge a distinct identity. Both the English and the French had admitted as much when in 1713 l'Acadie became Nova Scotia and when the Acadians decided to become British subjects and not move to Île Royale, Île Saint-Jean, or New France.[25] This identity, however, would be tested in a brutal fashion, and its impact is still being felt today.

SCATTERING THE IDENTITY TO THE WINDS

The Grand Dérangement has been well documented elsewhere. It will suffice to make the following points: Lawrence entrusted its implementation to Colonel Robert Monckton (Chignecto area), Colonel Winslow (Minas), and Major Handfield (Annapolis Royal). The City of Moncton and my own university, where I have spent the bulk of my career, are named after Colonel Monckton. The order was to capture the Acadians, deport them to the American colonies and points beyond, including France and England, and burn Acadian houses and villages and round up the livestock.

By the fall of 1755, over 6,000 Acadians had been deported and by 1763 over 10,000, or 75 percent of the entire population. They were dispersed among the American colonies (900 in Massachusetts, 675 in Connecticut, 955 in South Carolina ... and the list goes on). Some made their way to present-day Quebec; others were sent to France or England; and still more made their way to Louisiana (where they are today called Cajuns). The Spanish government offered some Louisiana land to Acadians in 1785, and about 1,600 took up the invitation.

My ancestors were sent to various points. Some of the Savoies were deported to New York, another was made a prisoner in Halifax, and yet another made his way to Quebec. My own direct ancestor, according to oral history, was made a prisoner in Fort Beauséjour, escaped, and fled north to the Miramichi River, with the help of the Mi'kmaq. His son Jean Savoie eventually made his way to Bouctouche, where he died in 1815 at the age of seventy-five. While the deportation order was being implemented, about 8,000 New Englanders came to occupy the rich agricultural land which Acadians had so successfully created from marshlands.

It is hardly possible to gain a full appreciation of the hardships Acadians endured. Families were split up, with men going one way and women and children another. Lawrence saw no need to unite families. He wrote to Monckton, "I would have you not wait for the wives and the children coming in but ship off the men without them."[26] Many Acadians to this day are still told by their parents and grandparents that the Grand-Pré shoreline was filled with the sounds of Acadians praying, crying, yelling and singing as they were pulled apart and forced onto boats to be shipped away like cattle to unknown destinations.

The deportation scene at Grand-Pré has been reproduced in paintings and was captured in Henry W. Longfellow's poem *Evangeline*. Published in 1847, the poem sold in the thousands and has become one of the most popular poems in American literary history. It tells the story of Evangeline, a young Acadian woman, who was torn from her lover Gabriel on their wedding day. She travelled far and wide in search of Gabriel only to find him on his deathbed in Philadelphia.

Even some of those charged with planning and overseeing the deportation felt remorse. Lawrence never showed any, but John Winslow wrote in his diary, "I believe that they did not then, nor to this day, imagine that they are actually to be removed. Things are now very heavy on my heart and mind. Met by the women and children, great lamentation. It hurts me to hear their weeping. The worst piece of service yet ever I was in."[27]

Acadians who escaped deportation, and many did, did so at great risk. Lawrence put a price on their heads, and they learned to live in constant fear, never knowing when the English would find them. A number of Acadians eventually turned themselves in to British authorities for fear of starving or freezing to death.

Those who were deported did not fare any better. Most Acadians were shipped to Britain's American colonies, which were hostile to all things French and Catholic. Many died before reaching their destination. Ships were overcrowded and some sank. Virginia rejected 1,000 Acadians, and they were subsequently shipped to England, but about 260 did not survive the voyage. One ship destined for Boston left Grand-Pré with 166 Acadians on board but arrived with only 125. Another left with 263, and only 205 survived the voyage.[28] Diseases, notably smallpox, typhoid, and diarrhea, struck hard. Those who made it to the American colonies arrived in a hostile environment, penniless and without family in many cases. Because they had refused to take the oath of allegiance, they were not considered British subjects.

They were deported to the American colonies because of the fear that if they were sent to France or French colonies, they would rearm and return to claim their land. It is worth quoting John M. Faragher at some length on how Acadians were coping in their new environment. He writes: "One group of exiles was forced to live for days without shelter in the snow-covered countryside, huddling together for warmth until a local minister secured housing for them. Many were reduced to begging from door to door. After complaints from local officials about Acadian vagabonds, in the spring of 1756 the Maryland Assembly passed a law authorizing local officials to jail indigent Acadians and 'bind out' their children to some person upon the best terms they can make … A majority of their children in both Maryland and New York were forcibly taken away and put out to service."[29] Many of the men were not able to find work because of widespread prejudice against Acadians, and a good number of them resorted to stealing to feed themselves.

Back in Acadia, British officials continued to hunt down Acadian fugitives and burn houses that had been left standing – again because of the fear that Acadians would eventually try to return. Lawrence and Shirley, meanwhile, established a process to divide the former Acadian farms among Protestants interested in relocating on the rich agricultural land in Nova Scotia. We know that the Earl of Halifax wrote to King George II to report that the deportation of the Acadians had made "available vast quantities of the most fertile land in an actual state of cultivation, and in those parts of the Province the most advantageously situated for commerce."[30]

However, the Protestants soon discovered that they were not able to repair and maintain the dykes. They simply did not have the knowledge or skill and had no choice but to call on Acadians for help. The British in 1760 held about two thousand Acadians as a result of mass surrenders and captures. They were now directed to help the newly arrived Protestants repair the dykes, not as equals but as labourers.

The Seven Years War came to an end in 1763, and the following year Acadians were formally given permission to return to l'Acadie. Moreover, James Murray, the military governor of Canada, issued an invitation in 1766 to Acadians to return home to settle "here upon the same footing with His Majesty's new Acadian subjects." Many did accept the invitation and returned to join the two thousand or so Acadians who had somehow remained. Some went to Lower Canada (now Quebec), others to Cape Breton, still others back to Grand-Pré, and many more in what is today eastern New Brunswick. But life would still not be easy. As Faragher writes, it

> signalled the end of a long and painful era. But the consequences of Acadian removal were permanent. The Acadians in the Maritime region would long remain a subject population. The provincial statute prohibiting Catholic landowner-ship and banning Catholic clergy was not officially repealed until 1783, and it was not until that decade that the authorities allowed the organization of Catholic parishes with resident priests. Catholics were not granted the suffrage in Nova Scotia until 1789, and they continued to be proscribed from holding public office by the Test Oath. Acadians remained poor and many remained landless, while the planters and their descendants grew prosperous on the fertile farms protected by old Acadian dikes.[31]

THE WANDERING YEARS

Post-deportation Acadie was vastly different from what l'Acadie had been before 1755. For one, its centre shifted from the Minas Basin in Nova Scotia to eastern New Brunswick, which was where most of those who escaped deportation had fled. Acadians had to begin rebuilding their lives and establishing new communities in a politically hostile environment. Relations with the English Protestants remained uneasy, and there was little help from outside. Relations with France were virtually non-existent, and were only slightly better with Quebec. The means of communication were primitive, not least because Acadians were for the most part illiterate, and because the Grand Dérangement had cut them off from their mother country New France and from various developments in the form of inventions and innovations.

To a very large extent, growth in Acadian communities in the three Maritime provinces has been the result of natural increase, though some French Canadians did migrate from Quebec to parts of northern New Brunswick. There has been some modest migration from Quebec and France to the Moncton area in more recent years, but nothing of any significance. Naomi Griffiths reports that the Acadian population in the three Maritime provinces in 1871, when the first Canadian census was taken, had grown to 87,000, of whom over half, nearly 45,000, were in New Brunswick.[32]

Historian Maurice Basque says that we still know precious little about Acadian life in the nineteenth century. The problem, he explains, is that we have a very limited number of documents available to consult and that a great deal of what we know from that era comes from oral history. We do know that Acadians, particularly in New Brunswick, voted against Confederation on the two occasions when they had the opportunity to do so (1866 and 1867). But we do not know precisely why. Some argue that the Acadians of that era were very conservative and resisted change of any kind. Others point out that Catholics in New Brunswick voted strongly against Confederation, which suggests that Acadians voted along religious rather than language lines. Still others maintain that Acadians, like Nova Scotians, saw little economic advantage for the region flowing from Confederation.

Maurice Basque writes that though Acadians became reluctant Canadians, things changed rapidly after Confederation. He maintains that they soon saw employment opportunities in the new government. Pascal Poirier, for example, was appointed a senator in 1884, which encouraged Acadians to run for elected office.

Acadians also had to come to terms with the fact that they had no territory to call their own. Their existence would always be a struggle for survival, somehow accommodating the wishes of the anglophone majority while carving out a political presence and an identity. The Roman Catholic Church played a crucial role, but even here there were problems. The pressure from Irish Catholic bishops on Acadians to assimilate into the anglophone community was no less strong than it was from anglophone Protestants.

A handful of the Acadian elite, together with the clergy, played a vital role in promoting a distinct Acadian identity at the turn of the twentieth century. Acadians held nine national conventions between 1881 and 1913. Some of these attracted as many as five thousand Acadians, a truly impressive number, not only for the period but also for today. They made a number of decisions: the selection of an Acadian patron saint (the Vierge de l'Assomption), a national day (15 August), an Acadian flag (the tricolour with a star), a national anthem ("Ave Maris Stella"), and a series of measures to promote an Acadian identity and a society that was capable of resisting assimilation.[33] The conventions also gave rise in 1881 to the Société nationale l'Assomption, later renamed the Société nationale de l'Acadie, and in 1887 to the well-known Acadian daily newspaper *L'Évangéline*.

Progress on the economic front was and remains slow. The co-operative movement, over the years, played a key role in many Acadian communities and still does today. The Assomption Society, founded in Massachusetts in 1903 but relocated to Moncton in 1913, now has all the trappings of a profitable medium-sized life insurance and investment firm. It is a mutual insurance company, which means that it is owned by policyholders, largely Acadians. It has grown in recent years and now manages over $1 billion in assets. There have been other economic development success stories, especially since the 1970s, and more will be said about this later.

LOOKING BACK

I have often asked myself what I would have done had I been Charles Lawrence. My answer has evolved in recent years. One can answer the question only by looking at it through the lenses of the 1750s. As Scotland knows full well, expulsion was not invented solely to deal with Acadians. Had I been in Lawrence's shoes, it is unlikely that I would have left well alone. From the British perspective, the situation was untenable. The Seven Years War, described by historians as the first global war, engulfed not just Europe but North America as well. As noted above, the war started earlier in North America – in 1754 rather than 1756 – and the British suffered significant losses in early skirmishes in Ohio under General Braddock.

Lawrence himself had to deal with flare-ups with the Mi'kmaq and some Acadians. He was a military man and war was at hand. Senior military officials are not known for leaving loose ends when planning their campaigns. I have come to recognize that Lawrence could not have left the Acadian situation unresolved as war began to raise its ugly head in the American colonies and Europe. L'Acadie was bound to be part of the battleground sooner or later.

One can fault Lawrence for not making an effort to impress upon the Acadians the advantage of taking an unconditional oath of loyalty to the British crown. He could have made it clear that the Acadians would have been able to keep their houses, their assets, their commercial interests, and their community intact if they accepted the oath. He did not do so. In fact, British forces, historians report, employed ruses to lure Acadian leaders to hand over their guns and to gather them together for deportation. Lawrence could also have established which communities were most likely to respect their commitment to neutrality (for example, those in the Minas Basin) and those that might not (for example, those around the Chignecto Isthmus). One can also fault Lawrence, as I do, for instructing Monckton to proceed with the deportation without regard to family relationships.

One could also, however, fault the Acadian leaders of the day. There were clear signs that war was about to break out and that the American colonies would become willing participants. They knew full well that priests from New France were stirring up the local inhabitants and that the British decision to establish Halifax was a sure sign that things would never be the same.

There is enough blame to go around, and painting Lawrence as the villain of the Grand Dérangement does not tell the whole story. But where the responsibility lies is, in my view, no longer the most relevant point. The Grand Dérangement cut off Acadian society and its development at the knees. Several generations were lost, economic assets and skills disappeared, and a promising process of peaceful accommodation between former Europeans and Aboriginal communities was abandoned. But that is not all. A largely peaceful people who wished to move away from both forces outside their own communities and their mother country in order to establish their own roots, their own identity, and their own interests would not be allowed to do so.

Acadians had to start all over again to establish new roots. They continued to rely on one language, one religion, and one symbol, the Grand Dérangement, to unite them through the ages. The deportation has dominated our history, our identity. I recall growing up in Saint-Maurice when the bicentennial of the deportation was celebrated. The hamlet, by any standards, was small and had precious few resources. Yet it was able in 1955 to mount a large white cross, well anchored in cement, to "celebrate" the deportation. I was present when the cross was raised and when many other celebrations, with people wearing various historical uniforms, were held. We were celebrating the expulsion of my ancestors, and to this day I am still struggling to understand why we would celebrate such a sad event. People usually celebrate victories and success, not a calamity.

The only possible explanation is that when the hamlet assembled on 15 August 1955, having pooled some of its limited resources for the event, it was celebrating our survival. We had been uprooted, cut off from all developments in the outside world for generations, and we had barely survived for over one hundred years. But now we were back, still clinging to our religion and our language. The land was less inviting than the one our ancestors had discovered in 1604 and started to cultivate some forty years later. Still, our parents and grandparents had persevered, driven by a deep sense of community and a desire to forge their own distinct identity.

2

Saint-Maurice: Where It All Began for Me

It is difficult to imagine a more inhospitable setting than Saint-Maurice. Yet it is also difficult for me to imagine a happier childhood than the one I had there. First, the community. Saint-Maurice today is a dying community, simply because it has no economic reason to live. It is several kilometres from the Northumberland Strait and from a main highway, thus away from any commercial fishing or traffic of any kind. It is impossible to grow anything of commercial value in Saint-Maurice, and the village is hidden away in the middle of a forest – and not a good forest at that. Saint-Maurice is not easy to describe because there is so little to describe. Perhaps the best description is to compare Saint-Maurice to the land that God gave to Cain.

Saint-Maurice is set at the end of a long and at times winding road that cuts through nothing except a forest that seems able to grow only small trees. At the end of the nine-kilometre-long road, there is nothing. There are some thirty-five houses today, somewhat fewer than there were in the 1950s. The houses, then and now, are modest by any Canadian standard. A good number of them abut the road. There are no shutters to decorate the windows and no lawns, so the roadside easily blends in right up to the front doors. There are no landmarks of any kind. In short, there is nothing special, nothing original, and nothing of any significance whatsoever in Saint-Maurice. It once had a decent brook that meandered through the hamlet. But even that is now lost. Some thirty years ago, the brook turned into a tiny stream. Today, one can still see signs of where the stream was because it comes alive for a while every spring when the snow melts.

As I remember it, Saint-Maurice was home to warm, generous, and unpretentious people, always willing to give a helping hand. They went about their lives with a minimum of fuss and expectation. They were not materialistic: content with meeting basic needs, perhaps because they could hope for nothing more. They were a threat to no one, nor did they want to be. I do not recall ever locking our front door. In fact, I don't believe that we even had a key to it. People came in and out of our house as if they were family members. No one knocked on the door, and we did not have a doorbell. If they had a reason to see any of us, they simply walked in. If they happened to come at mealtime, they sat down to eat with the rest of us. That is the way things were in Saint-Maurice in the 1950s. It had a deep sense of community, and we believed in collectivism, not because of its ideological merits but because we had no choice.

I lived in Saint-Maurice until the age of twelve, and I have very fond memories of those years. Life was unhurried and rather undemanding – at least for me, as the youngest child. I attended a typical one-room school: no running water, no electricity, and a wooden stove smack in the middle of the room. We took turns fetching wood in the shed at the back of the school to feed the stove. The teacher flipped her attention from one grade to another with relative ease, giving us several breaks every day. We could always tune in to what she was saying to the higher grades to see if we were smart enough to figure out what she was talking about.

The quality of education was acceptable for its time. At the end of grade 6, students from all the surrounding villages were brought together for regional exams before they entered what is now called junior high school. I came first in the parish, and the priest announced it during one of his Sunday-morning sermons. My mother was very proud and so was I, but for different reasons. The priest had announced that I would be receiving a prize. I waited impatiently for what seemed like weeks to receive it. I had time to let my mind explore what the prize could be – hockey equipment or perhaps a real baseball bat and ball. Imagine my disappointment when the prize finally arrived: a very slim book entitled *Nous qui faisons route ensemble*, by Henry Brifaut. I still have it but have yet to read it. I don't think I ever will.

Our house was in the very centre of the village, a large two-storey white house. It had a glassed-in front porch, a large living room, a dining room, a large country kitchen, a bedroom for our parents on the main floor, a sewing room, and another room that housed the local post office, which my mother ran. When television arrived at our house, my parents combined the dining and living rooms to make one large TV room. The children's bedrooms were upstairs, while the basement had storage rooms and a wood furnace. Since we did not have forced air, the heat generated by the furnace had to make its way up to our rooms on its own, without any encouragement. Some winter nights were very cold.

Immediately across the road (the *chemin du roi*) was the one-room schoolhouse that I attended, and next to the school stood a small white chapel that became every May the village's gathering point. Every evening during the month of May (*c'est le mois de Marie, c'est le mois le plus beau*), nearly everyone in the community came to the chapel to pray, sing, and celebrate the Virgin Mary. We also celebrated spring, and it was the time of year when we could take out our bats (homemade) and balls (the cheap rubber variety bought at the five-and-dime store in Bouctouche) and have fun. Attending church service, it seemed to me, was the price to pay to have fun.

At six o'clock every evening we were all rounded up – reminiscent of a military roll call – to come in to say the rosary. The archbishop of Moncton had a daily fifteen-minute program on French-language radio when he said the rosary and shared a few words of wisdom (*le quart d'heure marial*). None of us children had watches, but we always knew when it was time to come in because our neighbour opened her front door precisely at 5:55 every night and yelled at her children, in a voice so loud that half the village could hear it (and with words frequently laced with profanities), as she called them to come in and say the rosary. Those fifteen minutes were long, painfully long. We had to drop whatever we were doing and rush home. To make matters worse, Archbishop Norbert Robichaud had one of the most high-pitched, boring, and annoying voices in all of l'Acadie. I went through the motions of saying the rosary, but my mind was elsewhere, often on the ball or hockey game that we had been playing when we were so abruptly called to order.

Since my mother ran the local post office from our house, this meant that everyone in the community dropped by at least once a week. We were the first in the village to have a television set, which posed special challenges. The channels were all in English and, initially at least, we had a difficult time trying to make out what all these new faces were trying to tell us. Television in Saint-Maurice, as in thousands of small rural villages throughout North America, opened up the world to reveal fascinating images from far beyond our own community. We could see high-rises in New York, news from all over Canada, and, more importantly, our beloved Montreal Canadiens on Saturday nights.

Wednesday night at 8:00 PM was special. The Bunkhouse Boys had a half-hour program of country and western songs on the local Moncton channel. They sang in English, though many of the singers were in fact Acadians. They were the Myers Brothers. I was told that they were all originally from Kent County, or at least their parents were, and that their name was actually Maillet. They sang under the Myers name to make themselves more acceptable to the English-speaking owners of the local television station and Moncton's English-speaking community. I do not know to this day whether or not all of this is true, but at the time it sounded true enough for me and it made sense.

Wednesday evening was a very busy time in our house. People began to arrive for the Bunkhouse Boys any time after 7:00 PM.

On every Wednesday evening at least, our television set belonged to the community. I recall that Liberace was on for thirty minutes immediately before the Bunkhouse Boys. We never could understand why the English could possibly be interested in his show. He draped himself in extravagant costumes and sang songs that were quite unfamiliar to the folks of Saint-Maurice. We all waited impatiently for this bizarre spectacle of a man and his show to run its course, knowing of course that the Bunkhouse Boys were next. Chairs were lined up around the television set, and my sisters, my brother, and I, together with our parents, stood up at the back of the room – it was often standing room only at the Savoies when the Bunkhouse Boys were on. No other show, with the exception of *Les Belles histoires des pays d'en haut*, was able to grab the interest of the community, so we were usually left to enjoy television on our own for the rest of the week.

There was one exception. The evening of 10 December 1958 will remain carved forever in my mind. Yvon Durelle, one of our own, fought Archie Moore for the light heavyweight title of the world in the old Montreal Forum. I was eleven years old and was allowed to stay up and watch what has been described by sports columnist Greg Smith, among others, as the "standard by which great fights are measured." The sports journalists of the day, and even those of today, argue that that fight defined both skill and will in the boxing ring. Moore had plenty of boxing skills, while Durelle had plenty of will. The night before, I prayed to every saint in heaven who would bother to listen, to intervene so that Durelle would win. One year earlier, I had gone to the old Moncton stadium with my father (a rare and special treat, indeed) to watch Durelle knock out Gordon Wallace, a fighter from Ontario, in the second round to win the British Empire light heavyweight crown – no small achievement for the "fighting fisherman" from Baie-Sainte-Anne, another Acadian village on the Northumberland Strait.

I recall Yvon Durelle coming to Saint-Maurice to visit Jos à Calixte à Pisse Vite and the local bootlegger. I can hardly overstate the commotion that a Durelle visit to our village entailed. His very presence reverberated throughout the village – as if a demigod had just landed for a brief visit. I remember to this day Durelle driving by our home in his large black Buick at a speed much faster than anyone else ever went. I later told anyone who cared to listen that I had seen Yvon Durelle drive by our house. I was not, of course, revealing anything that everyone in the village did not already know. It was the age before the Internet, the fax machine, and even the telephone in the case of Saint-Maurice, yet somehow, within minutes of his appearance, everyone knew that Durelle was in the village. We had precious few things to boast about in our village, but catching a glimpse of Durelle speeding up or down Saint-Maurice ranked at the very top.

On the evening of 10 December 1958, Durelle jumped into the ring with Archie Moore with a big heart, strong arms, but little pre-fight training. Mike Dunn, another sports columnist, wrote that "Durelle did most of his training on the job, hauling lobster traps from the frigid waters near Baie-Sainte-Anne." The question was whether he was in good enough shape to last fifteen rounds in the ring against the crafty and well-trained Archie Moore. The thinking was that Durelle needed to get to Moore early, and he did. Early in the first round, Durelle knocked Moore to the canvas three times, and it appeared to everyone that the fight was over. We certainly did in our house. But a controversial "long count" followed one of the times he was on the floor, and Moore came back to win the fight in eleven rounds.

Moore said after the fight, "Durelle hit me harder than I'd ever been hit in my life."[1] That was one small consolation for us. Little was said in our house, and people quietly went home, heads down. We were left with the question, Why would the long count happen to Durelle? More to the point, Why to us? I wondered why all those saints to whom I had prayed the night before had been asleep at the switch when the referee stuttered and stumbled in such a simple exercise as counting to ten. I went upstairs convinced that there was no reason to say my prayers that night, given that all those saints had let me down, so I cried and went to sleep without saying a word to my brother, who shared the bedroom. He, too, never said a word. He had come home that night from the Collège Saint-Louis – a residential college run by priests not very far from Saint-Maurice – especially to watch the fight.

The next day, the talk of the village was that Durelle had been cheated out of the crown by a long count and that if only he had access to the right trainers and the right training facilities, he would be world heavyweight champion, let alone light heavyweight champion. It never occurred to us that things were probably no better, and more likely worse, for Archie Moore, a black American born in Mississippi in 1913, who had spent a great deal of time in a reform school until the age of twenty-one. In time, Moore and Durelle became close friends, and Moore later came to visit him in Baie-Sainte-Anne and Moncton. They probably concluded that they had a great deal in common.

My father often went away to Labrador, to Camp Gagetown near Fredericton, or to Moncton to work in the construction sector. Both parents attached a great deal of importance to education – the one ticket to get out of Saint-Maurice and into a good job. My three older sisters, Rose-Marie, Simone, and Claudette, became teachers; my fourth sister, Fernande, a nurse; and my brother Claude, a psychologist, who went on to become a highly successful entrepreneur.

I have an older adopted brother – Alfred Dowling. He left home when I was very young, so I never got to know him well. When I asked my mother why they had adopted Alfred, she explained that I had had an older brother, François, who died at childbirth, and adopting Alfred was one way of dealing with their loss. I asked, "Why Alfred?" She told me that he was from far away and had no one to take care of him.

I recently learned quite a different story. Although it is true that I had a brother who died, my sisters tell me that one of my aunts on my father's side got pregnant and had to leave the village temporarily. Unwed mothers in rural New Brunswick in the 1930s (as indeed across the country) were not to be seen. They had little choice but to hide in shame, and it seems that my aunt left Saint-Maurice to wait out her pregnancy in a home for unwed mothers in Saint John. The Depression years were harsh and devastating for Acadian communities, as they were throughout Canada. My aunt had little money and no intention of staying in Saint John any longer than she had to. So my uncle Calixte Savoie, who later became a senator and was already a well-known leader in the Acadian community, worked out a special deal with the home for unwed mothers. The Savoies would adopt someone from the home in exchange for the home taking care of my aunt and her child after she left Saint John. It fell to my parents – more specifically, to my mother – to raise Alfred Dowling.

I was very close to my mother but far less so to my father. In time, however, I came to appreciate my father and the time and effort he had to commit to build his business. My sisters and brothers have always insisted that I was my mother's "pet." Being the baby of the family held great advantages, which may explain why I was able to get away with things that my siblings were not. Growing up, I also had a very close relationship with my brother Claude and my sister Fernande, who were only slightly older than me. My three older sisters, Rose-Marie, Simone, and Claudette, went away to a convent in Bouctouche for schooling and then off to the normal school, or teacher's college, in Fredericton when I was very young. I love them all and now realize that compared to me, they got the bad end of the deal because they were older. They were expected to help with chores when growing up and help the family after graduation, and they did. Rose-Marie's automobile became available to everyone in the family who had a driver's licence. I enjoyed all the benefits of being the baby of the family, and very little was ever expected of me in return.

Claude, Fernande, and I played hockey in winter and whatever sport we could dream up in summer, with very little in the way of equipment. We built a hockey rink between our house and barn, and friends from up and down the village came to play. We had makeshift boards – two-by-fours strung in a roughly rectangular shape. In reality, the boards were shaped by snowbanks. It worked well, except that we lost a lot of hockey pucks over the course of a winter. As the snow melted in spring, pucks began to surface one by one, and by the end we were able to retrieve the pucks that had accumulated over the winter. The problem was that by late January we were always out of pucks, and we had to improvise for the rest of the season unless there was a brief winter thaw. We discovered that cow dung, once frozen hard, would do just fine.

There was also a serious shortage of hockey equipment in Saint-Maurice. Some of us had hockey sweaters; many more did not. Hockey sweaters were of one kind only – the Montreal Canadiens. I would venture to guess that to this day, a Toronto Maple Leaf sweater has never made its way to Saint-Maurice. Some of us had hockey pads; many did not. Feminism was still years away, which probably explains why Fernande had no pads. Hockey was a boys' game. Still, she was eager to play, and we were always short of players. We saddled her up with an old Eaton's catalogue on one leg and a Simpsons-Sears catalogue on the other. She was our goalie and a good one at that, given the state of her equipment.

I admired my mother, and there was much to admire. She raised seven children, taught school, ran the local post office, looked after our small farm, and gave back to her community in many ways; and when we left Saint-Maurice for Moncton, she continued to teach but also helped my father build a successful business. While in Saint-Maurice, she taught school in a neighbouring village – Saint-Gabriel – some six kilometres away. I can still recall her walking to Saint-Gabriel to teach at her own one-room school. In the winter, she left on snowshoes, braving the elements and any wild animals she might encounter along the way. This may be difficult to swallow for some readers in the age of all-wheel-drive vehicles, suvs, snowmobiles, and video conferences. But transportation and the means of communication in Saint-Maurice in the 1950s were still primitive.

There was only one dirt road in and out of Saint-Maurice, which meant that there were days in the spring when cars had to be put away because of the mud, which at times and in some spots could be almost thirty centimetres deep. Winter months were not much better. We were the last on the list of roads to be cleared, and in any event the snow-removal machinery in Kent County was not very reliable. No doubt, in our minds at least, the English communities had superior equipment.

The road to Saint-Maurice snaked through four kilometres of uncleared woodland before it got to any house, so the snow-plough had a tough go even before it could reach civilization again. The first house, set about one thousand metres back from the road, was home to one of the bootleggers in Saint-Maurice. The other bootlegger was on the other side of the brook that ran behind the house. The competition between the two was intense. Sunday afternoons were always the busiest time of the week for them, the equivalent of today's Friday night or Saturday afternoon shopping at Wal-Mart. Automobiles would be parked all round the two houses, a sign that would have been obvious to any RCMP officer had one taken the time to make the short drive from the Bouctouche detachment. They rarely if ever came to Saint-Maurice. In fact, I don't recall a single occasion when the RCMP showed up in Saint-Maurice. It may be because the two Bouctouche-based officers did not speak our language – which no doubt suited the two thriving bootleggers very well. Apart from a very small confectionery store, which was located in the living room of our neighbour's house and sold only cigarettes, candies, potato chips, soft drinks, and canned goods, the bootleggers were the only businesses in the village.

I recall well when the telephone was introduced in Saint-Maurice. We had one party line to which everyone in the village who had a telephone was connected. News always travelled fast in the village, but it travelled much faster from the day the telephone arrived.

There was a grumpy old man in the village named Siméon. As I recall, everyone found him a most difficult and contrarian man, and I always avoided him if I could. He lived only three houses from our home and I often had to walk behind his house to go fishing. I waited until he was indoors before I made my move, but he was unpredictable. If he was outside, it was never a good experience. Still, I went because some beavers had built a dam in the brook behind his house, and it provided the best fishing spot in the village. I caught more trout there than in all the other fishing places on the brook combined. It may well be that Siméon wanted the fishing spot for himself or that, as one of my sisters now claims, he was all bark and no bite. I never waited around to find out.

My brother Claude and I realized that with the telephone we could level the playing field with Siméon. Now, finally, we had the tool with which to get even. We could actually talk to him without going anywhere near his house. We turned the manual crank two turns and a half to ring his house. He answered. Without of course identifying ourselves (in hindsight, it must have been easy for him to guess who was calling), we said, "Siméon, we want to kill you." His response, roughly translated, was "You have the wrong number. Now piss off." We looked at one another and realized that the telephone had its drawbacks – one could answer back. We decided that we had to try some other way to get back at Siméon. But we were never able to get even with him.

Siméon was not without skills useful to the village. Although he had no training, he was a good (if unofficial) veterinarian and the person to go to when things went bad with farm animals. Complications with our cow surfaced once when she was about to calve, and my mother asked my sisters to go and ask Siméon to come and give her a hand. My sisters resisted. Siméon was not easy to talk to at the best of times, and they could not imagine how they would explain the problem to him. So my mother wrote him a note. Off my sisters went, note in hand, to fetch him. Siméon told them that the note was completely useless because he could not read. One of my sisters bravely read it to him. He came, and both the cow and the calf survived.

My Saint-Maurice years were simple, straightforward, and easy compared with what young Acadians now experience in Moncton. Peer pressure and what we wore were of no consequence whatsoever to anyone. There was no competition. There were exactly two students in my grade, and the other one had little if any interest in studying. So I always came first in my class with no effort.

Life was never demanding for me, though it was a different story for my siblings. They did all the heavy lifting, from helping with the cooking, cleaning, hauling in wood for the stove and furnace (here, I helped) to working in the fields and in the garden. I did learn how to milk our cow and became quite proficient at it. I shared this chore with my brother Claude. We always had trouble with the cow's tail, which kept slapping at us while we were milking, though the cow was only trying to flick the flies off her back. We decided to tie the cow's tail to a big hook hanging from the wall while we milked her. It worked just fine until the day we forgot to untie the tail. As was her habit after milking, she darted off with great energy to the open field. Off went the cow, but half her tail stayed behind, firmly attached to the hook on the wall. We had a problem. How were we going to explain this turn of events to our father? Somehow, we were able to rationalize the incident, and the only damage was that our cow had to walk in our field for several weeks with a large white cloth bandage in place of half her tail.

This was about the most excitement that we could generate in Saint-Maurice. My brother had a pellet gun which he let me have whenever he was not around. I went hunting, mainly shooting at small birds sitting on power lines. I do not recall ever nailing one, but I do recall putting a few holes in windows around our house. In winter, I installed several rabbit snares in the woods not far from our house. I was more successful in catching rabbits with snares than hitting any creature with a pellet gun. My success was such that I ate more than my share of rabbit stew – not my favourite.

On Saturday afternoons, we often went to the cinema in Bouctouche. By the time movies came to the Roxy Theatre there, they were hopelessly dated and had been seen in virtually every cinema in North America. The owners were from Rexton, an English-speaking community in Kent County. French movies did not come to Bouctouche, so we did not always understand what was said. Still, it was an event – meeting new people from Bouctouche and having soft drinks, chips, perhaps a chocolate bar. An old movie perhaps, but all in all, life could not be better.

My parents occasionally went shopping in Moncton, and they took one child with them in rotation so that all of us had a chance to go. I always enjoyed the trip, seeing large stores full of things, useful or otherwise. The Eaton's store still sticks out in my mind. The firm had selected Moncton to locate much of its regional operations and its catalogue services for the three Maritime provinces. It had several floors of goods, and that alone would have profoundly impressed any young Acadian from Saint-Maurice. I followed my parents when they shopped, and I can't remember being served in French even once.

There is one thing that I saw on my trips to Moncton that had a lasting impression. We had to drive by the first two holes of the Lakeside Golf Club. I was fascinated, my face pressed against the car window, trying to figure out what all those grown-ups were doing in the field where the hay was always cut down so short. My mother explained that they were chasing a little white ball and the goal was to put it in a tiny hole far, far away. The grown-ups had special instruments to hurl the little ball towards the tiny hole. Why on earth, I asked my mother, would they want to do that? Could they not think of something better to do? I remember her telling me that it was a game that the English often played in summer. This did not in any way enhance the image I already had of English people. I recall my father adding that it was people with money who played golf, which meant in my mind that golf was not for Acadians.

People with money were not Acadians. Bouctouche was our commercial centre which we visited far more often than Moncton – at least a few times a week. Bouctouche had some businesses, providing for the more essential community needs. We had a car dealership, Dodge-Plymouth, a five-and-dime store, and of course K.C. Irving. Irving had a general store that bore his father's name – J.D. Irving – and a gas station. K.C. Irving became the role model for any aspiring entrepreneur. Acadians in Kent County and the Irvings have had a good relationship that is still evident today. K.C. was never known as a bigot or to be anti-French, which fifty years ago was the only important sign that mattered to Acadians. It meant that we could trust him. He was known for hiring Acadians and giving them the same opportunities as any English New Brunswickers. At the time, we could ask for nothing more. There was a period when K.C. and Kent County Acadians went through a rough period – when he publicly declared his strong opposition to Louis J. Robichaud's equal opportunities program. But things came back to normal after the program was fully implemented and Robichaud left active politics. Bouctouche is proud of its native son and today honours K.C. Irving in many ways, including a statue-monument, a park, an arboretum, and an ecocentre.

I remember seeing K.C. at his gas service station. He used to drop by, especially in the summer months. One young Acadian from Saint-Antoine, a community near Bouctouche, got a job at the service station, selling gas. He had set his heart on becoming an entrepreneur, something not often seen among young Acadians at the time. One day, K.C. came to buy gas, and the young man saw an opportunity to impress him and ask for advice on how to become a businessman. He decided to give him the complete service and then some. He poured the gas, he washed not just the windshield but all the car windows, he cleaned the headlights and even wiped the front and back bumpers with a cloth. He was careful to do all of this with great care. All the while, K.C. stood by, arms crossed, watching this young man giving it his all. It is well known in New Brunswick that K.C. always dealt with everyone he met with great civility, no matter their standing in the community. He waited patiently until the work was done. The aspiring entrepreneur then went to K.C. to collect the money and said, "My goal is to be a businessman. Any advice?" K.C. calmly responded, "You will need to work a lot faster if you ever want to make money." I am happy to report that the aspiring entrepreneur did learn to work faster, and today he is a successful businessman producing and selling construction material.

My father decided in 1957 to break from Saint-Maurice tradition somewhat and start his own business. I remember going with him and my mother to Richibouctou to see a young lawyer to incorporate his business – La Construction Acadienne/Acadian Construction. My father went into the lawyer's home while my mother and I stayed in the car for what felt like hours. I remember as clearly as if it were yesterday, my father turning to my mother on the way home and saying, "This young lawyer will be premier of New Brunswick some day." His name was Louis J. Robichaud. I was hooked on politics from that moment on. Imagine what it would be like, I thought, if an Acadian ever became premier of New Brunswick.

Looking back, what impressed me most that day was not that my father was founding a private firm – one that would grow and prosper and continue to expand, even as I write this book, to become one of the most dominant construction and commercial real estate firms in southeastern New Brunswick. Rather, it was the possibility that a young Acadian from Kent County might become premier of the province some day. In time, of course, I came to appreciate the courage and foresight my father showed in starting his own business. It also took courage to give his company a French name, La Construction Acadienne, which was very rarely done in southeastern New Brunswick in the 1950s if one hoped to solicit customers from the anglophone communities. He did, and he made it work.

Although the Roman Catholic Church was hardly the only factor, the dominant role it played in Acadian society until the late 1960s did inhibit Acadians from launching new businesses. In Kent County, the parish priest was king and master of the parish, commanding tremendous respect and power. The church ran many things, from education to health care and even the economy to some extent. It permeated most activities, commercial or otherwise, and had a tremendous hold on all of us. I remember hearing about someone from Haut-Saint-Maurice who had moved away from the village and married an English-speaking Protestant. It rocked the village, and I recall thinking that the poor soul was throwing everything away and would burn in hell for eternity for taking the most stupid decision one could possibly make – marrying an English Protestant.

Like many Acadian boys at the time, I became a choirboy. Choirboys had to stay on the bench for a long time before being called to serve mass. They had to learn the ropes, memorize several prayers in Latin by heart, and learn how to serve mass. One learned by watching for a year or two before being brought into action. The senior choirboys were expected to teach the new recruits. Unfortunately, I had no such preparation. My family always went to early mass, and within only a few weeks of joining the choir, I was told that I had to serve mass: the two designated choirboys were sick. I told the priest that I was far from ready. He replied that we had no choice and added that he would be there to help.

Off we went, coming into the church, as always, from the back of the altar. I stopped at the right spot and bowed at the right time – so far, so good. The first prayer I had to reel off in Latin was the *Confiteor*. In a lowered, almost hushed voice, I rattled on, stringing one foreign-sounding word after another. The priest took a quick glance at me with a puzzled look on his face. The Catholics who attended mass knew that a choirboy had to ring the bells on three different occasions to signal, among other things, that the parishioners must bow their heads. I had no idea what signal I was to watch for to know when to ring the bells. I had to improvise. I figured that about ten minutes after mass started I should ring the bells. I did just that, but it was not yet time. The priest was rattled and the parishioners were confused. Another ten minutes later, I decided to try my luck again. Wrong, again. This time, the priest asked that I bring the bells to him and he took over. Very little was said in the car on the way home. I sat on the bench for a very long time before I was asked to serve mass again.

Small Acadian villages in the 1950s were relatively self-contained, and thus we had limited contact with the outside world. There was a Mi'kmaq reserve some sixty kilometres north of Saint-Maurice, but I only visited it many years after I left Saint-Maurice. It was a community to avoid. I remember from time to time seeing two Mi'kmaq walking through the village selling hand-woven baskets. They were dressed differently, were of a different colour, and their faces had a much rougher complexion than ours. My mother always bought a basket from them. My grandfather, she explained, had learned the Mi'kmaq language and used to assist the parish priest in the confessional box, translating Mi'kmaq into French so that they could confess their sins to a priest. Because of her father's influence, she said, she felt a great deal of sympathy for them. Others in Saint-Maurice bought baskets, but for different reasons. Some believed that the natives had the ability to cast a bad spell on their homes, and buying a basket was a kind of insurance policy to protect their houses. I remember asking my mother if the Indians from Big Cove could cast a bad spell on us. She replied as most mothers probably would have: "If you are bad, yes."

My maternal grandfather, Napoléon Collette, stood out in Bouctouche, though not because of his height. He was short but had a strong personality. Antonine Maillet tells me that she remembers him as a prosperous farmer, opinionated, and a devoted Liberal. I spent some of my summer vacations on his farm. He had what I then considered vast open fields, along with a tractor, horses, and all kinds of farm animals.

He often mentioned with deep regret that he had voted Conservative once in his life, when a highly respected friend from Bouctouche ran for the party in the early 1900s. His regrets ran so deep that he decided to confess his sin to a priest. But that, he maintained, was not sufficient in God's view. He had a visible lump on his forehead and insisted that it was punishment from God for having voted Conservative. He never voted Conservative again for fear that God would punish him even more severely. For my grandfather and for many Acadians, the Conservative Party was the party that belonged to the English. He left New Brunswick only once in his life, I was told, to go to Quebec by train to attend Sir Wilfrid Laurier's funeral. Napoléon did not hide his disdain for the English. He still lived the Grand Dérangement and resented all things English because of it. I recall him rubbing his stomach after a meal, saying, "This is one meal that the English will never get."

His farm was sold intact after he passed away. Today, it is home to the Bouctouche Golf Club. The *Canadian Golf Course Directory* describes it as a "well designed" course that "offers variety and beauty and everything is quiet." Noise has never been much of a problem in either Saint-Maurice or Bouctouche. I have played the course many times. As I do so, I cannot help wondering what my grandfather or mother would say, seeing Acadians and English chasing a little white ball around their farm.

By the end of the 1950s, my father had decided to move the family to Moncton. His construction business was starting to expand, and he felt that the move would generate new business and give him access to better suppliers. We kept our house in Saint-Maurice, so I told my friends that we would return.

It was not easy to say goodbye. Saint-Maurice was a comfortable, unthreatening environment. In addition, my friends were sad to see me leave because there were not many youngsters to play ball or hockey in Saint-Maurice – and also because they were worried about losing access to television. The boy next door said that his parents had told him they would be buying a television set. He wondered, however, what kind of programs would come out of a new television set, believing that individual sets had their own programs and fearing that he would no longer be able to watch the Bunkhouse Boys. In a few years, Radio-Canada would bring French television to Acadian communities.

My neighbour was not alone in lacking an understanding of new communication technologies. An elderly woman from Saint-Maurice went to visit relatives in Waltham, Massachusetts, and decided to pack the family radio in her suitcase. She believed that she could simply turn it on in Waltham at six o'clock to hear Archbishop Robichaud's *quart d'heure marial.*

I only returned to Saint-Maurice to visit old friends and relatives from time to time. Several years after we moved to Moncton, our house in Saint-Maurice burnt down. We do not know what caused the fire, though perhaps, as some suggested, it was because of old and faulty wiring. I inherited some woodland and the land where the house and barn once stood. I sold the land to an Acadian who was living in Massachusetts but wished to return to the Bouctouche area on his retirement.

The real estate market in Saint-Maurice has never been hot, let alone red hot as in some other parts of the country. There are no commercial activities left in the village: the two bootleggers have passed away, and the owner of the confectionery store moved down the road to Bouctouche. Indeed, if someone from Rosedale in Toronto decided to sell his house and move to Saint-Maurice, he would have enough money to buy the whole village, build a new house on land of his choosing, and have enough left over to buy a new car.

I received $2,000 for the land and turned the money over to the Théâtre l'Escaouette. The theatre is a cooperative, bringing together Acadian artists to produce live theatre in Moncton. I asked that the names of my father and mother be identified as the donors. I think they would have been pleased. Nearly a hundred and fifty years earlier, one of my ancestors, Maurice Arsenault, left Bouctouche to settle on land that held no promise and no opportunity, only hope and a place to establish roots. He registered the land – some forty hectares deeded to his name on 30 June 1858 – about a hundred years after the Grand Dérangement and nine years before Canada was born.

3

Moncton: Louis J. Robichaud
to the Rescue

Saint-Maurice in 1959 could hardly have been more different from Moncton. It was much like the old television program *Cheers*, where everyone knew your name, everyone
had a thorough knowledge of everyone else's news, good and bad,
and there was a deep sense of community, or *appartenance*. Saint-
Maurice had about 200 inhabitants in 1959 – all Acadian, French-
speaking, and Roman Catholic. Moncton had a population of
about 44,000, 67 percent of whom were English-speaking, and
the majority were Protestant.

Saint-Maurice and Moncton were different for other reasons.
Moncton was urban, home to many businesses, and all levels of
government had offices there. English was the dominant language,
a fact that was evident everywhere, from public buildings to private businesses, and there were more Protestant churches than
Roman Catholic ones. Indeed, a stranger arriving in Moncton in
1960 would have had every reason to believe that it was solely an
English-speaking city.

Acadians were reminded every day and in every way that they
were the minority. Without wishing to assign blame to anyone, it
is safe to say that our economic conditions were substantially

worse than those of the English-speaking majority. Scarcely any Acadians owned a business. In fact, it did not take long for Acadians arriving in Moncton to see who among them did own a business. There was only a handful of such people, and this situation didn't change until well into the 1960s. At the time, Acadians badly trailed English-speaking Monctonians, according to whatever socio-economic indicator one wanted to look at: unemployment was higher among Acadians, earned income and per capita income were lower, the level of education was lower, and so on.

But that was not all. Leaving aside our churches, which certainly compared well at least in size to any Protestant ones, our public institutions were clearly inferior. Our hospital was not as big and well equipped as the one for English-speaking Monctonians. With some exceptions, our schools were hand-me-downs that were no longer up to standard for the English-speaking majority. Although we certainly had a large enough population to warrant a French-language high school, we had none until 1967.

If you were to ask an English-speaking Monctonian in 1960 about the state of English-Acadian relations in Moncton, he would probably have answered that all was well. If an English-speaking Monctonian had put the question to an Acadian, the response would probably have been, "Things are fine." However, if an Acadian had put the question to another Acadian, the answer would have been vastly different, something like "Les choses vont pas bien" (Things aren't going well).

Relations were just fine from an English-speaking perspective because Acadians knew their place. Their place was to be happy with where they were in society; this meant that they should not agitate for language rights, be overly ambitious in the workplace, and above all that they should learn to speak English. There were very few Acadians to be found in mid-level, let alone senior, positions in either the public or the private sector. Moncton's large employers of the day – Canadian National Railways and Eaton's – had, for Acadians, something even more impenetrable than a glass ceiling. While Acadians had less education, less training, and

were less interested in business than their English-speaking counterparts, there were other factors at play. The Orange Order and
the Freemasons were reported to be very active in screening potential employees in many Moncton-based organizations. Acadians were welcomed in some places, but even there only up to a
point and only up to a certain level. There were many Acadian
janitors, bus drivers, and floor workers. But it was difficult to find
many Acadians at more senior levels.

Previous efforts to promote language rights and more economic benefits for Acadians had not always been successful. Calixte Savoie (my uncle) led the charge for Acadian rights when he
taught school in northern New Brunswick, and in 1926 he was
appointed head of the Assomption Society. He decided to promote Acadian interests by developing the economic potential of the
society and by securing educational rights. He launched a membership drive with the goal of selling 1,755 new insurance policies
over a few months. (As the reader will realize, the target 1,755
was hardly a coincidence.) By 1927, the society had sold 10,000
new policies, and this gave Acadians an economic base from
which to promote their political, economic, and linguistic interests. They now had a voice, with a degree of economic independence, to speak on their behalf.

Next on the agenda were educational rights, but this proved to
be a much more difficult challenge. It could not be acheived
through their own efforts alone. It depended on the goodwill of
the majority. In the age before the Charter of Rights and Freedoms, the English-speaking majority held the power to deny educational or other rights to the minority. The concern for the
Acadian elite of the day was twofold – a fast-growing Acadian
population and a serious illiteracy problem. What Savoie and his
associates wanted was for Acadian schools to be taught in French.
This required French-language instructors at the provincial normal school (teachers' college), French teachers for Acadian
schools, and French-language textbooks – in short, a bilingual
school system.

In the fall of 1929, Savoie led a delegation to Fredericton to meet with educational officials. The meeting did not go well. Savoie went back to his hotel room reflecting on what to do next. By chance, several cabinet ministers and two officials from the Department of Education, who also had attended the meeting, were in the next room, where they too were reflecting on the day's events. They left the door open, perhaps because of the coming and going of ministers and senior bureaucrats, not realizing who was next door. The debate, Savoie reported, became loud, and he heard one senior departmental official say to a cabinet minister, "It is by keeping them ignorant that we are best able to dominate them. Allow them to teach themselves and you place in their hands the most powerful weapon to wean themselves from their cultural and economic poverty."[1]

This only served to stiffen Savoie's resolve. He pressed on by making the matter a political issue and forcing politicians to take a position. The government responded within a year by implementing Regulation 32, which recognized the bilingual character of New Brunswick's schools. Regulation 32 established standards for bilingual teachers that would enable them to teach in French, but only for grades 1 to 3. Still, it was a start. This would apply in predominantly French school districts at the discretion of the local school board, and teachers would have up to five years to earn bilingual certificates.

Savoie and his associates soon learned that although they might be able to win the battle, they could not win the war. The provincial grand master of the Orange Lodge warned that English New Brunswick would not stand for this and that there was to be "no Frenchifying" of the province's school system. He saw the development as a threat to the English-speaking majority and insisted that it was being led by the "French Roman Catholic church."[2] The warning was heard loud and clear and the government decided to rescind Regulation 32 before the 1930 provincial election.

Savoie next turned his attention to securing more employment for Acadians in Moncton by circulating a letter in Acadian communities urging them to speak French when shopping. This, he argued, would force English business owners to hire more Acadians. The initiative backfired. English Monctonians reacted angrily, and some businesses actually laid off Acadians already on staff, albeit occupying some of the lowest positions in the organization. The economic depression of the 1930s was difficult enough for Acadians, and the letter made matters worse.

An English-speaking executive with a Moncton business recently shared the following revealing story with me. Not long after joining the firm, he recommended that one of his colleagues be promoted. The chair of the committee responded with a firm no. Undaunted, he pressed on, singing his colleague's praises. The chair replied in no uncertain terms, "He has gone as far as he will, he is French."

Acadians had limited capacity to challenge the English-speaking majority. They had no economic power, little political power, few institutions of their own other than the Assomption Society, and a Roman Catholic Church that was both conservative in its views and slowly but surely losing influence.

MY FIRST DAYS IN MONCTON

I had an idea of what to expect in Moncton because I was aware of some of the battles *mon oncle Calixte* had fought over the years. The head office of the Assomption was on the corner of Archibald and St George Streets in Moncton, the Orange Lodge was on the opposite corner, and Calixte lived about a kilometre away, also on Archibald Street. I was told that not long after the letter incident, someone from the Orange Lodge, or so my uncle believed, called him at home one evening to say that he would be shot driving to work the next day. They knew his car, he was told, and he had been properly warned. Calixte responded that he was not afraid of the Orange Lodge and to make the point said he would be walking to work the next day. He did, but nothing happened.

My transition from Saint-Maurice to Moncton was particularly painful in the first year. I had to learn English quickly, which

I was able to do. My adjustment to city life, however, was not so easy. I remember looking out of the living-room window of our rented house and seeing a man standing at the front door ringing the bell. I had never seen such a thing before. What was wrong with this man? If he wanted something from us, why on earth didn't he come in? My mother answered the door and later told me that this was the way things were done in Moncton. Nobody here, she explained, simply walks into a house without first ringing the doorbell or knocking on the door. It was something I would have to do, she said, even when visiting friends. How strange, I thought.

I went to the Aberdeen school, which was named after Lord Aberdeen, Canada's governor general between 1893 and 1898. The school had opened its doors in 1935 and for a number of years served as an English-language high school. By 1960, Moncton's school system had been sufficiently updated to allow schooling in French between grades 1 and 8. Aberdeen, by then an old building and with outdated facilities, had been turned into a French-language school, which I attended in my first year in Moncton.

I was miserable in grade 7. It was an altogether new environment, much less friendly than Saint-Maurice. Moreover, I did not like my teacher, Miss Cormier. Monday mornings were particularly painful, knowing that I would have to live another five days of hell. It was only much later that I discovered that Miss Cormier was one of the most disliked teachers in the entire French school system in Moncton. She was mean-spirited and took a particular dislike to boys. I came to believe that all teachers in Moncton would be like Miss Cormier.

On my first day at school I arrived on a shiny new bicycle. There were few of us at school who had a bicycle, let alone a new one. As I parked it, a student came over to ask if I had a lock for it. I asked why I would need one. I soon discovered why. Not long afterwards, someone from Lewis Street, which was a particularly rough neighbourhood on the poor side of town, decided to help himself to my bicycle. I told the school authorities my bike was gone, and within a few days I had it back. Apparently, someone at school, also from Lewis Street, had seen the boy with it and, perhaps out of jealousy, decided to report him. The bicycle had a few new scratches, but nothing serious. I met with the thief and told him that if he wanted to borrow my bicycle, all he needed to do was ask. He gave me a puzzled look, probably wondering where on earth I was from with my Bouctouche accent – which, incidentally, I still have. That is the way we did things in Saint-Maurice. But not, apparently, in Moncton. I saw him from time to time after that and always said hello, but he never once asked to borrow my bike. I did, however, purchase a lock. Had my parents asked after my first year in Moncton if I would like to move back to Saint-Maurice, I would have said, "Let's get the moving truck quickly."

The next year, my parents bought a house in Moncton's north end. I attended Beauséjour school, a relatively new school where the teachers were great and the environment was very friendly. It was also the year I discovered girls and gave up on hockey. In Saint-Maurice, I had played hockey on the homemade rink next to our house. Moncton was a very different story. I joined organized hockey and played Bantam at the old Moncton stadium. What a difference! Artificial ice, no need to remove the snow from it, warm dressing rooms, real boards, and you didn't have to bring your own puck. I played for the Red Indians team – that was before political correctness set in. We played once a week, and the next day the local paper, the *Times and Transcript*, had the results of every hockey game. I never saw my name in the game summary because I never got a goal or even an assist. More to the point, I was not a very good hockey player. I played on the last line.

We were heading towards the last game of the season, and I knew I would not be good enough to play in the next division, Midget, the following year. We were playing the Bruins and I had a good friend, Roger Léger, who was playing for the team. He was only a marginally better player than me and his name, like mine, never appeared in game summaries in the local paper. To remedy this I went to him and said, "If we are ever on the ice at the same time, I'm going to start a fight with you and will get a penalty. It would be nice to see our names in the paper just once." Sure enough, at some point in the third period (probably by then the coaches knew who was going to win the game), I skated up to Roger like an enraged Tie Domie or John Ferguson, dropped my gloves, and hit him. Off we went, and the next day, there we were in the *Times and Transcript*, a major penalty for fighting. I ended my hockey career on that note, but Roger kept going and eventually became a pretty good player.

All in all, my second year in Moncton was a good one, and the city started to make a great deal of sense. If my parents had asked after my second year if I wanted to move back to Saint-Maurice, my answer would have been a firm no. However, grade 8 was the end of the line in Moncton for Acadians wishing to pursue their education in French. The choices were limited – give up and get a job, which many did at that time, go to an English-language high school, or go to a private college run by priests. My parents wanted no part of the first two but were willing to pay for the third. So I did my high school years at the Collège l'Assomption. I have good memories of those years and made some lifelong friends. There was only one drawback – no girls – so we had to go to the local church-run youth centre to meet them. We did and had fun.

About this time, the face of New Brunswick was about to change. English-French relations would be shaken to the core, and l'Acadie would venture into a bold new direction. Acadians would become more secular, less patient, and more ambitious than at any time since the Grand Dérangement. The spark plug for all of this was Louis J. Robichaud.

THE ARRIVAL OF LOUIS J. ROBICHAUD

The new Acadian elite that emerged in the late 1950s and early 1960s wanted to see changes, and quickly. Members of the old Acadian guard, including Calixte Savoie, were asked, gently or not, to take their leave. Louis St Laurent appointed my uncle to the Senate, where he sat as an independent. Ironically, ten years later, the new guard of the early 1960s came under the same kind of criticism they were dealing out – that things were progressing too slowly.

As the saying goes, the right man at the right moment. In Louis Robichaud, Acadians had a new young, dynamic, and determined leader precisely at a time when they needed this kind of leadership. He was the type of politician, rather a rare breed these days, who knew exactly why he was in politics – to introduce sweeping changes. His election sent a bolt of electricity right through New Brunswick, especially among the province's English-speaking majority.

Many of them were probably asking themselves, on the morning of 28 June 1960, how they could have let it happen. How could they have permitted a thirty-four-year-old Acadian lawyer from Kent County to lead his Liberals to a majority victory? Only thirty years earlier, the grand master of the Orange Lodge had needed only to bark and the government had backed down from allowing French schools for grades 1 to 3. Now, the province had elected a premier who not only had a forceful personality but was not afraid to stare down the Orange Lodge or anyone else.

The outgoing premier, Hugh John Flemming, was a quiet businessman from Carleton County who had run the province well. "Steady as she goes" had been his approach, and he saw no need to poke into potentially controversial issues such as English-French relations. The Conservatives had been overconfident as Flemming went for a third mandate. There was no reason why they, or for that matter many New Brunswickers, should think that the people would turn Flemming out.

Robichaud had crafted a platform that would appeal to both language groups. He promised to abolish a provincial hospital premium tax that everyone had to pay regardless of the ability to do so, a commitment that proved to be a popular initiative, particularly in rural areas. In addition, he adopted many modern campaign techniques. Lastly, he had loads of what political observers now call "charisma." He was an inspirational speaker, a passionate orator who could fire up an audience at will.

There was another factor at play – *la revanche des berceaux* (the revenge of the cradle). The Acadian population was growing more rapidly than the English-speaking one, and its presence was increasingly being felt. The province's francophone population had grown steadily from 15.7 percent of the total in 1871 to nearly 40 percent in 1960.

Robichaud's victory came as a surprise even to a number of Liberals. The federal Liberal Party had the practice of alternating between English- and French-speaking leaders, and many Liberals thought that this practice should be extended to New Brunswick. Robichaud had been chosen leader in 1958 – many believed as a "token Acadian leader, to be defeated in 1960 and subsequently dumped."[3] Since Premier Hugh John Flemming (with the electoral slogan "Carry on Hugh John") was believed to be much too strong for any Liberal to defeat, it was thought best to let a young untested Acadian take the fall. This would solidify Acadian loyalty to the Liberal Party and later allow a strong leader to emerge in the post-Flemming era.

Conservative Party poll workers could hardly believe what they were seeing on the evening of 27 June. One Conservative-appointed returning officer from Charlotte County simply refused to announce, for a few hours, that a Liberal had won the election in the constituency for which he was responsible. Della Stanley in her work on Louis J. Robichaud writes that "not a single press reporter or photographer had followed Robichaud to Richibucto (his constituency) for the election night. They were all with Hugh John Flemming, believing that they would be on top of the news when it happened."[4]

It may well be that Flemming himself did not believe what he was witnessing. Today, the transition of power from one party to another in Western democracies has become a sophisticated exercise, with numerous briefing books prepared to assist the incoming government. Meetings between the incoming government and career public servants are held to map out a strategy for the government's first days in office. Transition planning was nonexistent in New Brunswick in 1960, but it is now an important exercise at election time, particularly when there is a change of government. I participated in three transition planning teams (Frank McKenna in 1987, Jean Chrétien in 1993, and Shawn Graham, in New Brunswick, in 2006).

Robichaud told me that he waited by the telephone for Flemming to call to congratulate him and set a date to hand over power. The call never came, so Robichaud decided to place a call. Flemming finally congratulated him, and Robichaud asked him if he had decided on a date. Flemming hesitated and then said, "What about July 12," some fifteen days away. Robichaud immediately saw the irony but believed that Flemming did not, and he quickly agreed to the date. Thus, Robichaud was sworn in on the very same day that the Orange Order held its annual parade through the streets of Fredericton.

I need to inform the reader at this point that I became a close friend of Louis Robichaud in the 1990s and remained so until he passed away on 6 January 2005. We met often, had many discussions, and I tried as best I could to be helpful to him in his later years while he was in the Senate and in his retirement. He retired from the Senate in October 2000 and spent the last years of his life in a modest bungalow by the sea in Bouctouche. I headed a research institute at the Université de Moncton from 1983 to 2005, and while there, I sponsored a conference entitled The Robichaud Era, 1960–70, which Robichaud attended. The papers tabled at the conference were later published. I also sponsored a biography of Robichaud written by a fellow Acadian, the well-known CBC Radio/Radio-Canada journalist, Michel Cormier.

When Robichaud died, I published an article in both the *Globe and Mail* and *Le Devoir* in which I wrote, "Robichaud put forward comprehensive reforms, fought for them in the public arena, played by the rules of democracy, and won. He then stayed to implement the changes, again, never putting his own interest before the public interest. If this sounds corny today, it is only because our age is more cynical. But it explains why New Brunswickers and historians will still be singing his praises 50 years from now." I mention all this for two reasons. First, in my many conversations with him, I picked up a great deal of information that I am now sharing with the reader. Second, the reader should be forewarned that I have a strong bias when it comes to Louis J. Robichaud, which may well colour parts of this book. More to the point, while Robichaud made mistakes and, like every human being, had weaknesses, the reader will have to go elsewhere to read about them.

DECIDING WHAT TO DO

Robichaud knew exactly what he wanted to accomplish – to transform New Brunswick society. High on his to-do list was an overhaul of the province's higher education system. In May 1961 he established the Royal Commission on the Future of Higher Education and appointed John J. Deutsch of Queen's University to lead it.

The Deutsch Commission held four public hearings and submitted its report in June 1962. At the Moncton hearing, Father Clément Cormier, head of the local classical Collège Saint-Joseph, stressed the bilingual nature of the province and then made the case that a French-language institution of higher learning was urgently needed.⁵ At the Fredericton hearing, Colin B. Mackay, president of the University of New Brunswick, said there was no need for a French-language university, arguing that one central university would be less costly and that New Brunswick should concentrate its limited resources on it. With respect to the question of providing French-language facilities to serve the French-language population, Mackay argued that the University of New Brunswick had always accepted French-speaking students. However, he proposed that some sort of bilingual system could be set up at the university to serve the French-speaking population better. But he did not explain in any detail what form of bilingualism would be introduced or why he had to wait for the Deutsch Commission to recognize the need.

To add insult to injury, Mackay concluded his presentation by urging the government to join forces with the University of New Brunswick in assisting less-developed countries to establish new institutions of higher learning. He suggested Indonesia, where the Government of New Brunswick "might direct some of its energies, however small, in the initial instance, to assist in the building of a newly created college."[6] It should be noted that by the time the Deutsch Commission was touring New Brunswick, francophones made up 38 percent of the province's population and accounted for about 7 percent of the student population at the University of New Brunswick.

Robichaud dismissed Mackay's recommendations out of hand and accepted Deutsch's recommendation to "establish the Université de Moncton as the sole degree-granting French language institution of higher learning in New Brunswick." On 1 March 1963, the Robichaud government presented a bill to the legislature to incorporate the Université de Moncton. Robichaud often said later that if he had to point to the single most important achievement during his tenure as premier, it would be the creation of the Université de Moncton.

Father Clément Cormier, a close friend of Robichaud and founder of the Université de Moncton, drove up to Fredericton on 12 March 1963 to sit in the public galleries of the legislative assembly to witness third reading of the bill. The opposition was crying "scandal" because the Robichaud government had negotiated a deal with Italian investors to build a new pulp mill in South Nelson. The opposition called for a public inquiry, claiming that Robichaud had not negotiated with New Brunswick's best interests in mind. Robichaud rose in the assembly and declared, "I propose to refer the matter to the electorate," and moved to dissolve the assembly. Robichaud told me that as he sat down, he looked up at the gallery and saw Cormier's face "turn white." Cormier rushed downstairs to see Robichaud and said, "Louis, what are you doing? We could lose our university." Robichaud responded, "Clément, Clément, do you really think for a moment that I called the election to lose it? I will win." Win, he did. He increased his majority, and the legislation establishing the Université de Moncton received final reading on 15 June 1963. Cormier described it as "one of the most important dates in the history of the Acadian renaissance."

But the establishment of the Université de Moncton was just the beginning for Robichaud. During his ten years in power, he completely rebuilt the provincial public service, launched an initiative to study the union of the three Maritime provinces, built an ambitious hydroelectric project on the Saint John River, passed legislation to make English and French the province's two official languages, and set in train the most controversial socio-economic reform package in the history of the province – the Programme of Equal Opportunity. Political scientist Robert A. Young put it well when he observed, "Sweeping as it was, the Programme of Equal Opportunity had profound effects. It was a model for other jurisdictions and was widely noticed by public-finance experts, officials, and politicians elsewhere. Its internal effects were manifest throughout the political, economic, social, and even cultural life of the province."[7] *The Canadian Encyclopedia* described the Robichaud reforms as "so rapid and fundamental as to be called revolutionary" and added that "the Acadians gained most from the program of equal opportunity."[8]

SEARCHING FOR EQUAL OPPORTUNITIES FOR EVERYONE

Robichaud never accepted that his Programme of Equal Opportunity was introduced mainly to benefit Acadians. He argued that there were poor people everywhere in the province, not just in the Acadian areas, and everyone, not just Acadians, would benefit from equal opportunities.

Robichaud asked Ed Byrne, a Bathurst lawyer, to chair a Royal Commission on Finance and Municipal Taxation. Byrne came back with a detailed report that outlined pronounced inequities between regions and communities. There were five hundred villages where education was provided in a one-room schoolhouse, and nearly half of the province had no access to secondary education. While the City of Saint John was able to spend $300 per year per student on education, the largely Acadian Gloucester County was able to spend only $144. Byrne found similar problems in health care, justice, and social services and recommended that the provincial government take charge of delivering services in these sectors and eliminate the role played by county councils. Byrne also recommended that the government increase the province's sales tax from 3 to 5 percent, that property taxes be made uniform across the province, and that many tax exemptions to private firms be eliminated.

The report raised expectations, particularly in Acadian regions but also in rural anglophone areas, and it aroused outright opposition in urban areas and from some of the province's leading businesses. Robichaud did not respond to the report immediately. He realized that a great deal of work was needed before he could endorse its findings. He wanted his ministers to appreciate what lay ahead for them if the government proceeded with the report. Morevover, he concluded that the provincial public service was not yet capable of implementing the report's recommendations. Thus, Robichaud first set out to rebuild the public service. He went outside the province to recruit new talent, especially from Saskatchewan. That was because Premier Ross Thatcher had rid the provincial government of many senior officials after he defeated T.C. Douglas and the Co-operative Commonwealth Federation (CCF) (forerunner of the New Democratic Party) in 1964. Robichaud recruited several of these seasoned bureaucrats, and they eventually played a critical role in implementing his equal opportunity program.

When Robichaud was good and ready, he declared that he accepted the bulk of the Byrne Report and its recommendations. The legislative agenda was mind-boggling – there were 130 bills, a number of new government bureaus and agencies, and sweeping tax reforms. County councils were abolished.

Robichaud's reform package unleashed a firestorm of protest. Some anglophone business leaders and the economically strong urban areas – notably, Saint John, Fredericton, and Moncton – and the English-language media went at Robichaud and his plan with all the determination and at times venom that they could muster. The *Telegraph Journal* happily published a letter to the editor which said that the plan was a plot to "rob Peter to pay Pierre."

Fredericton's *Daily Gleaner* produced a series of cartoons against it, one of which depicted Robichaud as Louis XIV, with rats crawling out from the bottom of his robe. Michael Wardell, the *Gleaner*'s publisher, never made any effort to hide his profound dislike of Robichaud. His words and actions often bordered on racism. He wrote in the *Atlantic Advocate* that Robichaud was "a little man with a violently-expressive mouth," and he circulated rumours in Frederiction that Robichaud's goal was to push the English aside and have the French take over.

Other rumours began circulating that Robichaud was lining his own pockets and that he used his position as premier to secure kickbacks from government contracts. Alan Reynolds, a Protestant minister from Fredericton, gave the rumours a public voice when he declared in a broadcast service that "issues of legislative reforms have been clouded by accusation, rumours and reports of corruption and evil doing in high places." He added, "Is it not true that our Premier was almost penniless when first elected and is now reliably rated as worth somewhere from $600,000 to $2,000,000?"[9] The accusation was given wide publicity. It was later found to be completely untrue, but the damage had been done. Feelings ran high in Fredericton in 1966 to the point that the RCMP had to provide twenty-four-hour protection to Robichaud and his family. Robichaud told me that he had received many death threats.

Robichaud was not known to back down before any individual, however powerful. Lord Beaverbrook, a New Brunswicker and major benefactor in the province who had achieved fame and fortune as a press baron in the United Kingdom, always sent a telegram to the premier before every trip back to Fredericton. Tradition required the premier to meet Beaverbrook at the airport with his chauffeur to bring him back to town.

Not long after Robichaud came to power, the premier's office received the customary telegram from Beaverbrook – and he decided not to go to the airport. He told me what happened next. Beaverbrook took a taxi directly to the premier's office, swept past his assistant, and marched straight in, barking at Robichaud, "Where were you?" Robichaud jumped up from his chair and shot back, "Who is premier here, you or me?" Beaverbrook answered "You," and Robichaud replied, "Don't ever forget that. Now, what can I do for you?" It is interesting that Robichaud and Beaverbrook got on very well after this meeting. Beaverbrook continued to endow the province with gifts, including the Playhouse, a theatre next to the Legislative Building. I would love to have been a fly on the wall that day when two such powerful personalities – each so very short in physical stature – had a clash of wills.

Robichaud and K.C. Irving had been friends in the past, and Irving had supported Robichaud in the 1960 election. Both were from Kent County, and both had been successful in their fields. Both shared the experience of being put down by the Establishment. K.C. Irving had been regarded by the city's business leaders as an upstart from Kent County when he arrived in Saint John to open an auto dealership, and Robichaud was viewed in the same way by Fredericton's political elite when he first arrived in Fredericton. But Robichaud's equal opportunity program was simply too much for Irving to stomach. How could Robichaud do such a thing? Robichaud would reply that there was only room for one democratically elected government in New Brunswick.

Robichaud established a committee of the legislative assembly to enable New Brunswickers to voice their concerns, including their support for or opposition to public or private bills. Irving's criticism of Robichaud's equal opportunity program served to draw the battle lines "between the gutsy, aggressive politician and the smooth, calculating industrialist."[10] Irving was never one to seek publicity, but he was prepared to pay the price to let New Brunswickers know that the Robichaud plan would badly hurt relations between the government and the business community. He flatly claimed that no "sane government" would proceed with what the government had in mind. Robichaud told me on more than one occasion that he was profoundly hurt by Irving's personal attacks.

Meanwhile, Cy Sherwood, the quiet and inefficient leader of the Conservative Party, resigned. Charlie Van Horne, a colourful, fully bilingual, former Conservative federal MP from northern New Brunswick, announced that he was returning to the province to run for the leadership of the Conservative Party. Van Horne easily won the leadership against a young lawyer, Richard Hatfield.

Robichaud then called an election for October 1967. For the first time in New Brunswick's history, two bilingual Roman Catholics would be leading the two major political parties. Van Horne's mother was an Acadian, also from northern New Brunswick. All in all, New Brunswickers were in store for the most entertaining (Van Horne hired Don Messer and His Islanders to tour the province with him) and bitterly fought election campaign in the province's history.

Van Horne was quick off the mark. He drove through the province in a white Cadillac with two speeches in his hands, one for anglophone communities and another for francophone. In the first, he pledged never to tax Peter to give money to Pierre. In the latter, he accused Robichaud of not doing enough to promote language rights for francophones and promised to introduce legislation to that end. Acadians, however, were not fooled by Van Horne's rhetoric, as the election results would reveal.

Robichaud campaigned hard and visited all areas of the province more than once. He took dead aim at Van Horne's credibility, often pointed to the bias of the English media, and stressed the advantages of his program of equal opportunity for "all" regions of the province. He argued that in a democracy everyone should pay taxes, including wealthy industrialists, "not just the little guy." New Brunswickers and indeed Robichaud himself saw the election for what it truly was – a referendum on the government's program of massive social reform.

I would like to reproduce here part of what I wrote for the *Globe and Mail* when Robichaud died. I wrote:

> In the dying days of the 1967 election, Louis Robichaud went to Tracadie, an Acadian village in northeast New Brunswick, to address a rally. We are told that there were more than 1,000 people packed like sardines, waiting for him in a hall that normally held 600. As Mr. Robichaud reached the parking lot, his organizers realized that they could not make any headway to the front door, let alone to the front of the hall. Acadians decided to improvise and they raised him above their heads and passed him from hand to upraised hand until he reached the platform. Few people anywhere could match Mr. Robichaud's oratorical powers and, that night, he touched the soul of everyone in the hall when he spoke about his Equal Opportunity program and what it would mean for them and their children. Later, some of his organizers wanted him to leave by a side door. But the crowd wanted none of that. It wanted their hero to go out by the front door and, indeed, he went out the same way he had come in. He suffered some scratches and his clothing was torn, but he went on to the next campaign stop.

Robichaud told me that he knew all along that this was the most important election campaign of his political life. The campaign gained national and even international attention. The focus was on the Robichaud–Van Horne battle, and the *Globe and Mail*, *Toronto Star*, *La Presse*, *Le Devoir*, and even the *New York Times* sent reporters to the province to cover the campaign. The *Globe and Mail* and *Toronto Star* both wrote editorials highly supportive of Robichaud.

Robichaud won the election, winning thirty-two seats to Van Horne's twenty-six. Predictably, Robichaud won heavily in Acadian areas, while Van Horne won more seats in anglophone areas. Still, the verdict was in, and Robichaud could now proceed with his equal opportunity program. He would also later introduce legislation to make English and French official languages in New Brunswick.

Robichaud said that he sensed early on during his last mandate that his job was done. He dealt with a number of things, including partisan political matters. He attended the 1968 national Liberal leadership convention that elected Pierre E. Trudeau. He was very close to Trudeau but decided to support Robert Winters, a Maritimer who had moved to Toronto. Robichaud told me that he favoured Trudeau and had a long conversation with him to explain his decision: it would be best for an Acadian to be seen supporting Winters rather than Trudeau. That said, he made it clear that his commitment to Winters was for the first ballot only and that from the second ballot he would support Trudeau, which he did.

Robichaud fought his last election in 1970 without the energy, commitment, or interest he had had in 1967. There was much less at stake for him. He had accomplished what he had set out to do, and his major initiatives were firmly in the implementation stage. In addition, disaster struck in mid-campaign. James Cross, the British trade commissioner, was kidnapped by Quebec extremists, and later Pierre Laporte, a minister in the Quebec government and a close friend of Robichaud, was murdered. Robichaud cancelled several campaign stops to attend Laporte's funeral. Liberal Party organizers realized that this would give rise to renewed English-French tensions in the province, which could hurt Robichaud's chances at election time.[11]

Robichaud told me that he was completely at peace with the 1970 election results. He had had enough, his job was done, and his family had already paid too high a price. He also reports that he had full confidence in the new premier, Richard Hatfield, a moderate Conservative who reached out to Acadians. Nor did Hatfield attempt to undo Robichaud's equal opportunities program, the Official Languages Act, the establishment of the École normale (French teachers' college), or the establishment of the Université de Moncton. Robichaud could ask for nothing better. His government had gone down to defeat, winning only twenty-six seats to Hatfield's thirty-seven. But Acadians had stood by Robichaud until the end, still voting overwhelmingly in his favour.

THE END COMES

In the fall of 2004, Louis Robichaud and his wife came to see me at my Université de Moncton office. Robichaud often dropped in when he came to Moncton, but this time it was different. In the past, he had always called ahead to see if I would be there. This time he came unannounced. He had just received some medical test results.

"Any problem?" I asked.

"Some," he replied, "but I think that we can beat it." He explained that his doctor had put him on medication and that he was pretty confident that things would work out just fine. That was it. I sensed that he wanted to talk about something else, and we did: the usual – politics, the state of the provincial economy, and a few jokes here and there. As he and his wife Jacqueline left, they had a chat with my assistant Ginette, as they always did when they came to visit. All things appeared normal; but they were not.

Louis and Jacqueline continued to call when in Moncton for Louis' medical treatment, and it became clear that things were not going well. He had cancer and it was spreading fast. His condition deteriorated rapidly, literally over several weeks. I talked to him on the phone and to Jacqueline from time to time to see how he was doing. I could tell from his voice that things were not good.

Jacqueline called me in December to say that Louis had asked to see me. Would I come down to Bouctouche? I drove down, and when I walked into the house I saw Robichaud sitting in his favourite chair, covered in a blanket. He had lost a lot of weight and his face was a pale greyish colour. The cancer had spread to virtually every part of his body, including his throat. He looked up and in a low, barely audible voice, said, "I'm sorry."

"Sorry for what?" I asked.

"Sorry that you have to see me like this."

I had a difficult time holding back my emotions, but somehow managed to say, "Louis, if there is one person on earth who does not have to say sorry to an Acadian, it is you." I added, "Please, do not say you are sorry. There is nothing to be sorry about."

I knew that he would tire quickly, so I let him do the talking. He told me that J.K. Irving (one of K.C. Irving's three sons) had heard about his state of health and had come to visit, bringing a small gift, a gesture that deeply moved Louis. He said, "You know, Jim Irving is a very good man." I nodded. Louis had often talked to me about Jim Irving. He liked him a great deal, and the two of them met from time to time after Louis left the premier's office. What a great story, I thought, and somehow and for some reason I believed that K.C. Irving would have approved.

Louis had talked to me about K.C. various times. There was a side of him that respected K.C., and the two had been good friends. What Louis never fully digested was Irving's remark that "no sane government" would countenance Robichaud's reform agenda. He took it personally, convinced that K.C. Irving was accusing him of insanity. However, although his disagreements and fights with K.C. were strong and intense, Robichaud respected Irving's accomplishments in the business world and his contributions to New Brunswick, as indeed I do too.

I would like to note here that Louis Robichaud did not, as a matter of principle, denigrate others, however strongly he disagreed with them. In all my conversations with him, he only made strongly worded negative comments about two individuals. I recall asking him one evening in Ottawa while he was still in the Senate, "Do you know if Michael Wardell is dead?" He replied, "Yes. Oh him. He waited too long to die." The second person is still alive and I've chosen not to reveal Louis' views about him. I think Louis would be grateful.

When I visited him in Bouctouche on that cold December day,

Robichaud looked up at me and said, "I have a favour to ask."

"Anything," I answered. "Just tell me."

"I want you to organize my funeral."

I did not know how to respond. I thought of saying, "Now, Louis, things could still work out with new medicine, one never knows." But who would I be kidding? Instead, I told him I would do whatever he wanted and asked if he had anything specific in mind.

"Make sure," he said, "that the Université de Moncton is involved somehow. I would like you to talk to Yvon Fontaine, the university president. Could you also let Paul Martin know and perhaps Jean Chrétien?"

"No problem," I said. "Anything else?"

"No, you figure it out."

As I left, Jacqueline followed me outside to say, "You know, Louis thought about this. It is important for him that you take this on."

"Jacqueline, I will do my best not to let him down."

My drive back to Moncton was difficult. I tried, with little success, to block out of my mind the last image I had of Robichaud. At the same time, I tried to focus on a new task, organizing his funeral. I had a little experience to draw from to take on this responsibility. A few years earlier I had organized my brother's funeral. However, Robichaud's funeral would mean a great deal, not only to Acadians but to all New Brunswickers. He had become an icon in the province, now widely respected if not always loved in every region. English-speaking New Brunswickers from Charlotte County (a rural region) and elsewhere had come to appreciate Robichaud's equal opportunity program. Many New Brunswickers also recognized in Robichaud a man of deep convictions, courage, and passion. The well-known author and former New Brunswick resident David Adams Richards expressed the views of many when he said, "He was our greatest premier."

I was reminded of two events that had occurred in the previous twenty months in Moncton. The Université de Moncton celebrated its fortieth anniversary in June 2003, and Robichaud was the guest speaker. After the event, I was standing next to him with others, chatting about the celebrations, when I caught in the corner of my eye an elderly gentleman walking towards Robichaud, eyes fixed on him. I guessed that he had once been a fisherman, given his clothes and his weather-worn face. He walked up to Robichaud, touched his arm, and without saying a word, backed away. He did not turn round; he simply stepped backwards, eyes still firmly fixed on Robichaud. He had driven to Moncton from a small Acadian village to see, hear, and touch his political hero, the one man who had turned things around for so many Acadians and their families.

After another event in Moncton, I walked with Louis and Jacqueline to their car. Robichaud had problems walking as he grew older, because, he told me, of knee injuries dating back to his hockey-playing days in college. As we approached the car, a man in his forties came up to me and asked if he could introduce his twelve-year-old son to Robichaud. I said, "No problem," and asked Robichaud, who by then was sitting in the passenger seat, with Jacqueline at the wheel as always. He said, "Sure." The father turned to his son and said, "I want you to meet the greatest New Brunswicker you will ever meet. Some day, you will be able to say that you shook hands with Louis Robichaud." Robichaud was most gracious. I asked the father, as I often do whenever I meet a New Brunswicker, "Where are you from?" He said, "Sussex." Sussex is in the heart of English-speaking New Brunswick, and that man did not, and very likely could not, speak a word of French. Robichaud, I thought, had been right all along in insisting that he was premier of all New Brunswick and that he wanted his reforms to benefit all those English- and French-speaking New Brunswickers who were in search of equal opportunities, a fair start in life.

I did not know how much time I had in which to plan Robichaud's funeral. The scope of what I had been asked to do would involve the City of Moncton and the provincial and federal governments. It would involve meetings with church authorities, the university, and the funeral parlour, as well as family and friends. As soon as I returned to Moncton, I contacted one of my very close friends, Maurice LeBlanc, and asked for help. Maurice had just returned to Moncton from Windsor, Ontario, where he held a senior executive position with Chrysler Canada. We first met in grade 9 at the Collège l'Assomption, and to this day we have remained very close friends. He is married to Robichaud's niece Monique and knew Louis and Jacqueline well. He agreed to handle the logistics and did a masterful job. He met with the undertakers and with government officials and looked after all the "nuts and bolts" of the funeral, including organizing bus services to and from the cathedral. In short, he made the buses run on time, as I knew he would.

I told Linda, my wife, that I should be fine through Christmas but after that would be focusing all of my energy on planning the funeral. She, as always, was fully supportive. She, too, had become very fond of Louis and Jacqueline. I told the same thing to my assistant Ginette, who also had had a close relationship with Robichaud, and she was very helpful with the arrangements for the funeral.

I contacted the prime minister's switchboard and asked that Paul Martin be informed of Robichaud's state of health. Similarly, I called Jean Chrétien's law office. He was out of the country, so I asked his assistant to explain the gravity of the situation the next time she spoke to him. Within days, both Martin and Chrétien telephoned Robichaud. Martin also called me to say that he wanted to attend the funeral. He did, which complicated things somewhat because of security requirements, but it was a gesture that Jacqueline and the Robichaud family deeply appreciated.

I met with Robichaud's son Paul, who came down from Ottawa. We mapped out a plan and took a number of decisions, which he passed on to his brother René and his sister Monique. I met with Yvon Fontaine, as Louis had requested, and one could not have asked for better cooperation. Fontaine agreed to close the university for a day to honour Robichaud, and he offered the Louis J. Robichaud physical education centre to be transformed into a funeral parlour, where everyone would be invited to come and pay their respects. He also made plans for the university to host a reception on campus after the funeral, to which, again, everyone would be invited.

A number of people wanted to give the eulogy at the funeral, which was to be broadcast on Radio-Canada television. We agreed on Robert Pichette, one-time chief of staff to Robichaud. It was without doubt the right decision. Pichette, with his deep baritone voice, spoke very well. When the time came, both the delivery and the substance of the eulogy were of the highest quality. Pichette also did extremely well in meeting with the media to explain Robichaud's contributions to New Brunswick.

Next came the selection of the pallbearers and honorary pallbearers. The first decision was relatively easy – Robichaud's nephews. The choice of honorary pallbearers was a different matter, as a number of friends and colleagues requested the honour. I consulted Jacqueline and Robichaud's son Paul as I prepared the list. All living former Robichaud ministers were invited. I then put together the following list to which Jacqueline and Paul gave their blessing: Antonine Maillet, Acadian author; Viola Léger, a senator and Acadian artist who portrayed La Sagouine in plays across Canada; Yvon Fontaine; former premier Frank McKenna; Wallace McCain; Suzanne Lévesque, daughter of Jean-Louis Lévesque, a Montreal financier and a close friend of Robichaud; Antonia Barry, a long-serving assistant to Robichaud; and J.K. Irving.[12]

The funeral took place on a bitterly cold January day. Many ordinary citizens braved the weather to attend the funeral at the Moncton cathedral. The city blocked off several streets and provided extra security and a number of buses to carry people from the university to the cathedral and back again. Numerous dignitaries attended with no incident, and the media reported the funeral as "the biggest in the province's history."[13]

Tributes poured in all week from right across Canada. Students in several Acadian schools and community colleges produced a book of condolences in which they could register their feelings about their hero. Conservative Senator Lowell Murray went to the heart of the matter when he commented, "There aren't many political leaders who have the opportunity to lead the rebirth of a people, but that's what he did. There are generations of Acadians who owe everything to him." J.K. Irving said, "His vision of equal opportunity and his commitment to the Acadian people of this province is a legacy that lives on today, and New Brunswick is the better for it." Denis Losier, the head of Assomption Life (formerly the Assomption Society), observed, "We would have a totally different New Brunswick had it not been for Louis Robichaud."

It was a great funeral as far as funerals go, and I felt certain that Robichaud would have been pleased. Hundreds of people walked by his casket in a building named in his honour on the campus of the Université de Moncton, the university he had established, his proudest achievement. When it was all over and as the buses returned to the campus, J.K. Irving asked me, "Where are they going to bury Louis?" I said that the family did not want to announce it publicly quite yet but that Louis would not be buried. He had asked to be cremated and for his ashes to be scattered over Bouctouche Bay. Irving looked at me, never said a word, but I saw his eyes swell with tears. He, like his father, spends his summers in Bouctouche, and he understood Louis' close attachment to the community.

A few weeks after the funeral, a friend came by my office to say that he had heard "some criticism" from "some Acadian nationalists downtown" about my choice of honorary pallbearers. Specifically, they asked whether it had been a good idea to include anglophones, in particular J.K. Irving, given his father's battles with Robichaud. I told my friend, "Don't tell me who has been saying this. I would rather not know their names from you. Instead, I would appreciate it if you would go back to them and ask that they come in to see me, and I would be happy to explain the decision." I am still waiting. Those people never understood what Robichaud stood for, only what they themselves stood for. Robichaud took great pride in the fact that his reforms were to benefit all of New Brunswick, not just Acadians. I also knew that I had been on safe ground inviting both J.K. Irving and Wallace

McCain, since Jacqueline, Paul, René, and Monique supported my decision.

Enough has been said about the relationship between J.K. Irving and Louis Robichaud. As for Wallace McCain, Robichaud had a profound admiration for him and his brother Harrison, who had since died. Harrison and Robichaud had been close friends, and I have first-hand knowledge of this. I arranged for both to meet on Canada Day in 2003 at Harrison's summer home in St Andrews. One could sense the warm friendship and admiration they had for each other. It was the last time they met. Harrison often said that he had one political hero, one photo of a politician in his office – Louis Robichaud. The McCain brothers always supported Robichaud through thick and thin.

The funeral gradually receded from my mind and from those of New Brunswickers generally as people went about their business again. The issue, however, surfaced again midway through the 2006 New Brunswick general election campaign. The premier, Bernard Lord, was ahead in the polls and things were going relatively well for him and his party. His party's election platform included a "regional development policy" for the province. The policy, Lord explained, would apply everywhere in the province, except in the cities of Moncton, Fredericton, and Saint John. The media contacted me for my views. I was critical of the proposed policy, suggesting that it was not a regional policy, since it would apply everywhere, not in one or two regions. Regional policy, by definition, I explained, must have a regional focus: "Call it what you want, but Lord's proposal is not a regional policy. How could northern New Brunswick possibly benefit from such a policy?" The media reported my views, and according to a journalist who was on the Lord campaign bus, northern residents responded by putting questions to Lord and his candidates in that part of the province.

Lord was asked for his reaction, but instead of dealing with the substance of my criticism, he took a different tack. "I have respect for Donald Savoie," he said, "for the work that he's done. But I recognize that he is a partisan person, who has written books on former New Brunswick premier Frank McKenna, and he planned the funeral of Louis Robichaud. But I still have to take his counsel and his advice during an election campaign with a grain of salt." The media immediately contacted me, and I had this to say: "I don't want to be involved in that kind of debate. I'll let people draw their own conclusion. People who want to engage in that kind of debate can go at it alone. I won't be part of it."

Robichaud's widow, however, didn't hesitate to get into the thick of things. She was livid that Lord would use her husband's funeral as a ploy in the election campaign. She wrote to the *Telegraph Journal*: "My husband, the honourable Louis J. Robichaud, greatly admired Donald Savoie, and it was as a personal friend and not for partisanship or political ends that a week before his death, Louis asked Mr. Savoie to take care of all his funeral arrangements. Mr. Lord, I am deeply offended that you would make such a comment, especially during an election campaign, and I ask, as wife of the greatest premier this province ever produced, that you publicly apologize for this inappropriate comment."

The *Telegraph Journal* gave the controversy plenty of coverage and on 31 August 2006 ran a front-page article above the fold, with the headline "Lord Regrets Remark." There was a large photo of Robichaud's coffin, with the caption "Lord has come under fire from the late premier's widow." I knew – as I immediately suspected every New Brunswicker did, for that matter – that the story would not play well for Lord, particularly in Acadian regions. The election pitted Lord, a francophone, a product of the Université de Moncton, fluently bilingual, and Roman Catholic, against Shawn Graham, an anglophone with some ability to speak French. Lord lost the election. I do not want to suggest that the above story explains his defeat. There were other controversies that hurt him, including one in which one of his candidates in Saint John openly contradicted him on energy policy. But the funeral fracas did shift the momentum away from Lord in the middle of the campaign.

I have never answered Lord's charge that I am a partisan Liberal. It is time to tell. Liberals have accused me of being a Conservative. I recall, for example, Stéphane Dion telling me in my office in Moncton that my name had been discussed in Ottawa (he did not specify where) and that the consensus was that I was a partisan Conservative. I should note here that Stéphane started his teaching career at the Université de Moncton and he and I worked together on several projects while he was there. We know each other well, and I had spent most of the day with him in Moncton when he made the comment. It was in 1998, and he was in the area as a minister of the Chrétien government to celebrate National Acadian Day, 15 August. He was to be the guest speaker at Le Pays de la Sagouine, and I accompanied him to the ceremony.

During our drive down to Bouctouche, he asked me for advice on what he should say. It is not unusual for politicians to seek such advice before a speaking engagement. I suggested that he remind Acadians that he began his career at the Université de Moncton and that perhaps he should simplify his vocabulary – maybe use the slang word "job" instead of "*emploi.*" Many Acadians had braved a very hot August day to come to the celebrations, and Stéphane gave a barn-burner of a speech – perhaps not the image of Dion the reader has in mind. He said that his first "job" was with the Université de Moncton, that he recalled leaving Montreal in an old beat-up Volkswagen which he and his wife had named *Pélagie-la-Charrette* after the book for which Antonine Maillet had won the Prix Goncourt, and he spoke at some length about Acadians and their contribution to Canada. He was heartily applauded, and I saw that day a side of Stéphane that I wish more Canadians could see.

There are two possible reasons to explain why Stéphane and others think that I might be a partisan Conservative. First, my work for Prime Minister Mulroney in establishing the Atlantic Canada Opportunities Agency (ACOA) has left the impression among some long-serving Liberal MPs from Atlantic Canada that I had a connection to the Conservative Party. Second, I served on Jean Chrétien's transition team before the 1993 election, which should make me a Liberal. However, while serving on the team, I was asked by Professor Andy Stark (a colleague and friend from the University of Toronto), who worked for then prime minister, Kim Campbell, to write a brief five-pager for her, outlining what I believed to be Canada's major challenges. He explained that they were asking, if my memory is correct, twenty-five Canadians to do the same to give the prime minister a sense of what policy prescriptions were needed. It was made clear that the exercise was non-partisan and that some high-profile Liberals had agreed to participate. I agreed, but I also informed the chair of the Chrétien transition team, because I felt that it was the right thing to do. No one ever told me directly, but I later discovered that some Liberals were less than pleased with my decision.

In addition, Preston Manning and some Conservatives took a shine to one of my books, *The Politics of Public Spending in Canada*, and they frequently quoted from it in the House of Commons debates and elsewhere, which probably led many Liberals to conclude that I must be Conservative. In addition, my book *Governing from the Centre* was interpreted in some quarters as a criticism of Chrétien's style of governing, which did not endear me to some Liberals. More will be said about this later. Stockwell Day, then leader of the opposition, referred to my work in a major address on Canadian federalism in May 2000 as being "forward looking and dynamic."[14] This alone would make some Liberals suspicious of my political allegiance.

The Graham government announced in March 2008 that it had decided to scrap the province's early French immersion in favour of a core French program, starting in grade 5. (It subsequently backtracked somewhat by making French immersion available to grade 3 students.) The media contacted me for my views, and I was highly critical of the decision. Eliminating early immersion is, in my view, a step backward in Canada's only officially bilingual province. I have seen first-hand the important contributions the province's early immersion program has made to my community. I am now served in my mother tongue by English

New Brunswickers in restaurants and stores in Moncton, something that happened very rarely, if at all, when I first moved to Moncton. That the leader of Robichaud's political party would now want to turn back the clock was both perplexing and very disappointing to me.

I decided in July 2008 to ask seventeen other New Brunswick francophones to sign a letter in support of anglophone parents who were fighting to save the province's early French immersion program. The list of signatories included Jacqueline Robichaud, widow of Louis J. Robichaud, Denis Losier, president-CEO of Assomption Life, and Bernard Cyr, a well-known Moncton entrepreneur. The media correctly identified me as "the instigator" of the letter. The reaction was swift and in some quarters partisan. A number of English-speaking parents made a point of thanking me personally, and several added that they hoped that some day they could return the favour to Acadians. I was taken aback by the level of support from English-speaking New Brunswickers. We have indeed come a long way in New Brunswick in promoting English-French relations since the days of Leonard Jones.

One well-known Liberal, however, expressed his disappointment that I had not resolved the matter inside "the family." I responded, "I know what family I am from, what family are you from?"

"The Liberal family," he replied.

"Which Liberal family?" I asked. "The Shawn Graham Liberal family or the Louis Robichaud family?" The point I was making is that it is increasingly difficult to tie political parties to overarching principles and policies. Partisans now identify with the party leader or aspiring leader all too often in the hope of reaping rewards as a lobbyist or getting a consulting contract, legal work, or the like.

I also became highly critical of the Graham government's lack of focus in pursuing a multitude of priorities without an overall and coherent strategy, and for losing sight of its most important election campaign commitment – to make every effort to put New

Brunswick on the road to economic self-sufficiency. The *Telegraph Journal* gave my comments front-page coverage, and suddenly I was a Conservative supporter, at least in the eyes of some Liberals. That said, I applaud Graham's energy and ability and his determination to sell New Brunswick as a place to invest and locate new economic activities.

Many Conservatives, meanwhile, are convinced that I am a Liberal. For instance, Greg Thompson, New Brunswick's representative in the Harper government, rose in the Commons on 26 March 2007 to say, "Donald Savoie is a nice man, I respect him at many levels, but he is a Liberal." Thompson was responding to an opposition MP who had quoted me in the House in his criticism of the Harper government's 19 March budget. I note here that I do not recall ever meeting Greg Thompson, so his belief that I am a nice man is very flattering!

Here are the facts for those who may be interested, beginning with my voting record, which I give only to make the point that political parties are fast losing relevance to me – and, I suspect, to many other Canadians. I have voted Liberal, Progressive Conservative, and NDP. (I voted NDP once, in 1972, while living in Fredericton when the party had a particularly strong local candidate.) I have been asked to serve under both Liberal and Progressive Conservative governments. I have served on three transition teams for Liberal governments. I was appointed a member of the Economic Council of Canada by the Trudeau Liberals and also by the Mulroney Conservatives. I was appointed to the steering committee of Canada's "Prosperity and Competitiveness" planning exercise by the Mulroney Conservatives, and I was appointed to the board of directors of the Canada School of Public Service by the Chrétien Liberals.

I have voted Liberal more often than Conservative. I have written only one book on the McKenna years, strictly from an economic development perspective – not "books," as Lord charged. The book was largely positive because McKenna pursued economic development with a missionary zeal and met with success.

I also readily and happily acknowledge that I consider Frank McKenna to be a good friend. I firmly believe that he had all the attributes of a strong leader and was able to inspire New Brunswickers to exploit their potential better. I also readily and happily acknowledge that I was very close to Roméo LeBlanc, a senior Trudeau minister, who later became Canada's governor general, and that we worked very well together over the years.

I voted for Richard Hatfield's Conservatives when Douglas Young was leader of New Brunswick's Liberal Party. Hatfield connected with me, as he did with many other Acadians, and made the Progressive Conservative Party more than acceptable to us. He did this by protecting the Robichaud legacy and by his genuine interest in Acadian communities. It will be recalled that he supported Trudeau's efforts to bring the Canadian constitution home and to add the Charter of Rights and Freedoms to it. He promoted bilingualism and Acadian cultures not just in New Brunswick but in other parts of Canada too. Robichaud told me on a number of occasions that Hatfield showed great courage when he stood up to the pressure from his essentially English-speaking cabinet and caucus when they wanted to turn back the clock and tear down the Robichaud reforms.

I voted for Brian Mulroney during the 1988 free trade election. I believed then, as I do now, that free trade was good for both my region and my country. I have never voted for Bernard Lord, not because I am a partisan Liberal but because I did not think that he pursued economic development for my province with the kind of commitment and energy that was required. My strong friendships with Louis Robichaud, Roméo LeBlanc, and Frank McKenna do not make me a Liberal. There are many Liberals with whom I would not want to be associated, nor would I vote Liberal if one of them were to lead the party.

That said, I strongly believe that political parties should be key instruments to a well-functioning democracy. I also believe that we should all be concerned with the dramatic drop in memberships in political parties everywhere in Western democracies. I am very reluctant, however, to ally myself firmly with one political party. Party leaders matter to me far more than their parties in shaping policies and in directing government if elected to power. Party platforms are now put together by party leaders and a handful of advisers, not by the rank-and-file members of the party. In short, today, party leaders matter a great deal and political parties far less so. As a result, political parties are now defined by their leaders, with the parties taking on their leaders' personalities, not the other way round. It should come as no surprise to anyone, then, that when a party leader is able to secure a majority mandate, the party is in his or her debt, not the other way round.

In my view, political parties in Canada and in many Anglo-American democracies have lost their soul. Gaining power is all that matters. The people who count are the pollsters, the lobbyists turned political advisers during election campaigns, the communications specialists, and a handful of advisers around the party leaders. There is a big payoff for all of them if their "horse" wins the race, and their sole purpose is to spin the right image to make this happen.

Political parties are today little more than election-day organizations. They stand for very little other than winning power. They have no defining principles and no sense of history or of what the party has stood for over the years. How else can one explain Graham's provincial Liberal Party doing away with New Brunswick's early immersion program or Harper's federal Conservative Party blocking the purchase of MacDonald, Dettwiler and Associates by an American investor? It is not possible for me, and I suspect many Canadians, to be loyal to a political party when they themselves have no loyalty to anything other than winning power.

Louis Robichaud was a partisan Liberal – let there be no doubt about that. He became a Liberal because the party best represented his own views and his progressive thinking. Moreover, he was motivated not by power but by a profound desire to change New Brunswick. As I have already noted, he often pointed to the Université de Moncton as his most important and proudest accomplishment. He often asked what its 25,000 graduates would be doing today if it were not for the university. And indeed, the Université de Moncton did create many economic and employment opportunities for its graduates. But it has done much more than that, as Robichaud realized it would. The next chapter explores what and how.

4

Université de Moncton: All Hell Breaks Loose

In my first week at the Université de Moncton, I met Bernard Imbeault, a fellow student from Quebec. Bernard is a soft-spoken man, unpretentious, and in the parlance of the Maritime provinces, "one hell of a nice guy." I had not until then met many Québécois, and I was fascinated by what he had to say and how he said it. The words he used were mostly – though not always – the same we used, but his accent was quite different. And there was another difference, one that shocked me. Bernard was an atheist! How could such a nice and smart guy possibly be an atheist? I went home that evening to tell my mother that I had met a real atheist. She advised me to help him. So I bought a case of beer and went back to convert him to Roman Catholicism. I have no idea if I had much of an impact. I suspect not. However, later in life, Bernard began to attend church regularly, while I fell out of the habit. I was soon to discover that the university was home not just to atheists but also to Marxists-Leninists, communists, and students who favoured Quebec leaving Canada. Saint-Maurice, the Collège l'Assomption, and Moncton had not prepared me for this.

The Université de Moncton blew fresh air, new ideas, and an independence of spirit that transformed the city. It brought new people to the community, young people who had no knowledge of Moncton's history or of English-French relations over the years. They were at a point in their lives when they were free to voice radical ideas and to challenge authority with little consequence. They were francophones from northern New Brunswick as well as from Quebec and France. In many instances, they had had little contact with anglophones. Many of them could barely speak English, if any at all. Added to all of this was the fact that we were smack in the 1960s, the decade that gave us Vietnam and student unrest throughout the Western world. The decade also gave Louis J. Robichaud to New Brunswick and the Royal Commission on Bilingualism and Biculturalism to Canada. In addition, there was CBC Radio/Radio-Canada, which had introduced French-language radio service in 1954 and extended French-language television service to Moncton in 1959. This gave the community another fresh voice, one that was largely indifferent to past grievances between English- and French-speaking Monctonians.

These developments came face to face with a society that was not well prepared for change – all in all, the making of a powerful brew. Hugh Thorburn, in his 1961 book *Politics in New Brunswick*, described an Acadian community that was timid and hesitant to press for more language rights:

> The Acadians are hesitant about asserting themselves for they are a simple and honest rural people who lack the leaders who normally come from such urban professions as law, medicine and business. They want above all to be left alone to live their lives as they wish. They are conscious of the superior power of their English-speaking neighbours and wish to take no action that might provoke them to retaliation. The history of the Acadian race is the history of helpless people, buffeted about by superior forces and somehow surviving by a non-violent acquiescence that meant no spirit of aggression, rather an element of humility, if not timidity.[1]

The age of humility and timidity was about to come to a crashing end, and the Université de Moncton was front and centre in this turn of events.

BUILDING THE UNIVERSITY

In June 1963, Louis Robichaud and Clément Cormier had got what they wanted – a university for the province's francophone community. But the hard part was about to begin. The new university had few resources to draw on and no private sector to turn to for a helping hand. The one asset it did have was Saint-Joseph College, operated by the Holy Cross fathers, of which Cormier was a member. Saint-Joseph was essentially a combined high school and classical college. It had operated near or in Moncton for about a hundred years. The religious community also had land, a 32-hectare site in Moncton's north end. Antonine Maillet tells me that Monsignor Norbert Robichaud decided to buy the land "because the English did not want it. It was part marshland, part hill, with no agricultural or commercial value." The archbishop is reported to have said at the time of the purchase, "Some day the land will be important for Acadians. This is where we will build our educational institutions." History would prove him right.

Saint-Joseph College, under the leadership of Cormier, transferred assets totalling $1.8 million to the new university, assets that included the 32-hectare site along with books, periodicals, and equipment. Cormier became the university's first *recteur* (president). Despite its limited resources, the university began an ambitious construction program, which took place in two phases, beginning in 1963 and ending in 1968.[2] During the first phase, four major buildings were constructed at a cost of $5,075,000: a library, a science building, an arena, and a gymnasium. The second phase, from 1965 to 1968, saw the construction of seven major buildings at a cost of $4,255,000.

The university's Board of Regents envisaged three major revenue sources to finance the capital construction program. Out of the total cost of $9,330,000, the federal government would provide $745,000 and the provincial government another $1,330,000. It was agreed that the remaining $7,255,000 would be financed through a fundraising campaign. Thus the board was assured of only 20 percent of the total cost of the capital construction program. The remaining 80 percent was to be financed by a fundraising campaign that had yet to be launched, let alone discussed at any great length.

If the financial estimates for the capital construction program appeared optimistic, the university's operations budget was also cause for concern. The operating budget for fiscal year 1964–65 provided for a deficit exceeding $90,000. The problem was that the university had little in the way of assets or financial reserves to deal with a deficit. So it simply put off the problem to another day.

The newly constituted Senate asked for an inventory of the professors at the university during the spring of 1963. The review revealed that the bulk of the faculty were Holy Cross fathers. The faculty consisted of twenty-seven professors, only one of whom had a PH D. There were fourteen MAs and the remaining twelve had only a BA or the equivalent.

The university intended to begin its first fundraising campaign in 1964, but delayed it by a year after learning that the University of New Brunswick was initiating a similar campaign of its own. The campaign was officially launched on 12 September 1965, with a $5,000,000 target to be reached within three years. It was chaired by Jules Brillant, a well-known businessman from Quebec. The campaign soon secured four substantial gifts: Jules Brillant, $150,000; Paul Desmarais, $100,000; Jean-Louis Lévesque, $500,000; and K.C. Irving, $500,000.

The campaign never came close to its objective, however. After three years, it had reached only $3,000,000. The capital construction program also hit a snag, which could not have come at a worse time, given its failure to raise the $5,000,000. The foundations of the new arena had to be constructed twice, at an added expenditure of $350,000. The arena was built on a part of the campus that is marshland. The first foundation began to sink into the ground, and the base had to be strengthened before construction could continue.

The university's financial situation was simply untenable, and at one point the bank served notice that it could not honour the university's payroll. The situation was such that senior administrators even started asking themselves if a university could actually go bankrupt. Médard Collette, the university's vice-president of finance, told me that immediately after the bank called him with the bad news, he went to see Cormier and found the president "in his office, kneeling before a crucifix, praying for help." Collette told Cormier, "That won't hurt, but we also need to do something else." They contacted Judge Adrien Cormier, a close friend of both Robichaud and the Montreal financier Jean-Louis Lévesque, who was originally from Gaspé. Judge Cormier in turn contacted Lévesque, who told him to go to the Moncton airport with Cormier and Collette and take the first flight to Montreal. Lévesque arranged to have the plane tickets waiting for them at the airport. At the meeting, Lévesque called the bank with instructions to honour the payroll, saying that he would cover it. He also told the bank executives never again to hold back the university's payroll without first talking to him. A financial crisis had been averted, but the university's future was anything but certain.

THERE IS TROUBLE BREWING

While the university was trying to cope as best it could with its limited financial resources, student enrolment doubled between 1963 and 1966, as did the number of professors. The university had by then become less and less dependent on the Holy Cross Order for its teaching staff. While members of the Holy Cross had represented over 40 percent of all teachers at the university in 1963, the proportion of members of the order to laymen was less than 20 percent by 1966.

Most of the new professors came from outside the province, mainly from Quebec and France. Among the twelve professors in Social Sciences, for example, six were from France and two were from Quebec. The other four were from New Brunswick and Nova Scotia and had done postgraduate work in either France or Quebec. At the risk of stating the obvious, the French faculty members had no experience of living as a minority, nor had they much knowledge of Acadian history.

When Charles de Gaulle famously proclaimed from a balcony at Montreal City Hall, "Vive le Québec libre!" – a rallying cry for Quebec separatists – Prime Minister Lester Pearson made it clear to the French president that his words were not acceptable to Canada, and de Gaulle returned to France without visiting Ottawa. But that was hardly the end of it. De Gaulle later invited four Acadian leaders to Paris to discuss how France could help Acadian institutions. One of the four was Adélard Savoie, newly appointed president of the Université de Moncton, who returned to Moncton with a firm commitment from de Gaulle to support the young university, including providing financial grants, scholarships, and still more professors from France. Another Acadian on the trip was Gilbert Finn, who later became president of the university. He reported from Paris, "The anglicization of New Brunswick is ended."

President Adélard Savoie, who was Robichaud's brother-in-law, got more from de Gaulle than he had bargained for. With the professors from France came dissatisfaction with the status quo and the will to challenge authority. Protests in one form or another became a regular occurrence on campus in the late 1960s. There were protests against members of the Acadian elite (including Robichaud and Savoie), against the provincial government for not providing sufficient financial support to the university, and against the City of Moncton for not providing bilingual services. Nothing was sacred any more. Even the Acadian flag was lowered on one of the university's buildings and replaced by the communist hammer and sickle.

Students took dead aim at the Acadian elite, claiming its members were self-serving and unwilling or incapable of standing up for their people. The main target was the Ordre de Jacques-Cartier (better known as La Patente), a secret society founded by Calixte Savoie and others of his generation to counter the influence of the Orange Order. The idea of La Patente was to establish a fraternal organization that would identify employment opportunities for Acadians. Robichaud had been a member but had resigned when he was elected premier. The students insisted that nothing should be decided in secret any more and that the time had come for l'Acadie to come of age and confront all situations and all groups, including the English-speaking majority, head-on and in full public view.

Monctonians, including Acadians, were hardly prepared for these protests. I recall attending a student demonstration on campus when one student with a clearly French accent addressed the gathering, stating, "We are all saying the same thing to one another here and we all agree. We need to do something different to let people know that we are serious. I suggest that some of us go downtown and blow up the CNR building on Main Street." We Moncton students could not figure out if he was serious or not, but none of us were prepared to volunteer!

Things came to a head on campus on 7 February 1968 when President Savoie announced plans to increase tuition fees in view of the university's ongoing financial problems. He explained that the university had applied to the government for extra funds, but the premier had told him that there was a funding formula that applied to all provincial universities by which they had to live within their means, no exceptions.

The student council called a general strike to promote awareness of the university's difficult financial position. All roads leading to the campus were blocked. Later, a number of students occupied the science building in an attempt to force the administration to secure more funds from the federal government. Later still, student leaders organized a march on Fredericton to press the provincial government for more funding. A delegation of four students met with the premier, also to no avail. Some of the students felt that Robichaud was turning his back on Acadians and their university. Robichaud, meanwhile, was walking a tightrope. There was a limit to how far he could push the anglophone majority. As it was, there were growing signs of a backlash and an unease in the province over developments on the Moncton campus. As one can imagine, the appetite to provide more generous funding to a French-language university that had recently flown a communist flag on one of its buildings was not very strong.

Without any prior warning, approximately 125 students marched into the science building on Saturday evening, 11 January 1969. They ordered the night watchman out and locked all the doors. Working in crews of twenty-five, students manned the doors with fire hoses, allowing no one but a few fellow students to enter. The following day, President Savoie stated, "The situation is very serious and it paralyzes everything on campus. Those persons responsible for the occupation will have to answer for their actions." Classes were postponed until further notice.

A student spokesman issued a statement early on Monday morning, announcing, "We want 32 million dollars aid from the government for the University of Moncton. The university received only one million dollars during its first year and we'll get only two million in the next two years, while the University of New Brunswick received in the neighbourhood of 22 million dollars last year alone." He added that it costs more to build a new university than to operate one that has been established for years. The figures were hardly accurate, but that did not matter to the students. They were occupying the science building to make the point that the Université de Moncton urgently needed a "catch-up" budget, and they had to get involved because the Acadian elite was not assuming its responsibility.

Michel Blanchard, one of the main leaders of the student demonstration, added that they would not leave the science building until the government committed the university to a catching-up grant of $32 million. He said that the students had enough food for three weeks, and more was available if needed, as well as a plentiful supply of sleeping bags, mattresses, and other necessities.

President Adélard Savoie had had enough. He was getting pressure from the provincial government and from Moncton residents to bring the crisis to an end. A week into the occupation, he asked the Moncton City Police and the local detachment of the Royal Canadian Mounted Police to eject the students from the science building. The police chief and the university's head of security entered the building and met with Blanchard and Rodrigue Fergusson, the other main leader of the occupation. The students were told that they had one hour to leave. After some negotiations over possible criminal charges, Blanchard led the occupants out of the science building, singing "Ce n'est qu'un au revoir."

The student leaders were mostly from northern New Brunswick and Quebec. Blanchard, a fiery orator, was from Caraquet, the son of Mathilda Blanchard, a labour union leader. The students involved in the occupation and in other major protests proudly called themselves the "new left." There were precious few Acadians from Moncton involved, either in the various protests or in the occupation.

The new left was busy planning yet another protest. While the student occupation was in full swing, a group of students were organizing a demonstration in front of Moncton City Hall to demand early implementation of the Laurendeau-Dunton Report on bilingualism and biculturalism. Fearing that the march would be met with outright opposition from the community, the president of the student council asked the leaders of the demonstration to cancel it, which led to a split among the students. "Recommendations on bilingualism and biculturalism have been made," he said. "Accordingly, there is no need for a demonstration at this time." Moreover, he argued that "it might detract from the prime concern of the student council to focus attention on the problems facing both university and students on the financing of higher education." But the leaders of the new left were not to be deterred.

University President Savoie, meanwhile, called a meeting with the organizers of the march on the day the demonstration was to take place. He asked them to call it off, arguing that there was already a great deal of friction between the two ethnic groups in the city and the march could only have a negative effect for the university. The march organizers disagreed with the president, but they accepted his suggestion that he select the spokesperson who would make the presentation. He feared that the students would choose Blanchard or someone else from either northern New Brunswick or Quebec to lead the delegation to meet Mayor Leonard Jones, who was widely known to be strongly against bilingualism, if not anti-French. The president was concerned that the mayor would dismiss out of hand any spokesperson who did not have parents living and paying taxes in Moncton, which in turn would only make things worst.

The president asked a Moncton resident, my brother Claude, a graduate student in psychology, to lead the march and meet Leonard Jones and his council. Claude was president of the university's association of graduate students, and our father was a local businessman paying taxes in Moncton. Both President Savoie and Claude agreed that it was important to remain calm, professional, and not to provoke any outbursts from either the students or the mayor.

Approximately 1,000 to 1,500 students took part in the march. The media reported that "the parade to City Hall was noisy but orderly and there were no incidents." The *Moncton Times*, however, added, "A group of men gathered on a street corner near City Hall and greeted the marchers with a chorus of catcalls. Nevertheless, a task force of 40 uniformed Moncton City Police, City Firemen, and plain clothes members of the Royal Canadian Mounted Police were stationed at City Hall in the event of trouble."

Once inside City Hall, the students met a cold and aggressive city council. Councillor A.L. Galbraith immediately called for the council to reaffirm its oath of allegiance to the monarchy. Mayor

Jones refused to hear the delegation in French because his council could only understand English. He then offered the students "some fatherly advice," suggesting that "they could accomplish more for the community if they would return to their classes and their studies."

Making due provision for brotherly love and for an obvious bias, I believe to this day that Claude performed remarkably well and showed more class than the mayor. I also remain convinced that in the end Claude won the day. He took the catcalls from those inside the council chambers ("Go home frogs" and "Speak white") as he walked into City Hall with dignity. The exchange he had with the council is captured on the film *L'Acadie, l'Acadie*, and you are invited to see it and judge for yourself. Claude was polite, to the point, and when told by the mayor to speak English, he switched languages with no fuss. He remained calm and respectful throughout his presentation and as he left the council chambers. It was a highly explosive situation, and one false move could have led to violence.

The next day, Claude and his delegation met the local press to share their impression of the meeting. Claude said, "It was certainly not a meeting of which Moncton citizens could be proud; it was not conducive to the dialogue which we had hoped to establish." Members of the delegation also expressed regret that the mayor had not allowed them permission to speak in their native tongue, and they charged that he had acted like an "aggressive crown prosecutor seeking a conviction."

The reaction of the delegation sparked anger among the students towards Mayor Jones. Students from northern New Brunswick and Quebec had seen enough, and they were looking for opportunities to express their frustration. The mayor was scheduled to drop the first puck, opening a hockey series between two local hockey clubs at the Jean-Louis Lévesque Arena on the Moncton campus that evening. A few minutes before game time, some 150 students walked into the arena without paying while about twelve policemen stood by without intervening. The students marched in file around the arena singing "O Canada," in French. The mayor was apparently rushed into a waiting police cruiser and escorted off the campus.

After learning that the mayor would not be present at the arena, two students from Quebec placed a pig's head in a large cardboard box with a card saying, "This is a gift from me to you," and signed it Jacques Belisle and Jacques Moreaux. The two marched directly to the mayor's house, backed by about fifty to seventy other students, and presented the gift to the mayor. They were immediately arrested and charged.

The next day the university was expecting the worst. The administration decided to have a few students standing by to answer telephone calls from the English-speaking community. Again, they were to be students from the Moncton area. I was one of them. I have never, before or since, been subjected to such venom. I heard most of the swear words ever invented in the English language, and I was told in no uncertain terms to go back to France. One irritated caller said, "Go back home, you goddam frog."

"Where is home?" I asked.

"France, you stupid frog."

It had been a long, long time since my ancestors left France for l'Acadie and I couldn't begin to imagine France as home. I bit my tongue more than once, knowing that provoking a debate with the callers would only make matters worse. Tension between university students and English Monctonians ran high, and any provocation could have easily tipped the balance.

Things started to calm down as end-of-year exams drew closer. Towards the end of the academic year, the university decided not to renew the contracts of four sociology professors from France on the grounds of academic incompetence. Many suspected, however, that the real reason was their far-left views. During the following summer months, the university told several students that they would not be readmitted. These students had all been directly involved in the student occupation.

LEONARD JONES

Leonard Jones had first been elected in 1963 and continued as mayor of Moncton for another eleven years. He won the Progressive Conservative nomination for the 1974 federal election, but party leader Robert Stanfield refused to sign his nomination papers because of Jones's opposition to the party's policy on bilingualism. Jones decided to run as an independent and won the constituency against the Liberals, the NDP, and the incumbent MP, who was the Conservative candidate. He was able to secure 46 percent of the popular vote. The message was not lost on Acadians – their presence and their fight for language rights were pressing against the wishes of the majority. Jones decided not to run in the 1979 general election. He was later charged with tax evasion and resigned from the Moncton Rotary Club in protest after the club decided to accept women as members.

Ironically, Leonard Jones ended up as one of the most powerful forces pushing Acadians to pursue language rights. His belligerent attitude towards the Université de Moncton students and his unwillingness to accommodate anything that resembled giving in to bilingualism (even a bilingual plaque on City Hall) led many Acadians who in the past had been reluctant to seek equality, at least in Moncton, to conclude that the time had come. Enough was enough.

There were not many Acadians from Moncton directly involved in the student demonstrations, but as we stood by watching events unfold, we understood what the students from away were trying to accomplish, though we may not always have agreed with the means. By the late 1960s, a few businesses in Moncton began to advertise in both English and French. A number of students who had come to study at the university decided to stay. Many started new businesses, including Bernard Imbeault, the Quebec "atheist." He never left Moncton and became a highly successful entrepreneur in the restaurant business (Pizza Delight and Mike's restaurants).

At about the time Jones was elected to Parliament, a group of young Acadians got together to establish the Parti acadien. The party knew what it was against: the politics of accommodation with the English majority, Maritime union, capitalism, and the traditional ideology of the Acadian elite. It envisaged an Acadian province so that Acadians would enter Confederation as a distinct people. The party never won a seat in the legislative assembly and was formally disbanded in 1986. However, one can speculate that Jones was a factor motivating young Acadians to come together to create a nationalist party.

Leonard Jones, reflecting on his years in politics, had no doubt who was responsible for the rise of English-French tensions in Moncton – the Université de Moncton. It is worth quoting at length from a speech he gave to the Alliance for the Preservation of English in Canada on 20 November 1978: "Back in the early sixties, peace, harmony and good will existed among the English and French persons in the City of Moncton of which I was then Mayor. We had all grown up together, gone to the same schools, the same boy scouts, or whatever the case may be. And this is not political jargon. But things changed in the City of Moncton with the setting up of a *University* there." He argued that English Monctonians had contributed funds to the university but the university was not open for persons of English-speaking origin. This, of course, has never been true – there have been and continue to be many English Canadians who attend the university. The language of instruction, however, is French, much as the language of instruction at the University of New Brunswick, Mount Allison, and Saint Thomas universities is English. Jones also claimed that "persons from the Moncton area were being turned down over and above the Québécois." This too is completely false. He never explained how he arrived at this conclusion. It may well be that he heard it on the streets of Moncton and decided that it must be fact.

Certainly, the Université de Moncton has had a profound effect on l'Acadie, Moncton, and New Brunswick. It gave Acadians a sense of identity, an institution through which to articulate their aspirations, and the self-confidence to chart a new course. It opened up Acadian society to new ideas, put pressure on public institutions to accommodate increasingly persistent demands for services in both official languages, and produced university graduates precisely at a time when the two senior orders of government were looking for qualified bilingual employees.

The university also generated impatience among the Acadian population. A new generation of Acadians considered that their political elite, the wheels of justice, and the operations of government were moving far too slowly. Some Acadians did not hesitate to hurl criticism at their own, including Louis Robichaud and his government. In hindsight, one can appreciate that it must have been somewhat unnerving for Leonard Jones and his generation to see the Acadian community transform in ten short years from a timid people to one willing to say that henceforth we will be taking more space in the community because we intend to take our rightful place in society. No wonder Louis Robichaud so often singled out the establishment of the Université de Moncton as his proudest accomplishment!

A NEW ACADIE

By the 1970s, the Acadie that I grew up in was no more. It was a new Acadie, more secular, more confident, and more ambitious. The impact of Leonard Jones and his supporters, if anything else had served to strengthen the resolve of many Acadians to rally behind the new Acadie. The balance of power between the two languages in Moncton and New Brunswick was changing. Jones could voice the same opinion as the senior Department of Education official did some forty years earlier to explain to ministers why Acadians should not be awarded their own schools. The opinion had mattered in 1930, but it mattered much less by 1970. The Department of Education official had been talking from a position of strength; Jones much less so.

I saw first-hand the Acadian community in Moncton come of age. However, Leonard Jones was right about one thing: the impetus for change came from students from away, not from Moncton Acadians. The great majority of the student leaders in the occupation of the science building, in organizing the student strike, and in planning the march on City Hall were from northern New Brunswick and Quebec. Although Claude Savoie led the delegation to meet the mayor and council, it was only after the president of the university had intervened to appoint him to the task.

It was also students from away who challenged the provincial court system to hear their cases in French after the province's Official Languages Act had been proclaimed into law. Michel Blanchard from northern New Brunswick, the leader of the student protest, gained considerable attention when he demanded that his trial be conducted in French, knowing full well that the province's judiciary was not up to the task. He persisted in asking whether the province's Official Languages Act had any teeth or whether it was just symbolic. He wanted to know whether being tried in French was a right or only a privilege. His position resonated with many Acadians and, in time, with the courts.

Moncton Acadians, however, were not prepared to challenge the status quo to the same extent. Denis Gautreau, from Pré-d'en-Haut, a small village near Moncton, was charged in the 1960s with impaired driving. He went to court on the appointed day and waited his turn without legal counsel. Finally, the judge called out, "Denis Gautreau versus the Queen." Denis bolted up from his chair and told the judge, "I have nothing against the Queen, me, she's all right. I am not versing (sic) the Queen. I only drank a bit too much. That's all." The last thing on Denis's mind was to ask the court to hear the case in French. He simply wanted to get out of there with a minimum of damages and costs. The court erupted in laughter, but Denis was making the point that he did not want to challenge the English-speaking majority. Back in Pré-d'en-Haut, he told his friends, "Hey, I was in enough trouble that I didn't want to start a fight with the Queen. God, the English would have put me in jail and thrown away the key."

I have often reflected on why it was students from away who took matters in hand. We Moncton Acadians lived at home while going to university rather than in a residence or an apartment, which probably made us less radical. We had to account to our parents at home in the evenings or at weekends, and few of them would have approved their sons or daughters spending time occupying the science building.

There were, I believe, other important reasons. We Acadians had been conditioned to accept our state in society and see the English-speaking majority as being on top. One long-serving teacher of second languages in the federal public service told me that the most difficult cases he has had to deal with are mature English-speaking Monctonians. He insists that there is a psychological block that inhibits their ability to learn French. We should not forget that Leonard Jones was elected and re-elected as mayor and then as an MP because a substantial majority of English Monctonians voted for him.

We had learned not to poke the big bear. Calixte Savoie's letter telling Acadians to ask to be served in French in stores in Moncton had a profound and lasting impact. That the initiative backfired with Acadians actually losing their jobs because of it was a lesson in itself. Acadians in Moncton in the 1930s, 1940s, and 1950s wanted little more than a job to put food on the table for what was, more often than not, a large family. That said, Acadians survived in Moncton and built their own institutions, including churches, because they had a strong desire to survive. "Leave well alone" was the best approach as far as most Moncton Acadians were concerned. Progress would be made, they believed, and more could be achieved by moving slowly and not upsetting the apple cart. Robichaud's election to power held promise, and it was best to let him take the lead.

Québécois and Acadians from northern New Brunswick, meanwhile, had had a vastly different conditioning. They would not hesitate to poke the bear, and what they saw in Moncton gave them every reason to poke it and poke it hard. I recall tensions between Moncton-based students and students from away. We knew that after we completed our studies, some of us would remain in Moncton while those from away would go home or elsewhere. In short, poking the bear would make him grumpy, and we would be the ones who would have to live with the grumpy bear. We knew, however, that relations between the English-speaking majority and Acadians in Moncton would never be the same. Part of us would be thankful for the actions of the students from away, but part of us worried about long-term implications. We were to discover that the benefits would far outweigh the drawbacks.

On a more personal note, I have very fond memories of my university days at the Université de Moncton. It was an eye-opener on many fronts: new ideas, professors from France, Quebec, and elsewhere showing me how to look at problems or issues from different perspectives. And unlike at the Collège l'Assomption, I had the freedom to watch a movie downtown or go to the tavern with friends.

Claudius Léger, a judge and part-time lecturer at the university, was from the old school – he held a roll call at the start of all his lectures. Victor Landry, a close friend to this day, and I decided that we wanted to see a movie, *North to Alaska*, which coincided with Léger's lecture. We came up with a plan: Shortly after roll call, Victor would say that he was feeling ill, and I would come to his assistance and help him out of the classroom. Then we would be off to the movies. But to my surprise, Victor stood up shortly after roll call and said, "I think that I am going to faint" and then fell flat on the floor. This was not in the plan, and the onus was on me to do something. I got up and said that I would take good care of my friend and then hauled him out of the classroom. On our way to the movie, I said, "Victor, a bit dramatic, wasn't it?" People who know Victor know well his mischievous smile and his sense of humour.

Leonard Jones was wrong about local students not being admitted to the Université de Moncton. There was no screening. If you were able to squeeze through high school or the Collège l'Assomption, you were in. Once in, some students turned to various means to try to get through university. I recall taking a course, Financial Mathematics, and doing fine. The textbook was in English, so I got into the habit of adding and underlining "ans" (short for "answer") after all my answers in essays and exams. In one exam, a Moncton friend, who never burdened himself with work while at university, sat next to me and decided to copy my answers. I was aware of this but decided to do nothing. However, in order to make his answers look different from mine, he decided to translate "ans" as years (*ans*), not realizing that I meant it to be short for "answer." The problem was that none of the questions had anything to do with years or a timeframe of any kind. One of my answers was wrong, so my friend's was too. The professor asked to see both of us for an explanation. My friend came clean and took full responsibility. The professor insisted, however, that I could have prevented the situation by being more careful in protecting my answers from his wandering eyes.

The following year, another professor announced that his Christmas exam would consist of forty true or false questions. Some of the Moncton-area students came up with what they believed to be a foolproof plan to do well. They asked Victor Landry, who had mastered this subject and quite a few others, to sit at the front of the class at exam time. The plan was for Victor to rub his left ear for the answer "true," the right ear for "false," and to go down the list until he had answered all forty questions. At that point, he was to rub both ears to signal that the exam was completed. Given my experience the year before, I decided to sit far from Victor at the back of the classroom on the opposite side. However, I watched the exam unfold with a great deal of interest. Whenever Victor rubbed one of his ears, something like ten to twelve heads behind him went down in sync. All went well. At the end, I saw Victor rub both his ears. Then I heard a voice, fairly loud and clear: "Shit, Victor, I only have thirty-four answers!"

As already noted, the great majority of the Moncton students stood on the sidelines as students from away decided to turn the status quo on its head. I was no different. I was not directly involved in student unrest other than agreeing to answer the telephone the day after the pig's head incident. I write with some regret that my university days were there to be enjoyed, for me to taste to the full my new-found freedom and to soak in fresh and provocative ideas from professors from Quebec and elsewhere and from my fellow students from away.

In the summer I worked for my father's construction company, at least for a while. Construction work is not easy, but it is particularly difficult when you wake up with a serious hangover. My father often (though not always, thank God) dropped me off at one of the job sites in the morning. I doubt that he ever believed in sleeping in, even in his youth. "Rise and shine and off to work" was his motto. On that difficult morning, he decided that I would work on a school construction project in Saint-Norbert, a small Acadian community some thirty kilometres from Moncton. The "roll out" call came at 6:30 AM and we were off by 7:00 AM. I don't think that my father was ever late for anything in his life. On the drive to the project, I said nothing, simply nodding yes or no and trying to catch a few minutes of sleep.

I knew that once there, life would be much easier. Gérard à Johnny, from Saint-Maurice, was the project manager. Gérard was highly competent and was sought after by other construction firms. He was one of my father's top foremen. He was also friendly, always had a smile and was always relaxed.

My father dropped me off, put me to work, and had a quick word with Gérard à Johnny before he left for another job site. As soon as he left, I explained the situation to Gérard and said, "Look, I need an hour's sleep and I will be able to work twice as hard afterwards." He understood. So I folded my jacket into a pillow, found a good-sized closet, and prepared myself for a good sleep. Unfortunately, my father returned after only a few minutes. Noticing that I was nowhere to be seen, he asked for me. Gérard tried his best to protect me, suggesting that I had probably gone outside to get something. My father would have none of that. He caught me sleeping in the closet and fired me on the spot. He was not about to give me a free ride in front of other employees, and he was right. The drive back to Moncton was the longest, most painful thirty-five minutes I have ever experienced before or since.

The only thing that he said, as we approached Moncton, was, "We will have to find you another job in Moncton. You have to work." I was put to work at Sumner's, a local construction hardware store.

In short, my Université de Moncton student days were hardly my summer of discontent. They were not by any measure my most serious years. I recall Aurèle Thériault coming to me one day to see if I would be interested in leading a party of three or four students who were going to Ottawa to attend a meeting of the Progressive Conservative Students' Association. Aurèle, a classmate and a good friend, is the son of Norbert Thériault, who was one of Robichaud's senior cabinet ministers. "What's the catch?" I asked. "No catch," he said. He was head of the Liberal Students' Association on campus, and the Tories in Ottawa had contacted him to see if he had any counterparts on campus who might be interested in attending a policy conference.

Perhaps, just perhaps, things were less partisan back then. I suspect, however, that no one on campus was willing to identify with the Conservative Party, with Louis Robichaud in power in Fredericton.

"What do we need to do?" I asked Aurèle.

"Nothing much," he replied. "Just say that there are three or four of you willing to go to Ottawa. Some of your expenses will be paid, you will meet MPs and probably see Parliament, and you will see Ottawa." I remember leaving Moncton with three friends on a DC-9. We had a most interesting trip and we all learned a great deal. The Conservatives were warm and welcoming.

I also remember that to the extent that my three friends had an interest in politics, they were probably more Liberal than Conservative. They were certainly ill-prepared to engage in political or policy debates. We were in Ottawa to see the city and Parliament and to experience politics for the first time. Two in the group had never been outside New Brunswick and one, Donald LeBlanc, always maintained that he had more important things to worry about than politics. As luck would have it, he was asked for his views on an issue being debated at a plenary session of the conference. I looked at LeBlanc to see how he would respond, thinking, Why hadn't the chair asked me or someone else? I figured that I, or anybody but LeBlanc, would have been better at bluffing our way through the issue. LeBlanc, always the straight shooter, stood up, took a few seconds to clear his throat, then said in a confident voice, "I am a man of few words," and then promptly sat down. Others at our table looked at him, eyes wide, jaws dropping, trying to see if there was somehow, somewhere, a deep message that was being shared. One in our group probably added to the confusion when he said in a solemn voice, "Well done, LeBlanc." It took everything in me not to explode in laughter.

Donald LeBlanc later became a leader in his community. He understands better than most that roots matter, and he has given back to his community in many ways. He is largely responsible for the building of one of the best community golf courses in southeastern New Brunswick, which sits right in the middle of Memramcook.

NEW FORCES AT PLAY

In the 1960s, l'Acadie was being bombarded by new forces both from within (the Université de Moncton) and from outside (professors and students from away). But there were other no less powerful forces pushing Acadians to occupy more political and economic space.

Pierre E. Trudeau came to power in 1968 with definite views on Canada, particularly the role of French Canada in Ottawa. He fought French Canadian nationalism in Quebec to the very end, but at the same time he fought for French Canadian interests in every facet of Canadian society. French Canada, for Trudeau, was not Quebec. It was bigger than Quebec. It included St-Boniface in Manitoba, Moncton in New Brunswick, and Pointe-de-l'Église in Nova Scotia. Trudeau argued that if you limited French Canada to Quebec, you were simply asking Quebec to leave Canada at some point. René Lévesque responded by arguing that francophones outside Quebec were dead ducks, and the well-known Quebec author Yves Beauchemin maintained that we were little more than *des cadavres encore chauds* (warm bodies).

The national unity debate was born, and Acadians became the pawns of federalists and separatists in Quebec, much as they had been in 1755 between the English and French forces. The issue at play in 1755 had been clear: which power, England or France, would have the upper hand in Europe and North America? L'Acadie was caught in the middle, in the wrong place geographically (a strategic location between the English colonies in New England and New France). The same could be said in 1968. This time, the issue was which view would prevail – a united Canada or Quebec going its own way?

Once again, the battle lines were drawn. This time, however, politics, persuasion, political spin, and government spending – not guns and brute military force – were the instruments of choice. Trudeau and his advisers sought to arm francophones outside Quebec to become comrades-in-arms for the looming battle by giving them the resources to organize and articulate their demands. He believed that Acadians needed a greater capacity to stand up to the English-speaking majority and to governments, of whatever level, in order to expand their rights and their economic interests.

Federal funds started to flow our way to set up all manner of protest movements. It may be recalled that Ottawa established the Company of Young Canadians (CYC) in 1966 to generate a "radical change for the better in Canadian society."[3] CYC had a stormy first year, during which newly minted university graduates went out to organize the poor and the disadvantaged to take power over their own lives. War was declared on poverty, on past injustices, and on the oppressors. Trudeau's call for a just society resonated in l'Acadie as much as, if not more than, anywhere else. Acadians saw the evening news – Quebec navigating through the turbulent 1960s, ending with FLQ bombings and kidnappings. Federalists in Ottawa believed that what French Canada outside Quebec needed above all was radical change.

New organizations were established with federal funds with the goal of securing language and economic rights for Acadians. CRANE (Conseil régional d'aménagement du Nord-Est) and CRASE (Conseil régional d'aménagement du Sud-Est) were established, giving Acadians a forum in which to voice their views, and a degree of economic independence in New Brunswick society. It will be recalled that a high-profile Acadian pushed for language rights to the point that he lost his teaching job, but he was soon hired by the Société nationale de l'Acadie (SNA), which was receiving federal funds to operate. There was a time when Acadians volunteered their time and effort to promote the cause, but no more. Now, they are put on a public payroll to be Acadians.

From the 1960s to today, Acadians wanting to promote Acadian interests have been able to turn to the federal government. Ottawa, willingly or not, has created a fully funded parallel bureaucracy pushing and pulling governments to do more in all economic and social sectors. In brief, Ottawa has institutionalized Acadian lobby groups to push its own departments and agencies as well as provincial and municipal governments to do more, much more, to promote development in francophone communities.

LOOKING AHEAD

The 1960s have been described as the radical decade, the decade of change when the baby boomers began to make their presence felt. The decade of Camelot, the Beatles, Trudeaumania, marijuana, and student unrest. It was also the decade when the church began to lose its grip on its parishioners. Acadians experienced the full force of the decade as much as others and probably more so, because they came from farther back. Hugh Thorburn captured the essence of Acadian society at the time when he described us as a simple and honest rural people who wanted above all to be left alone and who had no wish to provoke the English-speaking majority. We looked to the Roman Catholic Church for guidance and to 1755 to anchor our beliefs, our identity, and our roots. The 1960s radically transformed this world. We would become less rural, less religious, and less simple. And we would be drawn into the national unity debate successively by Prime Ministers Trudeau, Mulroney, and Chrétien. Public funds would be sent our way to establish or strengthen our institutions and enable us to secure a stronger presence in Canadian society. While these leaders' objective may have been to promote Acadian interests, they were all hunting bigger game – keeping Quebec in the Canadian family.

Meanwhile, my university years at the Université de Moncton were coming to a close. They were the best of times. I saw, first-hand, a society being transformed and a university taking root, built from the dream of two men – Louis J. Robichaud and Father Clément Cormier. What next? The English-speaking Monctonians who told me the day after the pig's head incident to go home to France had left me completely unfazed. I had other things in mind – pursuing graduate work in political science. I decided to enrol in an MA program at the University of New Brunswick in Fredericton – the very university that had presented a brief before the Deutsch Commission to oppose the establishment of the Université de Moncton.

On the Inside Looking In

Fredericton and its university was of course vastly different from Moncton and its university. This English-speaking community was divided and uncertain about Robichaud, bilingualism, and the sudden arrival of Acadians in their midst. Robichaud's election, combined with Moncton graduates coming to work in a growing provincial public service, saw a sudden influx of francophones in a community that hitherto had largely been the preserve of English speakers. The old guard in the provincial public service looked on bilingualism as an improper idea that some unreasonable politicians had brought into Fredericton for purely political purposes, much like dropping a baby on a doorstep. The University of New Brunswick, however, was different from the city. Some professors probably felt some guilt for the way Acadians had been treated down the ages, while most wanted to show that UNB could accommodate the province's new political reality.

I have long believed that Acadians, especially those from Moncton, have an instinct for sizing up an English-speaking individual's views on francophones and bilingualism. For myself, I can sense this within hours if not minutes. I was able to test this skill on many occasions. In some instances, there was no need. I had a professor, Patrick Fitzpatrick, who exploded with rage in a seminar and once called me "an emotionally gutted Frenchman." I learned to ignore him despite his prejudices, and I am happy to report that in the end I did very well in his course.

Fitzpatrick, however, was an anomaly. All the other professors I had dealings with at the University of New Brunswick were both competent and highly professional, and I learned a great deal from them. Sydney Pobihushchy was particularly demanding, and I have fond memories of him even though he pushed me to the limit. In our first class, he announced, "There are six of you here. I am fairly certain, based on past experiences, that three of you will succeed and three will fail." I looked to my left and I saw a young lady with glasses thicker than mine. She was a new Canadian from Eastern Europe and was the image of a studious, bookworm librarian. I thought, "I have my work cut out here."

At the end of the year, I was on the receiving end of one of the best put-downs I have ever experienced. I was looking at some exam results posted on a bulletin board, and I said to a group of fellow students, "Hey, I think that I came first." Pobihushchy happened to be there as well. He turned to me without a second's hesitation and, for all to witness, shot back, "Don't let it go to your head; it will get lonely up there."

On campus, things were great. I met very interesting students and learned a great deal from them. Graduate students had their own cubicles and access to a lounge. The difference between a university with substantial resources and one with very few struck me forcibly. I had a graduate scholarship, access to a good library and to professors, some of whom had actually published some interesting and provocative papers. The University of New Brunswick was a mature university, one of the oldest in North America, while the Université de Moncton was in the middle of growing pains, at times almost forced to close its doors because of lack of money.

I met students not only from New Brunswick but from other Maritime provinces, and even other parts of Canada, doing graduate work in various disciplines. We engaged in fascinating debates about anything and everything. Many wanted to know more about Acadians and Acadian history. I began to see English Canada in a new light. We talked openly and often about Louis Robichaud, Pierre Trudeau, and bilingualism. Often we agreed, but sometimes we did not. For me, things were no longer black or white; they began to take on shades of grey. I also learned to appreciate research, to enjoy a good library, and how to hunt for information from the archives and Statistics Canada. In addition, Pobihushchy, in particular, taught me how to think outside the box, how to challenge conventional wisdom, and how to marshal arguments.

University administrators were not what I had expected, in that they actually wanted to be supportive of francophone students. For example, I was told that I could write all my term papers and exams in French. I declined the invitation but certainly appreciated the gesture. I never had any difficulty getting to see university administrators, including the dean of graduate students, even at short notice.

I did very well in my courses: my MA thesis was about student unrest on university campuses in the 1960s, with an emphasis on the Université de Moncton. I hoped to go on to a doctorate, but after completing my master's thesis I decided that I first wanted some practical experience in government.

GOING TO OTTAWA

In the early 1970s the federal government held a series of competitions on university campuses to staff its new administrative trainee program. I applied and won a spot. Once admitted to the program, one could shop around to see which department had most appeal. Provided the department agreed, one was in business. I got lucky. I signed on to the Department of Communications as the administrative assistant to Allan Gotlieb, the deputy minister. The word in Ottawa was that Gotlieb had been promoted prematurely by his friend Trudeau and that he had not spent sufficient time learning the ropes on the way up. The point here was that if I were to learn as much as I should early in my career, I should have sought out a well-seasoned public servant.

To be sure, Gotlieb was young to be in the deputy ministers' club (appointed when he was forty), but I was hardly in a position to assess whether he was up to the challenge. History would prove the doubters wrong: he was up to it and then some. As is well known, he went on to a very distinguished career in External Affairs, including a stint in Washington as Canada's ambassador to the United States during the Reagan years.

I thoroughly enjoyed working with Gotlieb. He was patient with me and often made time available to meet with me. When I asked him if I could be involved in substantial policy issues, he cleared the way. I was asked to write a paper on Canada's participation in the space program. He took the paper seriously and circulated it to senior departmental officials for comment. I also recall that he had to deal with a most difficult situation with one of the department's senior officials who had a Quebec-only perspective. Members of the department had every reason to believe that he was a closet separatist, and history proved them right.

Over the years, I have been short-listed for the Donner book prize on three occasions. Gotlieb is chair of the Donner Foundation but not, I hasten to add, a member of the book jury committee. I attended the 2007 event (for my *Visiting Grandchildren*), and Gotlieb said some very kind things to the gathering about our work together and my contribution to the Canadian public policy and public administration literature. We had a private chat, reminiscing about our time together in the Department of Communications.

A CALL TO COME HOME

On 27 October 1970, Acadians woke up to the realization that Louis J. Robichaud would no longer be sitting in the premier's chair. Historians now report that an "English backlash" was one factor explaining Robichaud's defeat.[1] Robichaud himself had this to say about it: "I'd been there for ten years. A change was inevitable. I'd done too much for the Acadians and the English wanted a break."[2] Acadians had continued to stand by Robichaud, with only Edmundston, in the northwest of the province, going to the Progressive Conservatives' Richard Hatfield. The vote was lost when one of Robichaud's cabinet ministers from the community was convicted for tax evasion.

Acadians were uncertain about what to expect next and wondered what form the "English backlash" might take. In time, they discovered that Hatfield was a moderate leader who made sustained efforts to gain their trust. He made it clear to his party supporters that he would not turn back the clock and undo Robichaud's work, whether it was implementing the Official Languages Act, continuing with the equal opportunity program, or supporting the Université de Moncton. One only needs to think back to 1970, after ten years of a strong activist government led by an Acadian, to appreciate that it took considerable courage and political will to do what Hatfield did. He again demonstrated political courage in supporting Trudeau's repatriation of the constitution and incorporating in it the Charter of Rights and Freedoms. To this day, the Hatfield legacy is highly valued by most Acadians.

No Acadians were more concerned about the arrival of the Hatfield government than those in Fredericton working in the public service. Most of them had arrived during the Robichaud years, and if there were to be an English backlash, they would be the first to feel it. They had no way of knowing that they had nothing to fear. As far as they could see, Hatfield was English-speaking, with almost no French. He was a Protestant and a Progressive Conservative from Carleton County, the very heart of the English Protestant enclave. As well, there were only two francophones in Hatfield's first cabinet (one from Edmundston and the other from a multimember constituency) – hardly a reassuring sign, especially to those in the provincial public service.

David Smith, a well-known Moncton lawyer, who was a friend of Hatfield and a colleague of Paul Creaghan, the new health minister, contacted me in Ottawa to encourage me to return to the province. I had first met David, a soft-spoken gentleman, while we were both students at the University of New Brunswick. He had established an excellent rapport with Acadians during his Fredericton years and would later become New Brunswick's chief justice (Queen's Bench). He told me that Hatfield and some of his senior ministers wanted to establish early on that Acadians were in Fredericton to stay and that the objective was to attract more. "Would you come back?" he asked.

I met with Gotlieb to explain the situation and to seek his advice. Gotlieb understood French Canada well and appreciated Trudeau's vision of French Canada being more than just Quebec. He assured me that I would very likely have an interesting and rewarding career if I stayed in the federal public service but that in the end I would have to look inside my soul for the decision. The federal public service, he explained, was not about to go away, and I could always return if things did not work out in Fredericton. I decided to return to New Brunswick. It was not an easy decision. One can hardly imagine doing better than having Allan Gotlieb as your first boss and role model.

MY FREDERICTON YEARS

Fredericton has often been described as a mini-Ottawa. Both are government towns. Fredericton is a one-company town. Public servants the world over are not only cautious by nature, but they have learned not to have a public face (hence the term "faceless bureaucrats") by keeping a low profile. Public faces belong to politicians, not bureaucrats. Communities take on the personalities of their residents. Thus, Fredericton is physically handsome, stoic in nature, but without much excitement.

Here I was, all set to become a faceless provincial bureaucrat in an English-speaking setting. I worked in the Department of

Health and later as a program analyst in the Treasury Board Secretariat. I want to stress once again and with more than the usual emphasis that Hatfield did all he could to ensure that Acadians would have a smooth transition from the Robichaud years. Still, tensions surfaced between the two language groups, with francophones often alleging slights, real or imagined, from their anglophone colleagues.

I write "imagined" because, looking back, I have come to believe that some of the tension was often the result of Acadians' uncertainty in a post-Robichaud world. This is not to suggest that all anglophone public servants had Acadian interests at the top of their minds. Of course, there were some English-speaking public servants who wanted and expected things to get back to the pre-Robichaud days, when Acadians scarcely had a presence in Fredericton, let alone in the provincial public service. They had come to regard the public service as their domain and Acadians as intruders.

However, the majority of the public servants I worked with in the early 1970s went about their work focusing on the task in hand. They managed programs, carried out transactions, and came up with policy initiatives – all with limited interest in what was going on outside their own departments, including how well Acadians were faring.

Still, we wanted more. We were always on the lookout for some reassurance that francophones would be welcome in the Hatfield era. I recall getting together with Acadians in social gatherings when the matter of how we were doing in the public service inevitably came up. It was easy in these gatherings to believe that unintended slights had been intended and that the failure of a colleague to get a promotion was because of his Acadian roots. Some even became convinced that the Orange Order was alive and well in Fredericton, once again blocking Acadians from promotion.

I also got together with Acadian colleagues to discuss how best to promote new school facilities or the construction of a francophone community centre. We were impatient and blamed the anglophone majority for the lack of progress. Meanwhile, the Hatfield government, quite properly, was waiting for a cost-sharing agreement with Ottawa before committing to the project. In due course, it did get off the ground: for some time now, Fredericton has been home to a first-class school-community centre for its francophone population.

To be sure, there was quite an adjustment to be made from my Ottawa days and my work with Gotlieb. Trudeau and his two senior Quebec lieutenants, Jean Marchand and Gérard Pelletier, were aggressively pushing the federal public service to hire more francophones and to promote bilingualism. Quebecers in Ottawa were also more persistent in pursuing linguistic rights in the public service than Acadians were in New Brunswick. I soon discovered that federal public servants were more open to change and more creative than their New Brunswick counterparts. That said, I had the good fortune of working directly with excellent people while in Fredericton. I want to single out Marcel Massé, whom Hatfield brought down from Ottawa to be the deputy minister of finance. We worked together on a number of issues and have been friends ever since. Marcel returned to Ottawa, where he became clerk of the privy council and secretary to the cabinet in Joe Clark's government and later a senior cabinet minister in Jean Chrétien's government.

My work in Fredericton some thirty-five years ago speaks to the reality that governments deal mostly with permanent problems. Quick fixes or easy solutions to what are invariably complex problems only make sense during election campaigns. The fact is that society's problems can be improved, but they can never be resolved. We have never won the war on poverty, are still trying to achieve a just society, and there is no end in sight.

I worked on two major initiatives while in Fredericton – the development of a new health-care model and attempts to overhaul the government's expenditure budget process. I do not want to burden the reader with a review of the finer points of public policy underpinning these two initiatives. A brief look in the rearview mirror, however, will help the reader appreciate the notion that when it comes to government and public policy, *plus ça change, plus c'est pareil.*

The search for a new health model was based on the obvious need to cut costs. As today, the government considered that health-care costs were eating far too much of the government's total budget. Our task was to come up with less costly ways of delivering health-care services. I recall our group asking how we could attenuate our reliance on costly hospital beds and how we could make more efficient use of medical staff, particularly the nurses. We also looked at promoting home care as a way of cutting costs. We are still at it in New Brunswick and in the other nine provinces too.

At the Treasury Board Secretariat, we did what virtually all treasury boards or budget offices were doing throughout much of the Western world in the 1970s – trying to recast the budget process to focus on program objectives and the performance of government managers and programs. The thinking was that it was possible, through sophisticated evaluations, to establish which programs were performing well and which were wasting taxpayers' money. No more simply counting pencils: the way ahead was to focus on evaluating how well programs were doing and then to tell the politicians which ones should be terminated. The new approach would produce a more rational budget process and substantial savings for taxpayers.

No government has ever been able to deliver the goods. In March 2008 I attended a briefing in Ottawa prepared by the Office of the Comptroller General and the Treasury Board Secretariat on a new management accountability framework for the federal government. The officials making the presentation spoke about new concepts, new approaches, and new instruments that held great promise. It was the very same language that we had employed back in the 1970s or, to quote the American philosopher Yogi Berra, it was "*déjà vu* all over again." How, I asked myself, can public servants stand up and pretend that they are introducing something new when all of it has been tried more than once over the past thirty years or so? However, while in Fredericton in the 1970s, I did produce an administrative manual that documented for the first time administrative, financial, and personnel policies to guide managers in their work. The manual has been up-dated substantially over the years, but it is still in use today.

MEETING LINDA

I was asked to interview a young UNB student, Linda Dempsey, for possible summer employment in the Department of Health. All I knew was that she was from Moncton and that her parents were well-known supporters of the Conservative Party. Her mother was a poll or area captain for the party in Moncton's west end. Partisan politics was an important factor for students looking for summer employment with the New Brunswick government in the 1970s. It probably still is.

It would not have mattered had her parents been members of the Communist Party. One look and she was hired – so much for an objective hiring process. It was a classic case of love at first sight. I had gone out with far more girls than my looks warranted. The fact that I could borrow my father's Chrysler on weekends – back then, having a car in Moncton held great promise when looking for girls – no doubt helped my chances on this front. But this time with Linda it was different. I had never experienced such a feeling before, and I decided quickly that she was the one. It was the best decision I have ever made.

Linda has done all the heavy lifting over the years. She aban-doned a career as a schoolteacher to follow me around the world, to look after our home, and to concentrate her energy on raising our children. She has lovingly looked after her husband who, through tenacity and hard work, had overcome a learning dis-ability and also is colour-blind.[3] I can hardly imagine how I would have dressed over the years had she not been around to double check as I left for work or when packing my luggage. She is incred-ibly patient and has spent her life giving to others, in particular to me and our children.

There was, however, one major drawback – she was English, Protestant, and her parents supported both the Toronto Maple

Leafs and the Conservative Party – no small obstacle for a Bouc-touche boy. I had to weigh finding the love of my life against the values – as well as the prejudices – that had shaped who I was. It was no easy struggle. Would our children be brought up in English or French? What would happen to their Acadian heritage? At one point I decided to break off the relationship, telling Linda that I needed time to reflect on a number of things without being too specific.

Before long, I was back knocking on her door. This was it, no more second thoughts, at least not from my end. We decided to get married, and we drove to Moncton to inform our parents. My father was fine with our decision, but my mother was not. She said, "I do not know which is worse, that she is English or that she is Protestant." I must add that in time Linda and my mother became close friends, spent a great deal of time together, and shared many interests.

We decided to be married by a Roman Catholic priest and a United Church minister. We also decided on a first for Moncton – we would have a completely bilingual wedding. I would take my wedding vows in French, Linda in English, and the ceremony itself would be carried out half in French, half in English. There were a few delicate moments, but to appreciate their significance, one must think back to the prevalent values of the 1970s. One of my aunts was a Roman Catholic nun, and one of Linda's uncles was a United Church minister. Linda's grandfather was from Albert County, long perceived by Acadians to be decidedly anti-French, and he was one of the leaders of the Orange Lodge in Albert County.

We heard that my aunt was going to give us a crucifix as a wedding present. I had not realized that there was such a thing as a Roman Catholic crucifix and a Protestant one. It could become extremely awkward. What would Linda's grandparents think? What about her uncle, the United Church minister? We did receive a crucifix, and we opened it in front of the gathering, but to our surprise and delight it was neither Roman Catholic nor Protestant, just a Christian crucifix. It has a silver cross with two wedding rings and doves in the middle. Suddenly, all those on both sides who had been apprehensive about how the guests would react to a Roman Catholic crucifix felt very foolish, as they should have. Here was an elderly nun showing everyone that there was something far more important and meaningful than the narrow perspective of a single religion. We have always kept the crucifix in a highly visible place in our home.

One evening, we invited Linda's grandparents for dinner. In the hallway leading to the dining area, I had put up an old photograph of Sir Wilfrid Laurier in an antique picture frame. As Linda's grandfather walked by, he stopped, took a good look at it and said, "What a nice picture of Sir John A. Macdonald." I said, "No, no, that's Sir Wilfrid Laurier." We had a pleasant dinner and as he left, he walked by the photograph once again, paused and said, "What a nice picture of Sir John A. Macdonald." I also knew that he was not a fan of Robichaud. On my side of the ledger, my grandfather had a habit of rubbing his stomach after a good dinner and saying, "There's one meal that the English won't get!" As for myself, I took great satisfaction when the Montreal Canadiens had a string of Stanley Cup wins in the 1970s. The Toronto Maple Leafs could not compete.

Linda's family has a link to Stephen Harper, the current leader of the Conservative Party and Canada's twenty-second prime minister. Harper's grandfather taught school in Moncton and was principal of Prince Edward School. He taught Linda's uncle, Ron Dempsey. And Stephen Harper's father, Joseph Harper, went to school with Linda's mother, Corena, who has fond memories of him. She reports that "Jos" was a very good student, very intelligent, and well liked by everyone.

There is a story well known to elderly Monctonians but not to many Canadians. Stephen Harper's grandfather, when he was school principal in Moncton in the early 1940s, disappeared one afternoon, never to be seen or heard from again. To this day, no one knows what happened to him, and Linda's uncle remembers walking the marshes around Moncton with his father, looking for his school principal, "Puffy" Harper. I met Stephen Harper in Ottawa when the Institute for Research on Public Policy celebrated its thirtieth anniversary and reminded him that he had "Maritime roots" through his grandfather. He acknowledged this and said that his grandfather's disappearance remains a mystery to the Harper family.

I have long believed that Harper has been unfairly criticized in my region for his comment that the Maritime region suffers from "a culture of defeat." Taken in isolation, one can appreciate why the comment was not well received by Maritimers. It may be recalled that he made the comment in May 2002 when he was leader of the opposition. But he went on to say that the culture of defeat was born "because of what happened in the decades following Confederation." He pointed to national political institutions and national policies as the cause for the region's culture of defeat, and I happen to agree with him on this point. In addition, I have always applauded Harper's commitment to reforming the Senate to make it a more effective voice on behalf of the regions in national political institutions and policies.

I am pleased to report that there has never been any tension between the Savoie and Dempsey families, linguistic or otherwise. My father-in-law Lloyd Dempsey played an active role in Moncton politics to stop Leonard Jones from being elected to Parliament. He was both vocal and visible in his opposition, insisting that it would be an "embarrassment having Jones representing us in Ottawa." His strong opposition to Jones meant a great deal to me.

RETURNING TO MONCTON

The federal government decided to decentralize its Department of Regional Economic Expansion (DREE) in the aftermath of the 1972 general election. It will be recalled that the Trudeau government narrowly averted defeat and the search was on for new approaches to win favour with the voters. One of them was to establish four large regional and several provincial DREE offices across Canada.

The government picked Moncton to house Atlantic Canada's regional DREE office and asked Don McPhail, a Maritimer and a senior External Affairs official, to head the new operation. He arrived in Moncton with nothing more than an administrative assistant and plenty of boxes. Shortly after his arrival, he asked to meet with me. Someone, perhaps Gotlieb, had told him about my work in Ottawa. McPhail outlined the government's new approach to regional economic development, his objectives for the region, and how he planned to set up departmental operations in Moncton and the four provincial offices. He asked if I would be interested in joining him as his chief of staff.

Within days of moving back to Moncton, I was putting in twelve to fourteen hours a day. The agenda was very demanding, but there was hardly any staff around to get the work done. We had to hire people, set up new offices, get equipment, establish policies and procedures, define a new policy agenda, sign federal-provincial agreements, and sort out a new relationship with the departmental head office in Ottawa. I wasn't involved in all of these activities, but there was never a shortage of interesting work, and I could focus on issues that were of particular interest to me. I also made certain that qualified Acadians would compete for the new positions. I am happy to report that many did and a good number were hired, including my good friend Victor Landry.

It was a great learning experience for me. I saw how an organization takes shape, how policies are packaged, and how senior public servants deal with ministers. I saw how federal-provincial negotiations are carried out, how agreements are struck and programs implemented. I also saw how tensions can surface between regional offices and Ottawa and how key ministers close to the prime minister can have their way. This is not to suggest that government made sense to me, but I did gain an understanding of how it operates.

Don McPhail was extremely hard working and always put in more hours than anyone else. We developed an excellent working relationship. One day, while working well into the evening, McPhail said that we ought to be planning my next move in the federal public service. He suggested that I should return to Ottawa and gain experience in a central agency. He said he would be happy to promote my candidacy. But I had other plans in mind, having decided that I would return to university. Linda and I both worked, and we had agreed that we would put away funds to support us through a PH D program. I explained my decision to McPhail, making the point, however, that I was greatly enjoying the work with DREE. I had no strong objection to working in Ottawa in a central agency, but I had made up my mind to return to university.

His response was, "I will make a deal with you." He would strongly recommend to the department that it assume part of the cost of my study program provided that I would commit to several things. First, I would need to spend two years with him to develop the organization and also continue to put in long hours without claiming any overtime; and I would have to be prepared to travel at short notice and to undertake tasks that were clearly outside my job description. Second, I would need to return to the government for at least two years after I had gained my doctorate. Third, he would support me provided that I went outside Canada for graduate work.

McPhail had been an External Affairs official and had served abroad in various embassies, including as ambassador to Venezula. He believed that Canadians generally lacked a proper understanding of Canada's position in the world and in the international economy. He insisted that I would greatly benefit by studying in a foreign country, by reading the great newspapers of the world, and by gaining insight into how people in other countries view the world and Canada.

My response was unambiguous: "We have a deal." I had always assumed that I would be going to a Canadian university, but why not go abroad? Linda was fully supportive the moment I raised the possibility with her. We had no children and were renting a townhouse from my brother, so leaving the country was not complicated for us.

I applied to Oxford, Cambridge, the Sorbonne, Harvard, and Yale. Entrance requirements were not quite as demanding in the

1970s as they are today, and I thought that at least one of them would accept me. I assumed that the fact that I had work experience would help my candidacy. My first choice was Oxford for reasons that were not clear to me then or, for that matter, now. I suspect that it had to do with its reputation and the fact that a few Acadians I knew or knew about had been there. I got my wish. On a Friday evening at about 7:00 PM, I received a telephone call from the local telegram office. The official read the telegram, and sure enough, I was in. To make certain that there was no misunderstanding, I drove to the office that evening to pick up a copy of the telegram from Oxford. It was for real: I was now a D PHIL student at Queen's College, Oxford.

On Monday morning, first thing, I sent a telegram to Oxford saying that I would definitely be there in the fall. There would be no change of mind or heart on my part. I also wrote to all the other universities to tell them that I was withdrawing my application. No sense, I thought, wasting their time or resources when I had already decided where I was going. I told Don McPhail, who immediately wrote to the department's director of personnel to request some financial assistance to support my study program. The request was approved.

Within a few days, however, I developed an acute attack of self-doubt. How would I do at Oxford? I had attended only two universities in one province, neither of which was exactly the gold standard for universities. We had never visited Europe, let alone studied there, so why would I think that I could pull it off? When I confessed my doubts to my brother Claude, he replied, "I wouldn't worry about it. Go there and do your best. Remember, if you fail, it's no big deal. The way I see it, it's better to go to Oxford and fail than get a degree from the Université de Moncton or UNB." My mother fiercely dismissed the possibility of failure: "If people from Toronto or anywhere else can do it, so can you. You are as good as they are."

6

My Oxford Days

We left Montreal for England in August 1976 on the *Alexander Pushkin*, a Russian ship. It was hardly a luxury liner, but it attracted a number of young people, particularly students. It had a number of advantages: it was inexpensive, drinks were very cheap, and it enabled students to compare notes before arriving at their new universities.

We enjoyed crossing the Atlantic. The passengers included Canadian students studying abroad and others taking a year off to see Europe before entering university or graduate school. There were also a number of American students, some North American tourists, and various European families returning from a summer holiday in North America. Groups of eight were assigned to specific tables for dinner, so by the end of the eight-day crossing we knew our tablemates fairly well.

At our table most of us were Canadian students, but there was also a young woman travelling on her own. She told us that the night before she was due to be married, her fiancé had left town without so much as a telephone call, let alone an explanation. She was devastated, and only a few weeks later she decided to go to Europe on the *Pushkin*. I never saw her smile, and I only saw her at dinner. She was skinny, not particularly attractive, and never well dressed, even for the captain's dinner. We all tried to cheer her up, but with little success. She didn't seem bitter, but there was a tremendous sadness in her face, and tears were never far away. We didn't see or hear from her after the crossing, and I have often wondered what became of her.

I looked on the trip as my last week of freedom before Oxford consumed virtually every moment of every day of every week. The ship's bars, where one could have a beer or other drink for all of fifty cents (after we got into international waters), became the students' favourite gathering place. We met someone who claimed to have met Charles Manson, another who had worked as a summer intern for a US senator, and a young couple who were planning to teach in Canada's Northwest Territories after touring through Europe for a year. Someone said that there was nothing more spectacular than seeing the sun rise above the Atlantic Ocean. Why not stay up all night to see it? Why not indeed? A number of us did precisely that – chatting, drinking, and patiently waiting for the sun to rise. It didn't work out quite as planned. Dawn arrived wet, dark, and cloudy, and I chose not to repeat the experiment, although others did.

The *Pushkin* pulled into the Tilbury docks in East London. I went through immigration with little difficulty, but Linda took exception to the immigration officer who hinted that she was "a kept woman." This was the first of many signs that Europe needed and still needs to make progress in promoting gender equality and sensitivity. Once through immigration, we came face to face with Cockney English. I asked for directions to Oxford but didn't understand a single word of the directions I was given. I turned to Linda and said, "You're English, try your luck at understanding this guy." She didn't do much better.

It's often noted that the French spoken in l'Acadie is different from Quebec French and that both are different from the French spoken in France. There is, of course, a sharp difference between French spoken in different parts of the world because accents are different. In the case of Acadians, we still use words from old

French (words from pre-1755) because we were cut off from both Quebec and France for a long time. Many of us sprinkle English words into our conversation. That said, the difference between English spoken in Moncton and Cockney English is far greater than French spoken in Moncton and French spoken in Paris. Cockney not only has a distinct accent, but it also has its own rich vocabulary.

Based on Linda's understanding of how to get to Oxford in Cockney, off we went with four suitcases in tow. We took a train, then the tube and finally we were there – Oxford Station. We surfaced onto an extremely busy street and knew that something was not right. There were no Oxford colleges in sight, so we flagged down a taxi to take us to Queen's College.

We had no difficulty in understanding this gentleman. We also understood that we were in downtown London at the Oxford Circus tube station. The city of Oxford was still some sixty kilometres away, northwest of London. The taxi took us to Paddington Station, where there was a London-Oxford train every hour on the hour. We were off again, this time on the right train. I asked a fellow passenger how we would know when we arrived in Oxford. "No need to worry," he replied, "you will see the dreaming spires of Oxford." Sure enough, within an hour we were staring out of the window at Oxford's dreaming spires. It is an incredibly beautiful sight.

Our first job was to find a place to live, and here the university was very helpful. We decided to rent a duplex on Abingdon Road, about one kilometre from my college. Our landlady lived next door, a charming woman always ready with entertaining stories. She was extremely active in Britain's Conservative Party and became an energetic supporter of Margaret Thatcher. She recounted many stories from her experiences in the Second World War, including the day in 1940 when the Germans bombed the cathedral city of Coventry. "I knew," she said, "that someone was getting an awful trashing because of the constant roar overhead. It was only later that we learned that it was Coventry – those poor souls."

We could not have asked for better lodgings or better neighbours. The local pub was just round the corner, and every Monday evening I joined three or four neighbours for our pub night. Linda and I had the best of both worlds. We experienced life in one of the world's great universities and at the same time mixed with people who worked in manufacturing plants, carpentry, and the service sector. It gradually dawned on me that in class-based England, where everyone could tell by everyone else's accent precisely where in the class hierarchy they stood, Canadians were privileged. No one could "place" us by our accent, and consequently we were welcome among all classes.

MARSHALL AND JOHNSON

Within a few days of our arrival, I went to Queen's College to meet my tutor, Geoffrey Marshall. What a pleasant surprise! Marshall was a leading authority on parliamentary government, very friendly, and always available to students. He retired as provost of Queen's in 1999 and died in 2003. The *Guardian*, in its obituary, described him as the "foremost theorist of constitutions in general and of the British one in particular." He was also interested in Canadian political institutions and visited Canada on several occasions, spending some time at McGill University where, he once told me, one of his former students teaches law.

He was generous, had a keen sense of humour, and an extremely sharp intellect. I enjoyed his company and always came away from our sessions encouraged and enthusiastic about my work. He had a way of encouraging at the right moment but pushing hard on certain issues when he felt it necessary. I came to consider him a friend, and so did most of his students. He was short, built like a jockey. What he may have lacked in physical appearance, however, he made up for with his personality, determination, and intellect. He was never flamboyant or pretentious, and he disliked those characteristics in others. He was, according to the *Guardian*, "unobtrusive and effective."[1] He served on

Oxford City Council and represented Queen's at university and intercollege meetings. It never bothered him to be in a minority of one on issues if he felt it was the right thing to do.

Marshall published a number of books and many articles on political and administrative institutions, and his work is widely respected on both sides of the Atlantic. He was never one to blow his own trumpet or to pursue glory and honours. One of the most prestigious posts available to a political scientist in the United Kingdom, if not in the world, is the Gladstone Chair of Government at All Souls College, Oxford. Marshall was offered the chair but turned it down. His reason? Unlike Queen's, All Souls does not have a squash court.

He went out of his way to welcome me to Queen's. He urged me to take three courses – Political Theory, Comparative Politics, and Political Economy – and to attend as many guest lectures and seminars as possible. The doctoral program at Oxford is built around the thesis, but Marshall urged me to focus on these courses for several months.

I next met Nevil Johnson, my thesis tutor at Nuffield College. He was the polar opposite of Geoffrey Marshall, though they were friends. Johnson had a far more imposing physique. He looked German, with yellow hair, broad shoulders, and no fat. I don't remember ever seeing him smile. He never saw a joke, except by appointment. He was dour, sour, and stern. His office, unlike those of other Oxford tutors, was always neat, everything in its place. He had positioned his desk so that he faced the wall. He would swivel around in his chair to talk across a coffee table that separated him from any visitor. One invariably felt that Nevil was impatient to kick his chair back and continue working on whatever had occupied his attention before he was so inconveniently interrupted.

Nevil was a top scholar, and his work was widely respected everywhere by students of federalism and political institutions. He was a leading member of Britain's Conservative Party and an adviser to Margaret Thatcher. Thatcher appointed him a member of the Economics and Social Research Council and also as a civil service commissioner between 1982 and 1988. His work on German federalism and the British constitution has been widely quoted. He became my thesis tutor because I wanted to write my thesis on federalism from a Canadian perspective.

Our first meeting, shortly after I arrived, was brief and to the point. We agreed that I would not start work on my thesis for some time. We also agreed that I would write a twenty-five-page paper on policy coordination in federal states. I returned a few weeks later with what I believed to be a solid paper.

A few days later, Nevil summoned me to his study. There was little in the way of "Hi, how are you?" or "How are you enjoying Oxford?" He looked me straight in the eye and declared, "This is an awful paper. I have rarely seen such a poorly written paper. I really do not understand what you are trying to say."

I attempted to employ a strategy that had worked for me while at the University of New Brunswick. "Oh," I said, "I am an Acadian."

His response: "What on earth is that?"

"My mother tongue is French."

"I see," said Nevil. "Well, you know, there are some very good universities across the channel in France. Why not go there?"

"No," I protested. "I want to be here at Oxford."

"Well then, here is an English grammar." He tossed a book on the coffee table and added, "Read it very carefully and until you do, do not come here wasting my time." With that, he kicked his chair around to face the wall. I was left staring at the back of his head and at the grammar resting on the coffee table. I picked it up and left without saying another word.

A few days later, I was invited to a garden party organized to welcome all new doctoral students. It was not a pleasant evening, at least for me. I met two Americans, one of whom was the son of a senior executive at Chase Manhattan Bank. He had just completed his master's degree at Harvard. The other was from California, a graduate of Stanford. The Harvard man asked where I had studied. He gave me a very puzzled look when I said the University of New Brunswick. He had never heard of the place.

So this is Oxford, I thought. I was intimidated. Being Acadian was not going to help me here. I thought perhaps Nevil was right, maybe I should have gone to France. I went home and told Linda that I could do one of three things: go home; take Claude's advice and enjoy Oxford and not worry too much about getting a degree; or buckle down and do it. I gave serious consideration to the first and third possibilities but not the second. I decided to give it my best shot.

The next two years were all about work. I started at seven o'clock every morning and carried on until ten every evening, except on Sundays, when I started at noon, and on Mondays, when I stopped at six. Sunday mornings were always set aside for reading the *Sunday Times*, and Monday evening was pub night.

If I were to work such long hours, I knew that I would need something to strengthen my stamina. I had heard that transcendental meditation (TM) had been of help to a number of Oxford students. Linda and I decided to enrol in the course. I remain convinced to this day that without TM I would never have been able to complete my studies at Oxford. Not only did it give me more energy, but I believe that it was a substantial help with my learning disability. I soon discovered that I was able to concentrate better, to stay on a topic for hours, and to capture more fully the meaning of the material I was reading. I hear present-day politicians talk about the need for "transformative" change in society. When I look back to my pre-Oxford days, I recognize that I was then different in many ways – less confident, less serious, less able to concentrate, less able to challenge authority. Oxford represented for me a transformative change.

I read Nevil's grammar and it did help. But it was not enough. I went to Blackwell's, Oxford's famous bookstore, and bought a kit – *New Course in Practical English*. It was a 350-page, twelve-week course that included a number of exercises to improve one's grammar and writing style. I still have the kit, which I consult from time to time. I patiently completed every single exercise and read and reread all the material in about twelve days rather than twelve weeks. It proved invaluable, and it has had a lasting effect.

Several years ago a colleague at Carleton University told me that in reading one of my articles he was certain that he had found a grammatical error. After checking with his own grammar, he realized that I was right. He suggested that people who learn English grammar as mature students always master it better than those whose mother tongue is English. In my case, it had everything to do with Nevil Johnson.

I decided to write another essay for Nevil, again on policy making in a federal system. I took it over to Nuffield College with a note asking to see him. Within a few days, I was there waiting for the verdict. The tone was not any friendlier, but his message was. He said it was "much improved." He added that while there was still room for improvement, there was "some" evidence that I could write a thesis. But he added, "I have important advice." It was to use fewer words to express what I wanted to say. "In English, unlike in French," he said, "we do not need as many words to write down our thoughts." (Ouch! I thought). "Second, please do not employ complex or rarely heard words to convey a thought. Simplicity and clarity of style are highly valued at Oxford." He explained that one must have an accessible style of writing, otherwise what was the point in writing? (Conrad Black never attended Oxford.) Nevil had little else to say. I thanked him, placed his grammar back on his coffee table, said that it had been helpful, and left. He again swivelled his chair to face the wall.

By Nevil's standard, this was a positive assessment of my work. I went home, told Linda that we were staying, and that evening we went out for dinner, a rare treat. Linda enjoyed Oxford. She made many friends, including several who became very close to her. She did what she most enjoyed – art, including batik, painting, weaving – and one of her favourite pastimes, shopping. She also took up gardening, becoming very proficient at it. She later won the sunflower award in Moncton for her flower gardens.

I went to courses and seminars and began thinking about my thesis. We both bought bicycles, and most days I did my rounds – to Queen's College, Rhodes House, and back home by dinner time. I spent a great deal of time at Rhodes House because it had an excellent library on the British Commonwealth and federalism. I soon settled into a pattern of work and more work.

A few months after our arrival in Oxford, my parents and my brother Claude came to visit. My mother had been diagnosed with cancer only a few weeks after we left Moncton. She very much wanted to see Oxford for herself. Claude and I went to a pub to talk in private about our mother's illness. We went to the Fox and Hounds. The bar was dark, noisy, and full of cigarette smoke. However, I could see another room with fewer people in it, no smoke, and better furniture. The two rooms were divided by a half-door, probably to enable staff to move food between them. I went up to a man who was apparently in a state of advanced intoxication, pointed to the half-door, and asked if there was a way to get to the other side. He looked at the door, looked back at me, looked at the door again – all the while weaving on his feet – and as he rocked back and forth with his eyes lost in a daze, he said in a thick Irish accent, "Oh! there must be!" He then turned on his heel and staggered away. I realized that I needed to be more precise in my question.

We eventually got to the other room by going outside and entering the pub through another door. What Claude had to report was not very encouraging. Our mother was under good care, and Claude said that he would stop at nothing to get her the best treatment available. He wanted to be positive, probably thinking that being more brutally honest would hurt my studies at Oxford.

Linda toured the colleges with my parents and Claude. Like all Canadians, they were struck by Oxford's rich history. Claude, in particular, couldn't get over New College ("*New*?" he said) which had been founded in 1379. We talked about Oxford's role in the British Empire and wondered how Oxford had viewed the Grand Dérangement in 1755. We doubted that there had been much sympathy for our ancestors at New College or any other Oxford college.

I took a few days off to visit Dublin with my family. European cities are all well stocked with large churches, and Dublin is no different. We visited St Patrick's Cathedral, where my mother decided to kneel down and pray. As I looked around, I began to doubt that this really was a Roman Catholic cathedral as we had assumed, so I asked a priest and he said no, it was not. How could we guess that St Patrick's was a cathedral of the Church of Ireland? In other words, Anglican. I slowly made my way back to my mother and sat next to her to report the bad news. "It doesn't matter," she said, "it's the same God." We were making progress.

PROBLEMS IN FEDERAL-PROVINCIAL COLLABORATION

I read as much as I could on federalism generally and everything that I could lay my hands on about Canadian federalism. The broad outline of my thesis was starting to take shape. I had a number of discussions with both Nevil Johnson and Geoffrey Marshall, and I became increasingly convinced that I was on to something. I saw a hook for my thesis, one that was somewhat original. The federalism literature, in my view, did not pay sufficient attention to the role played by public servants in shaping federal-provincial policies and programs. Modern government was making it more difficult for citizens to determine who was doing what and which politicians were responsible for what policies and programs. To make my case, I would look at the work of my former department, DREE.

The new Canadian federalism was effective in sidestepping our rigid constitution (amending our constitution, as we now know all too well, was not an easy task) and in developing federal-provincial programs. I argued that it came at a cost. Politicians were losing some of their policy-making capacity, voters could no longer tell which level of government was responsible for what, bureaucrats were asked to extend their reach beyond the traditional model, and the federal government was not getting the kind of visibility that its spending warranted.

This was a new perspective, and both my Oxford tutors saw merit in it. Like other authors, I found it exhilarating to write something original and something that resonated with the likes of Nevil Johnson and Geoffrey Marshall. From that moment, the question was no longer how I could be motivated but how I could ensure balance in my life, between my writing and everything else. (This has been a struggle over the years, and I fear that my writing has won far too often.) At some point in my second year at Oxford, I knew that I would be able to get it done. The only question was how long it would take. I gave myself a three-year deadline. I met the objective.

I was able to take some time off, and Linda and I went to Paris one weekend, Rome another, and Brussels yet another. We also decided to visit the Soviet Union, curious to see what life was like under a communist regime. We spent four days in Moscow, three in Leningrad. We enjoyed the visit immensely, though the hotel and food services in the old Soviet Union were memorable mostly for being terrible. One day, I placed a wake-up call with our hotel in Moscow. The call arrived an hour earlier than requested, and the voice at the other end of the line said, "Stand up, please."

We visited as many museums and art galleries as we could squeeze in. I saw the famous painting in the Museum of the Revolution that features Lenin, Stalin, and other revolutionary leaders. Historians tell us that Leon Trotsky once also figured prominently in the painting but that Stalin had him painted over after Trotsky fell out of favour. Here I was, standing in front of the famous painting and sure enough, no Trotsky! I asked our tour guide why Trotsky was not in the painting. He gave me essentially a non-answer. I persisted. He again avoided the question. I was not about to let it go, and the guide became agitated. Finally, a museum official came over to me and said, "We have arranged to have the museum curator meet with you to discuss the matter and answer all your questions. He will be waiting by the door on the way out." Off we went to meet with him. We waited and waited – no curator. We no longer had our guide, and there was little we could do except return to our hotel. I recall that Linda was not too pleased with me that afternoon.

ENJOYING OXFORD

Once I knew that I would be leaving with my degree in hand, I began to enjoy Oxford. We went out with friends, something we had never done in my first year. We joined the traditional May Day celebrations at the crack of dawn on 1 May, again something we hadn't done before. And I often had dinner at my college, where I met other graduate students, which I had seldom done in my first year.

I was invited to dinner at the home of Charles Taylor, the well-known Canadian-born philosopher. He had taught at McGill University for years and now held the Chichele Chair of Social and Political Theory at All Souls College. A true gentleman and a great scholar, he was one of the most pre-eminent Canadians to hold a professorship at Oxford. That evening ranks as one of the most enjoyable during my student days at Oxford. Twenty-five years later, we were both finalists for the Social Sciences and Humanities Research Council (SSHRC) Gold Medal for Achievement in Research, and we met once again for dinner.

I used to ride by All Souls on my bicycle on my way to Rhodes House. All Souls sits in the very heart of Oxford, on the High Street, next to the Radcliffe Camera (one of Oxford's favourite tourist sites) and the Bodleian, one of the world's finest libraries. I used to peek through the iron gate on the college's west side to look at the beautiful Codrington Library. All Souls has no students, just fellows. It is one of the richest of the Oxford colleges, where fellows are able to pursue their research free of distractions. During my student years, it was home to Charles Taylor, Isaiah Berlin – regarded by many as one of the leading liberal thinkers of the twentieth century and recently retired but still present at the college – and John Hicks, the 1972 Nobel laureate in economics. All Souls is special, as everyone who has attended Oxford comes to appreciate.

We also made lifelong friends with other Canadians studying at Oxford. We attended many social gatherings, where we met John A. Chenier, Robert A. Young, Andrew Cooper, and Paul Guild. All have made important contributions to their discipline and to the academic literature.

JULIEN ARRIVES

We learned at the end of my first year that Linda was pregnant. Our first-born would be British, what Acadians call a "flat foot." I couldn't help but wonder what my ancestors would make of all this – my going to Oxford, the very centre of imperialism, where leaders of the British Empire were trained, rather than to France, and our first child being a British citizen. This was all very far from Bouctouche.

Julien's birth was extremely difficult. I was present at it, or at least tried to be. Linda was in labour for several hours and then things really got out of control. The medical team became agitated and there was blood everywhere. One of the doctors asked me to leave the room, and as he walked out with me, he said, "I don't know how you could remain so calm, given the situation in the room." He added that we could lose either Linda or the baby. We lost neither.

I went home exhausted around 1 AM and called Moncton to let my parents know the good news. Claude answered, and while happy at my news said, "If you want to see our mother alive, you need to come home right away. It is pretty well all over." I went to see Linda that day and told her about my mother. She urged me to go home, and the hospital staff said they would be happy to have Linda stay on until my return. Given the complications with Julien's birth, they added that it would not be a bad idea to have both mother and child stay longer so that they could keep an eye on things. I then went to see Nevil. His response was the first sign of many that revealed there was a tender heart beating inside that man. "Go see your mother," he said. "If anything should happen here, I will take care of your wife and child at this end."

I took a flight home the next day. As luck would have it, I sat two seats away from a crying child and arrived in Moncton completely exhausted. I immediately went to see my mother who, for some reason, was sleeping in my old room. Ravaged by cancer and weighing perhaps only thirty-five kilograms, she was barely recognizable. Claude was right; it was pretty well over. Still, as always, we had a lovely chat. She asked what name we were thinking of for our son. I told her Julien Zachary Savoie. She was very happy about Julien – an ancestor of hers in the Grand Dérangement had been named Julien. However, she did not like Zachary. There was a Zacharie living near Saint-Maurice who was, as she put it, a bum. People would make fun of him, she feared, and urged me to "just call him Julien." I wanted Zachary because of Zachary Richard, the well-known Cajun singer from Louisiana. I have always felt that Cajuns from Louisiana had it a lot tougher than us, and Richard's songs, especially "Réveille," speak to this reality.

I was glad to be able to come home to say goodbye to my mother. It was a very painful goodbye, but at least we were able to talk, and for that I shall always be grateful. Within a few days, I was back on a flight to England. My sister Rose-Marie tells me that she was in the room with our mother when they heard an airplane go over the house. She says that our mother said, "There goes Donald," closed her eyes, and went into a coma. She died a few days later.

Back at Oxford, I went to the Radcliffe Hospital to bring my family home. We soon discovered that Julien was not a sleeper. Wide awake, always curious, active, he kept us going day and night, sleeping for only a few hours at a time. It was our first child, and we were away from grandparents, aunts, and uncles who would have known how to cope. We responded to every cry, every sound, and his every beep for attention. This is when I discovered the level of Linda's patience – there is simply no end to it.

I continued to press on hard with my studies, knowing that in a few short months we would be returning to Canada. Looking back, I now realize that I sank into depression. I had never experienced depression before – or, for that matter, since – so I didn't know how to deal with it. Losing my mother had affected me deeply. Nothing made sense any more, and I simply couldn't stop thinking about her. I tried to imagine the physical pain and mental anguish she had suffered, with no success. Why was I at Oxford? What was the point of it all? Why her? I had no answers. I will always be grateful to Linda for her warm understanding in seeing me through that dark period.

TIME TO GO HOME

By June 1978 it was time to go home. I went back to Moncton a very different person from what I had been when I left. I was a father, and I had learned how to think and write. I had lived with the enemy for two years and discovered that there is much to admire about Britain and the British. My views on them had changed by 180 degrees as I had come to appreciate their immense contribution to the world.

England gave us Shakespeare, the world's best political and administrative institutions, the industrial age, Sir Winston Churchill, and some of the best minds that the world has ever produced. If one compares British history with any other, one quickly sees that British civilization did more good than harm in the world. The British Empire compares very favourably with other empires, be it the Americans or even the French in their treatment of other ethnic groups. I have developed a very strong attachment to Oxford, one of the few communities in the world where I truly feel at home. I love everything about Oxford – its ambiance, its unparalleled architecture, its charm, and its civility. I visit Oxford regularly, and it has truly become my second home. It is no exaggeration to say that Oxford was the most transformational experience of my life. I am in debt to it, and a part of me will always be there. It gave me confidence, lifelong friends, and a deep appreciation of the written word.

I have been careful in voicing my admiration for Britain over the years for fear that it would be misinterpreted at home. My grandfather, the one who rubbed his stomach after every meal because "this is one meal that the English will never get," would never have understood. I doubt whether my mother, father, brothers, and sisters, or even all my colleagues at the Université de Moncton, would understand. However, my regard for Britain does not in any way diminish my attachment to my roots, my heritage, or my strong desire to help Acadians and Acadian communities whenever I can.

My thesis was not finished, but we were returning to Moncton because some of the research material I needed was available only in Canada. I went back to my department, DREE, and explained the situation – Don McPhail had by then returned to External Affairs and Harley McGee had taken over. Senior management agreed that I could spend some time working on my thesis but stipulated that I must also work in one of the policy units. This was fine with me. But I soon discovered why Nevil Johnson had reacted so strongly to my first paper. Reading some of the files and policy papers, I was aghast at the sloppy drafting, at the bureaucratese. While full of words, the sentences said very little.

At the risk of sounding Olympian, I knew that I could do better. The question was whether policy papers were deliberately written in bureaucratic language to obscure the message. There are days when I still believe that sloppy drafting of government documents is deliberate. Our public servants are well trained and they, like everyone else, are familiar with well-written articles and columns in our national newspapers. Clarity in prose is a two-edged sword for bureaucrats: it can make policy options come to life, but it also makes clear a departmental perspective, which ministers (and now anyone, because of access-to-information legislation) can see and consequently hold the authors accountable. One thing I decided: I did not want to write like that.

By spring 1979 my thesis was done. I sent the required copies to Nevil, and a date for my *viva* (oral defence of my thesis) was set. Nevil wrote to say that Sir K.C. Wheare would chair the committee, and Vernon Bogdanor would be one of its members. Wheare had been the Gladstone Professor of Government at All Souls in the 1940s, and he had written the classic book on federalism, *Federal Government*. He had also drafted the definitive statement on academic self-government. An Australian, he was the first non-British vice-chancellor of Oxford University, and the university flourished under his leadership in the 1960s.

This would not be an easy *viva*. I decided to take a two-week holiday to read everything Wheare had written on federalism, which was quite a lot, and also to read Bogdanor's contributions. When I walked nervously into the examination room, Wheare was sitting at the head of the table with Bogdanor to his left. A number of graduate students were there – maybe to hear what I had to say or, more likely, to see the great man. Wheare, in his beautiful red and grey D LITT gown, was seventy-two years old and looked very distinguished. I had never seen him before but had been reading him, it seemed, for years.

I hardly expected what happened next. Wheare began by asking, "Did you come here all the way from Canada?"

"Yes," I replied.

"I am not at all certain that it was necessary," he said. "It is obvious to me that your thesis more than meets our standards. There is no question in my mind that you have earned the degree."

My jaw dropped. I thanked him and immediately looked to Bogdanor to see his reaction. He simply nodded his head in agreement. This is it, I thought. After three years of working twelve to fourteen hours a day and a final two weeks of intense reading, and the verdict is in after only a few minutes! I looked at the graduate students in the room and all I saw were smiling faces.

Wheare then said, "I want to discuss federalism with you, however. I understand that you are an Acadian."

"Yes," I replied.

"Well," he went on, "I know Canada well as I was an adviser when Newfoundland joined Confederation, and I have always marvelled at the history of the Acadian people. Tell me about your people."

The *viva* lasted well over an hour and, as I remember it, we talked about l'Acadie for some fifteen to twenty minutes. Many years later, I asked Bogdanor if he also had been surprised at

Wheare's opening remark. He said no, that they had met before and agreed that the role of public servants in federal-provincial relations had not been given the necessary attention in the literature and that my thesis did break new ground, however modestly.

A few days later, Nevil invited me to dine with him at high table at Nuffield College. I asked him if he remembered our second meeting, when he had said that I should think of going across the channel to France.

"Yes, of course," he said. He added, "What you were looking for was a crutch and I was not about to give you one. You would either meet the standards or you would not." To my surprise, he then talked about l'Acadie, revealing a fairly deep knowledge of our history. On the many occassions I returned to Oxford, I always visited him. Nevil died in 2006, the year that he left Nuffield College.

Back in Canada, the head of DREE Atlantic, Harley McGee, asked to meet with me. He had read my thesis and was visibly upset. He saw it as a condemnation of DREE. He gave me very specific instructions, to put the thesis in the bottom drawer of my desk, never to see the light of day.

"We have a problem," I said. "The thesis has been formally accepted at Oxford and it is available to anyone through the Bodleian Library." I added that Richard Hatfield had asked for a copy and I had already sent him one. McGee became even more upset and said, "This is completely unacceptable."

It was my turn now to be upset, and I told him, "Harley, this thesis has nothing to do with you. I went to Oxford, wrote a thesis that I happen to be very proud of, and if you have a problem with it, then there is an easy solution – just tell me that I don't have to honour my two-year commitment to stay with the federal government and I'll be gone." He did not respond. As I left him, I told him that like it or not, I fully intended to see if someone was prepared to publish my thesis.

Other than Hatfield, the only person I sent my thesis to was Ted Hodgetts, the dean of Canadian public administration and a man for whom I have great admiration. He was at the time editor of the *Canadian Public Administration* series with McGill-Queen's University Press. I do not know if it was Hatfield, McGee, or rumours circulating in DREE about my encounter with McGee, but word got around Ottawa that I had written a provocative thesis. What I did not know, given that I had been out of Canada for a few years, was that DREE had become quite unpopular with politicians and a number of senior public servants. This, perhaps more than anything else, explains McGee's reaction.

Hodgetts wrote back to say that the anonymous reviews were in and that both were very positive. McGill-Queen's University Press would be publishing my first book. I was, of course, delighted, but it also meant that my position with DREE Atlantic was no longer tenable. However, McGee refused to release me.

In his retirement, Harley McGee wrote a book on his life as a DREE bureaucrat. He titled the book *Getting It Right,* and in it he takes issue on many occasions with the findings of my first book. I was asked to respond, but I never did. I saw no need. DREE was disbanded in the 1983 federal government reorganization. A number of DREE employees, however, retitled McGee's book *Getting Even with Savoie.*

Before Oxford, if a senior bureaucrat had told me to step in line, I would have probably done so fairly quickly. But no more. Among many things, Geoffrey Marshall and Nevil Johnson had taught the importance of standing up for your beliefs even if you are in a minority of one. I soon discovered that I was anything but in a minority of one.

7

Ottawa: It's Really about Ontario and Quebec

In 1980 Pierre Trudeau put an end to his planned retirement and led his party back to power. The Liberals had been in purgatory only for a few months before they ousted the Clark government and came roaring back with a majority mandate and ambitious plans to bring our constitution home from Britain. There were sure signs that there would be other changes as well. During their brief time in opposition, some senior Liberals had begun pointing their fingers at bureaucrats for having too much power and for having held back change when the Liberals were in power in the 1970s. While Trudeau focused his energy on the constitution, some of his senior ministers focused theirs on changing the machinery of government, rebalancing the relationship with bureaucrats in their favour, and securing more visibility for federal-provincial programs. Federal-provincial relations were about to undergo a dramatic change.

Word soon spread in some quarters in Ottawa that I had written a thesis that challenged Ottawa's long-standing role in regional economic development policy, particularly from a federal-provincial perspective. Some senior ministers – notably, the newly appointed DREE minister Pierre De Bané and the fisheries minister Roméo LeBlanc, a fellow Acadian – called to find out what my thesis was about. Before long, I was in Ottawa meeting with De Bané and LeBlanc.

De Bané made it clear that the government wanted to overhaul its approach to regional economic development and asked if I would be willing to work out of his office as senior policy adviser to assist in overseeing the change. I explained my dilemma – I was required to honour my two-year commitment to the public service. I expressed strong doubts that the department, and in particular Harley McGee, would agree to let me go.

The next day, the department's deputy minister, Robert Montreuil, asked to meet with me. To my utter surprise, not only did he support the proposed assignment but he strongly encouraged me to accept it. He did not agree with McGee on DREE's future, recognizing that the status quo was no longer sustainable. He said that the department was about to undergo massive change, whether some in the department agreed or not. He was sure that I would gain a great deal from the experience of seeing government from inside a minister's office. He said that if I agreed to join De Bané's team, not only would I do so as a public servant but I would still be meeting all my obligations to the government that were tied to my Oxford study program.

Of course, I agreed on the spot. Back in Moncton, Linda and I made plans to move to Ottawa as soon as possible. We now had two children. Margaux Caroline had been born in Moncton in January 1980. This birth was by caesarean section, given the complications with Julien. Margaux's second name, Caroline, was chosen because of Queen Caroline, who has been perched under the cupola at the entrance of Queen's College, Oxford, for nearly four hundred years. Margaux has been a joy to us both. She has inherited her mother's kindness, if not her patience.

THE TOPPLING OF DREE

My work in Ottawa was to provide advice to the minister on restructuring the department and to provide an Atlantic Canada perspective to federal regional development policy. I worked closely with De Bané on the first issue and with Roméo LeBlanc and Allan J. MacEachen on the second. It soon became clear to me that Trudeau and his senior ministers wanted to put the surgical knife to DREE. They were convinced that the federal government was not receiving anywhere near the visibility or political credit that Ottawa should be receiving, given the generous transfer of federal funds for regional development to provincial governments. MacEachen, then finance minister, went public in 1981 to say that "the federal government has a particular problem of program visibility because the programs [he had DREE in mind] are delivered by the provinces and because little is done to acknowledge publicly the important federal role."[1]

Ontario ministers and the powerful Department of Finance, meanwhile, had other problems with DREE. Finance officials have never been enamoured of Ottawa's regional development efforts. It will be recalled that Ottawa became concerned with the economic slowdown of the early 1980s, especially its potential impact on central Canada. It was the age of energy megaprojects in western Canada and the East Coast (Hibernia), and the thinking in Ottawa was that both western and Atlantic Canada would experience significant energy-driven growth while Ontario and Quebec would see increasing softness in their manufacturing sectors. DREE, with its traditional emphasis on Atlantic Canada, had outlived its usefulness. De Bané wrote to Trudeau asking for a review of the department. This, as much as anything else, sealed DREE's fate. If the minister could no longer support his own department and if no one else in Ottawa was prepared to go to bat for it, its future was bleak indeed.

Change to the machinery of government is the prerogative of the prime minister and the Privy Council Office, not individual ministers or even the cabinet. The director of the machinery of government unit was asked to take the lead in defining a new approach. We were in constant communication and had lunch once a month so that I could brief De Bané on how things were progressing. On 12 January 1982, Trudeau unveiled a major government reorganization that put an end to DREE.

New economic-development machinery was introduced, based on a 1981 Department of Finance paper and the need for more visibility for federal government spending. The Finance department maintained that Canada's regional balance was changing as a result of buoyancy in the West, optimism in the East, and "unprecedented softness" in key economic sectors in central Canada.[2] The new machinery allowed Ottawa to deliver economic development directly to clients rather than having to go through provincial governments. In speaking about the merits of the new structure, Trudeau said that the new agencies and departments would review all federal policies and programs to assess their regional impact. This, however, was never done. The new machinery did not last long, and more will be said about this later.

ONTARIO AND QUEBEC MATTER

Ottawa was an eye-opener for me in several ways. It does operate in a bubble in the sense that much of what matters in Ottawa does not matter anywhere else. Politicians, political assistants, and public servants can spend hours speculating on a pending cabinet shuffle or changes in the ranks of deputy ministers. People outside Ottawa are generally inclined to yawn over such matters.

But what struck me most about the Ottawa system is its inherent bias towards Ontario and Quebec; and what I find most amazing is that the system does not recognize its inherent bias. I have seen more than enough evidence that Ottawa is always quick to react at the first hint of economic slowdown in either province or when Quebec rattles the national unity agenda. Ontario and

Quebec issues are invariably viewed as national issues requiring urgent attention, while western or Atlantic Canada issues are viewed as regional ones.

The senior ranks of the public service, most of the senior ministers, and the national media are concentrated in Ontario and Quebec. The country's manufacturing sector is concentrated in Ontario and Quebec, and the powerful financial sector is in Ontario. This was done largely by design, not by market forces. I know that Ontario and Quebec and their apologists do not like to be reminded that all thirty-two crown corporations established as part of the war effort during the Second World War were located in those two provinces. As well, the bulk of ammunition factories and associated activities were in Ontario and Quebec (the Maritime provinces received only 3.7 percent of these investments). Many Maritimers left their communities, never to return, when told that it was in the national interest to work in those factories. As is well known, the thirty-two crown corporations played a pivotal role in the development of central Canada's manufacturing sector in the postwar period. Economists in Ottawa point to market forces to make the case that the federal government ought not to intervene, conveniently overlooking Ottawa's role in shaping its National Policy (circa 1880s), the Canada–US Auto Pact (which created jobs in southern Ontario, but also made automobiles more expensive in the rest of the country), the building of the St Lawrence Seaway – and the list goes on and on.

Parliament and all that accompanies and supports it straddles the Ontario and Quebec border. While the United States, Australia, and Germany all have credible and effective upper houses to speak for the political and economic interests of the regions, Canada has not. Ontario and Quebec have resisted and will continue to resist such a development, for they continue to dominate the House of Commons, the one chamber that establishes who has political power.

Not only does Canada lack an effective upper house to speak on behalf of the regions, but its federal public service is more centralized than that of either the United States or Australia. Where one stands on policy depends on where one sits. The Canadian civil service has offices in all provinces and regions. So where do federal bureaucrats actually sit? Their numbers in Ottawa-Gatineau went from 93,640 in 1996 to 112,234 in 2003 and in Toronto from 19,724 to 22,171 (an increase of 2,447). Calgary went from 6,049 to 6,548 (an increase of 499).[3]

Ontario gained 13,353 federal public servants between 1996 and 2003. Quebec gained 2,316 during the same period, and Alberta, 344. The losses? 346 for Manitoba, 46 for British Columbia, 853 for Saskatchewan, and 2,381 for Nova Scotia. Ontario was home to 42.8 percent of federal civil servants in 2003, Quebec had 21.2 percent, Atlantic Canada 13 percent, and western Canada 22.5 percent.

Numbers tell only part of the story. On the whole, civil servants operating in local and regional offices deliver government programs and services but they do not play much of a policy advisory role, whereas the senior executive category, which does, is concentrated largely in Ottawa. Deputy ministers (with four exceptions) are all in Ottawa, but even the four located outside that city do not spend a great deal of time away from the capital. One Treasury Board official reports that "now over 70 percent of the Executive category is located in Ottawa." He adds that this trend can be traced back to the program-review exercise of the mid-1990s. Moreover, a significant portion of federal policy work is contracted out to consultants and research groups, and something like 70 percent of cabinet documents are now prepared by outside consultants – a practice that would have been unthinkable forty years ago. The great majority of these consultants and think-tanks are, of course, located in Ottawa.

By contrast, in the United States, over 80 percent of all federal civil servants (non-military) are located outside the District of Columbia, Virginia, and Maryland.[4] In Australia, the number is close to 70 percent. These countries have elected senates to provide a regional voice at the centre of government.[5] This may in fact explain why the civil service in these two countries is more decentralized than it is in Canada. One senior Treasury Board official reports that the percentage of federal civil servants located in Ottawa has gone up further in recent months and is now very close to 40 percent. Since both the United States and Australia have elected senates, there is probably less need to have the civil service speak for regional circumstances and interests, just as there is a greater need for such a role in Canada.

I attended a meeting in 1981 to review Ottawa's regional economic development policy. Among a few others, it was attended by Pierre De Bané, Allan J. MacEachen, and Gordon Osbaldeston. Osbaldeston was one of Ottawa's senior bureaucrats and highly respected in both political and bureaucratic circles. He made an observation that has stuck with me ever since. I cannot reproduce his exact words, but using a hockey analogy, he said that the system is designed for Ontario and Quebec, and once in a while Atlantic Canada will manage to get a breakaway. His point was that the Ottawa system generates policies and programs that correspond to central Canada's economic circumstances but that this is not so for Atlantic or western Canada. Once in a while, a powerful minister from one of these regions – for example, Allan J. MacEachen (Nova Scotia) or Ralph Goodale (Saskatchewan) – will strong-arm his way to secure a project for his region, hence the "breakaway" analogy.

I was to learn, however, that even breakaways are sometimes not permitted. Hector Hortie, the head of DREE in Nova Scotia, met with me when I was senior policy adviser to report some good news. He and his office had initiated negotiations with Deutz Diesel to locate some of its activities in Nova Scotia, and the early negotiations held promise. Although he saw merit in informing MacEachen, his regional minister, he asked when DREE Nova Scotia should brief DREE head office on the negotiations. My response was, "As soon as possible." The problem with doing so, Hortie explained, was that DREE Ottawa and other ministers and departments would try to bring Ontario and Quebec into the equation. "Unlikely," I insisted.

The next week, a briefing note went up through the hierarchy, informing senior management in Ottawa and the minister on the efforts to attract Deutz to Nova Scotia. Within a few weeks, I learned that DREE Quebec was in the process of making an offer to Deutz to locate in the Montreal region. I asked both De Bané and Robert Montreuil, the deputy minister, how this could happen. They saw no problem. Offers could be made from whatever office, and it would be up to Deutz to decide where to locate its activities. I saw many things wrong with this turn of events. DREE was disbanded before any firm offers could be made, so Deutz did not locate any activities in Nova Scotia.

Ottawa invariably argues that its role is to pursue the national interest through national policies. People outside Ontario and Quebec have come to recognize that "national policy" is code for Ontario's and Quebec's interests. The thirty-two crown corporations established during the Second World War are a case in point. But that is hardly all. National museums, the National Arts Centre, the National Gallery, the National Ballet – or, for that matter, the national anything and everything – must, it seems, be located in Ontario or Quebec. The Canadian Space Agency, national aerospace strategy, and national research and development measures are also centred on Ontario-Quebec (though Alberta's oil wealth has begun to tilt the research and development balance west).

Some years ago, I participated in a round table in Ottawa that brought together policy analysts from across Canada, but mostly from Ontario. A number of them expressed deep concern over the North American Free Trade Agreement, saying that we could well see "the Maritimization of Ontario's economy." Ontario activities, they worried, would flow to larger centres in the United States. We knew all about the Maritimization of our economy, and until someone can demonstrate otherwise, we in the Maritimes will continue to believe that over the years national policies, more than market forces, explain our economic difficulties.

National politicians (here, read those from Ontario and Quebec), such as Jean Chrétien, insist that it is simply the "Canadian way" when one region maintains that it has been shortchanged by Confederation. This is a vapid argument that simply sidesteps the issue. It is an easy way out for "national politicians." Over the years, the federal government could have documented the impact of its policies and programs on all regions. It has never done so. I recall, however, that both Pierre Trudeau in 1982 and Brian Mulroney in 1988 firmly committed Ottawa to undertaking a thorough review of the regional impact of national policies and programs. However, what the Department of Finance and the Ontario government have often done is to document the flow of federal transfer payments to the regions. This is easy to do; and, sure enough, on a per capita basis, more federal transfers flow to the Atlantic provinces than to Ontario. The Harper 2007 reforms to the equalization program did, however, tilt the flow of payments to favour Quebec.

People forget that federal transfer payments, notably the equalization payments, were established in the late 1950s at least in part to compensate regions for the uneven effect of national policies. Policy makers in the 1950s recognized that the National Policy of the 1880s, the war effort, and national industrial policy have not been applied evenly across Canada but have favoured some regions at the expense of others. Accounting for transfer payments by region is relatively straightforward, but it says nothing about other federal spending: salaries for public servants, tax incentives, which largely favour Ontario and Alberta, investment in research and development, and so on. It takes only a moment's reflection to appreciate that when it comes to economic development, a dollar spent on research and development is worth a great deal more than a dollar spent on equalization or employment insurance. Indeed, a dollar spent through transfer payments can actually inhibit economic development.

FRIENDS

I worked very closely with Roméo LeBlanc while in DREE Ottawa. We met often and established a close and lasting friendship. He understood Ottawa, having worked there as a journalist, later as a senior official in the Prime Minister's Office, and later still as a senior minister in the Trudeau government. Although I never became as close to Allan J. MacEachen, I also worked well with him, a powerful political minister from Cape Breton. I learned a great deal from the two men, including how to generate a breakaways.

I fondly recall a breakaway for New Brunswick. DREE decided in 1981 to establish a unit with a mandate to identify firms with high-growth potential and see if they would be willing to locate some of their planned activities in slow-growth areas. I had an excellent working rapport with DREE's senior managers, including Robert Montreuil, the deputy minister, and the new head of the unit who was from the Maritimes. He came to me with an exciting prospect concerning Mitel, which in the early 1980s was one of Canada's leading high-growth hi-tech firms. It was led by two high-profile Ottawa-based entrepreneurs, Michael Cowpland and Terry Matthews. Mitel produced telecommunications equipment and registered 100 percent growth year after year during the late 1970s and had sales of $100 million by 1981.

Mitel was looking to expand, and DREE decided that it should employ some of its resources to influence the firm in deciding where to locate the expansion. The head of the new unit came to me with the news that Mitel had decided to locate a new plant in Renfrew, near Ottawa, but had plans for two other new plants, and it was open to a site in Atlantic Canada.

"Any suggestions?" he asked.

"Sure," I replied, "Bouctouche."

He knew New Brunswick, but he was not at all certain that Mitel would have any interest in Bouctouche.

"We will only know if we try," I said.

A few weeks later, I attended a meeting with DREE's senior management and Michael Cowpland, and we put forward the Bouctouche possibility. Cowpland had, of course, no idea where on earth Bouctouche was, but he said that he would be happy to take a look.

Cowpland came back the following week to report that he had a strong interest in locating in Bouctouche. He had visited the community, flown overhead, and said that the area had a striking resemblance to the village where he was born in the United King-dom. In addition, he said that his staff told him that there would be little difficulty in attracting employees. Not only was unemployment high, but apparently some of the locals had the skills Mitel was looking for. Mitel needed people who were dexterous with their hands because of the need to assemble telecommunications equipment. Fish plant workers had such skills, and it would be easy to attract them to work at the new plant. I was also told that Cowpland had already selected a Bouctouche site to locate the first of two plants. We were in business.

All parties agreed that this had to be done in great secrecy. Other ministers and other federal departments should not be told until the last minute for fear they would try to entice Mitel elsewhere. We agreed that we would not even inform the Hatfield government in New Brunswick. This was the era when the federal government wanted greater visibility for its spending and wished to deliver more and more initiatives directly rather than going through the provinces. I readily admit that at the time I was a strong proponent of this view.

I made it clear to all that I had to inform Roméo LeBlanc, if only because Bouctouche was in his constituency. In any event, anyone who knew LeBlanc knew that he was one of the most discreet politicians in Ottawa, having honed his communication skills when working for the CBC and in Trudeau's office. I met with LeBlanc to tell him that DREE was on the verge of striking a deal with Mitel to locate two plants in Bouctouche. He was, of course, delighted, only asking if we had looked at Memramcook, his home village.

"No," I said, "it was Bouctouche all the way, and Cowpland was most pleased with what he saw. In any event, Bouctouche is part of your constituency, and there are no fish plants for miles around Memramcook." He understood the need for secrecy, probably better than anyone else.

Negotiations progressed very well, and soon DREE had a firm deal with Mitel. Press releases were prepared, and the date 16 July 1981 was fixed for making the announcement in Bouctouche.

LeBlanc would make it on behalf of the federal government. The day before the announcement, he called to go over the press release and to see whether it would not be better to announce just one plant rather than two. He feared raising expectations and not being able to deliver all the goods. I said that we had a firm deal with Mitel and that it was hardly possible to negotiate anything at this late hour. Besides, he would be the main spokesperson for the government and was free to focus his comments exclusively on the first plant.

I made my way to Bouctouche for the announcement. I sat with my brother Claude and some of our friends discreetly at the very back of the room. The word of new plants for Bouctouche had spread quickly in the community that afternoon, and a good number of residents attended the announcement, if only out of curiosity. LeBlanc talked about the progress Acadians were making everywhere and asked that I stand up because, he reported, "this guy from Saint-Maurice, down the road from here, worked hard to make this initiative a reality for Bouctouche." Then he proceeded with the big announcement – "two plants for Bouctouche, 1,000 new jobs, with a total investment of $48 million. DREE would invest $15.7 million."[6] I remember Bouctouche residents walking around after the announcement not quite believing what they had heard – a case of too good to be true.

Construction on the first plant was to begin immediately, and LeBlanc made it clear that the project was strictly a federal initiative. Indeed, the Hatfield government first learned of the project through the media, like everyone else. The federal Department of Industry also learned of it only as a *fait accompli*. But the Department of Industry considered the high-tech sector to be its own, not to be shared with DREE. It was busy promoting the sector in such areas as Kanata, Montreal, Toronto, and Waterloo, and it saw no reason why DREE should elbow its way in to bring jobs to a small Acadian village.

I remain convinced that the Mitel decision was one factor in the government's decision to do away with DREE. Ottawa could hardly allow a rogue department running around trying to attract new investment in the manufacturing sector in far-flung communities such as Bouctouche. The sector, particularly the high-tech sector, belonged to Ontario and Quebec.

Mitel did build two new and highly attractive plants, one in Renfrew and one in Bouctouche. But the company began to encounter serious financial difficulties even as the plants were being constructed. It was slow in introducing its new products, the competition was now hot on its heels, and the economic recession of the early 1980s forced Mitel to cut jobs. In the end, Mitel Bouctouche hired a director of personnel but did little else. He now works as chief of staff to Dominic LeBlanc, MP for Beauséjour and Roméo LeBlanc's son. The Renfrew plant did open, however, did hire staff, and did operate briefly. But although the Bouctouche plant was completed, it lay vacant for a long time. It is now home to Kanalflakt AB, an international company that manufactures ventilation systems primarily for the industrial market. Ottawa, meanwhile, came to the rescue of the Renfrew plant when Mitel left town, and it is now home to the National Archives.

LeBlanc called to ask me to meet him for breakfast one day. *L'Évangéline*, New Brunswick's only French-language daily newspaper, which began publishing in 1887, closed its doors in 1982. Management and labour were embroiled in controversy, and with little advance notice, the paper closed down. LeBlanc asked what could be done. I saw no role for government, let alone the federal government, in running newspapers and said so.

"What are Acadians now to read?" he asked.

"Someone, somewhere, will be coming forward with something," I answered.

"When?" He feared that Acadians would start reading local English-language dailies, that they would get used to it and would lose their language.

History has proved LeBlanc right, because many Acadians, particularly in the Moncton area, were quick to switch to English-language dailies. However, governments decided to intervene, and both senior orders of government agreed to establish an endowment fund to support a French-language newspaper in New

Brunswick. The fund was designed in part to underwrite part of the circulation costs so that the newspaper would be available in all French-language communities in the province. The newspaper, *L'Acadie nouvelle*, began publication on 5 September 1989.

On another occasion, LeBlanc called with a specific assignment in mind. He said that his political career was coming to an end and he wanted to do something for the Université de Moncton before leaving political life. He had worked at the university for two years after he left Trudeau's office and before he ran for Parliament. The federal government, he reported, had supported all manner of initiatives in virtually every Canadian university while he sat in the cabinet, and he felt that the Université de Moncton had already waited too long for its turn. Further, he had discussed the possibility with Trudeau, who had given him his go-ahead. Trudeau had always been vocal in support of the Université de Moncton, pointing out that it was one of the first universities that had granted him an honorary degree. For Trudeau, the Université de Moncton was an important symbol of his vision of a French Canada that extended beyond Quebec.

LeBlanc talked about a possible initiative to promote research at the university. He had nothing specific in mind but asked if I would meet with Gilbert Finn, the university president, to discuss the possibility. Finn welcomed LeBlanc's initiative, which came as no surprise. We talked about the possibilities and settled on a research institute. Finn, former head of the Assomption Society, had a strong bias in favour of economic development, and before long it was agreed that the proposal would focus on regional economic development.

LeBlanc came up with a level of financial commitment that he could support – Ottawa would commit $5 million, provided the university contributed $1.5 million. I acted as the go-between, which was not difficult, since Finn soon gave his approval. Trudeau later told me that he had chaired the cabinet committee meeting at which the government agreed to the proposal. Unknown to me, Finn had called Roméo LeBlanc with one more demand – that I would come home to head the new institute – or no deal. LeBlanc once again called for a breakfast meeting and asked if I would go to Moncton to set up the institute, at least for a few years. I said I would think about it, talk to Linda, and get back to him. However, I had by then moved on to new responsibilities.

FROM DREE TO PCO

Trudeau's decision to abolish DREE in January 1982 meant that I had to move on. Montreuil was appointed deputy minister to the new larger Department of Regional Industrial Expansion (DRIE) and asked if I would be interested in joining that department. I declined. By then my first book, *Federal-Provincial Collaboration*, was out, and before long, a number of people in Ottawa had taken notice.

The reaction of Gérard Veilleux, a senior official with the Department of Finance, to my book was a far cry from Harley McGee's. He congratulated me on it. In June 1982 I met with the prime minister. He, too, had read the book and quite liked it, saying that it shed new light on Canadian federalism. I was tongue-tied and was hardly able to stammer an awkward thank-you. I never expected for a moment that the prime minister would have had time to read my book, let alone appreciate it. I did not stay around long enough for him to change his mind.

This was all heady stuff for me. I recounted Trudeau's reaction to one of his senior associates and asked if Trudeau had actually read the book. He answered, "If Trudeau said that he read it, then he read it. You know, the prime minister likes to read, and he reads a great deal more than some people think." On reflection, I realized that my book supported all that Trudeau stood for – a more visible and distinct role for the federal government in federal-provincial relations and in delivering public services, and a stronger role for senior politicians in shaping public policy. Had my first book argued the opposite or approved of the DREE federal-provincial model, which so clearly favoured provincial governments in their dealings with the federal government, Trudeau would not have noticed the book; or if he had, he would likely have dismissed it out of hand. Still, it was not lost on me that Harley McGee, a senior DREE bureaucrat, had instructed me to put my thesis in the bottom drawer of my desk, never to see the light of day, whereas the prime minister was telling me that he quite enjoyed reading it.

Veilleux, meanwhile, saw merit in the book because he had also written on federal-provincial relations and because he headed federal-provincial efforts in the Department of Finance. He felt that Ottawa was all too often put on the defensive by provincial governments in their constant demands for more. He strongly endorsed my book's call to rebalance the relationship between the federal and provincial governments. I often met Veilleux in Ottawa, and we forged a close friendship that has lasted to this day.

Trudeau appointed Veilleux as his deputy minister for federal-provincial relations in the Privy Council Office (PCO), and before long, Veilleux suggested that I compete for the position of director of provincial analysis in the federal-provincial relations section. I won the competition. Not long after I began work in the PCO, Veilleux told me that he had just had lunch with Roméo LeBlanc and that they had talked about the new institute at the Université de Moncton. He said that the institute was important to some senior politicians in Ottawa and there was a view that I should go to establish it. His advice: "Go set it up, spend a few years to make sure it is running fine and then come back to Ottawa." He said that he would see to it that the PCO would lend me to the Université de Moncton so that I could return to Ottawa in a year or two after the institute was up and running.

I went down to Moncton to meet with Gilbert Finn again before making any decision. Finn has always been a no-nonsense business-oriented individual. Within minutes of my walking into his office, he came to the point. He said that he had told LeBlanc that I "had to" return to Moncton to set up the institute, otherwise there would be no deal. Then he told me that one university official had suggested that someone be brought from France to lead the institute. Finn would have none of that, nor would the university's two vice-presidents agree to turn things over to *un Français de France*. Surely, he argued, we have made enough progress in twenty-five years or so that one of our own can lead a new research institute. What message would the university be sending to Acadians or to the community if we had to turn the keys over to someone from France? He explained that he would have no difficulty having someone from France head a second, third, or fourth institute being established at the university, but not the first one.

I told Finn about Veilleux's offer, and he was pleased and relieved. He suggested that I set up the institute and find someone to take over in three or four years. In his opinion, it would be less of a problem if the second director came from away. Linda greatly enjoyed Ottawa and was reluctant to move back to Moncton, but if that was what I wanted, she would go along with my decision, she said.

I met with LeBlanc and said that I was prepared to take up Veilleux's offer. However, I had one condition, and I wanted to make it clear to LeBlanc, Finn, and anyone else who had an interest in the institute and its future. I said that I wanted above all to give the institute an academic mandate that would be as credible as any at Queen's University or the University of Toronto. This meant that I would not engage in community initiatives or sponsor local round tables or conferences. I made the case that the Université de Moncton now needed to compete in academic circles, and it needed to be much more than a community development agency. LeBlanc, like Finn a few days earlier, said that he had no problem with where I wanted to take the institute. He did, however, have some advice. He told me to make certain that I establish very early on what I wanted to do with the institute and stick to it, because what I did in the first six months would set the direction for the institute for a long time. He told me that when he went to work at the university, he decided to get to the office by 7:30 every morning for two weeks. That was it. From then on, he had the reputation of being an early riser. It didn't matter what time he came in after those first two weeks, his reputation was set. He advised me that if I set the parameters of the institute very early and stuck to them, things would work out.

In making the announcement on behalf of the federal government, LeBlanc reflected: "I, for one, saw from Victoria to St John's a large number of research institutes or centres, located on university campuses, looking into all kinds of issues. But none was designed to study regional development. We decided to correct this by combining our efforts with the Université de Moncton to create a first-class research institute." For his part, Finn said that his wish was to see the new institute "meet the highest possible academic standards." I had the mandate I was looking for, and now I had to get the job done.

8

Going Home

I arrived at the Université de Moncton in the summer of 1983 and went straight to work. I knew the campus well, of course, having been a student there. As well, I had taught there when I was working with DREE. I followed Roméo LeBlanc's advice and made it as clear as I could in the first weeks that my objective was to establish a research institute that was the equal of any in Canada and that the litmus test would be our publications.

The Trudeau government endowed the Canadian Institute for Research on Regional Development (CIRRD) with $5 million of federal funds over five years, provided that the university make a $1.5 million contribution. Before long, I began to get a reaction – some of it cynical, some disparaging. John Meisel, a distinguished political scientist at Queen's University, called to say, "This institute at the Université de Moncton is really a form of patronage." Meisel has always been a good friend, an extremely generous and gentle man, as anyone who knows him will readily attest. My response was, "John, would you rather see patronage build a few more kilometres of road here in New Brunswick or try to develop the Université de Moncton?"

"You have a point," he replied.

I heard that a few academics at Carleton and Dalhousie were somewhat upset that the institute would be located at Moncton rather than at their own universities. I only heard this through the grapevine, and no one from either of the two campuses had Meisel's courage to call me directly. I wasn't surprised by the criticism – it comes with the territory. I have, over the years, come to the conclusion that there is nothing in government too small that you can't wrap a process around it, and there is nothing in academe too small that you can't fight over it. Meisel, however, called a few years later to say that he and a colleague-friend, Jean Laponce from the University of British Columbia, were about to retire and wanted to set up a research institute on language, ethnicity, and political conflict. They were looking for federal funding and asked if I had any advice.

"Ah, John, you are looking for patronage, are you?"

"Touché," he said, with a hearty laugh.

I suggested that he contact the Department of the Secretary of State, which had at the time the federal government's mandate for both post-secondary education and minority language rights. I don't know if he was ever successful.

Meanwhile, at the Université de Moncton, some of the faculty and even some in the administration thought that I was setting the bar a bit too high. The university was still very young, and many of the faculty members were still working on their PhD theses. One faculty member told me caustically that we all have to learn to walk before we can run and that the university had only just begun to walk. His point was that I was setting the institute up to fail, since it would not be able to deliver the publications I envisaged.

None of this shook my resolve. I made only one concession. I agreed that the institute would provide typing services to faculty members who were working to complete their doctoral theses. Otherwise, we would concentrate on one thing: to "publish or perish," much like universities the world over. I was adamant, however, that the institute would not support community projects or entertain financial requests from faculty to attend conferences and the like.

I looked for faculty members with publications in the social sciences, but they were thin on the ground. Rodolphe Lamarche had a PhD in geography, and I invited him to the institute. He worked there for several years and was very helpful in defining a research agenda. I hired Maurice Beaudin, a young Acadian from northeastern New Brunswick, who had just completed his MA in economics at the Université de Moncton. I encouraged him to enrol in a doctoral program, which he eventually did. Over the years, he has produced solid research reports for the public sector, and by all accounts he is now an excellent professor of economics at the Université de Moncton – Shippagan campus.

The institute sponsored a number of young Acadians to undertake graduate work. Pierre-Marcel Desjardins completed his doctorate at the University of Texas and now teaches in the Department of Economics at the Université de Moncton. Sébastien Breau did his doctorate at the University of California at Los Angeles and he is now on faculty at McGill University, where he shows strong potential as a scholar.

It soon became apparent that if the institute were to make its mark, I would have to roll up my own sleeves and get busy researching and writing. The institute's early years were productive years for me. I published *Regional Economic Development: Canada's Search for Solutions* with the University of Toronto Press and co-authored a book on economic development for the Presses de l'Université du Québec. I published an edited book with Methuen Press and co-published a book of essays on regional economic development at the Presses de l'Université de Montréal. I also published a number of articles in the *Canadian Journal of Political Science*, *Canadian Public Policy*, *Canadian Public Administration*, the *Journal of Canadian Studies*, and the *Canadian Journal of Regional Science*. I was not about to perish. More important, I greatly enjoyed the research and working at the institute. My publications had the added bonus of answering those who were critical of the institute's being located at the Université de Moncton. I recall Meisel calling to congratulate me on my publications and on the institute's progress in the early years.

BEN HIGGINS

I had no choice but to call on outside scholars to lend a hand at the institute until faculty members were in a position to contribute. Ben Higgins, a Canadian living in Australia, came highly recommended, and I invited him to spend time at the institute as a visiting scholar. He came in the summer of 1985 and returned every summer for the next ten years. It was one of the best decisions I ever made. Ben's contribution to the institute was immense. He did everything – published an important body of work, made himself available to faculty and students, and produced a number of research reports for governments. Ben and his lovely wife Jean became part of the family at the institute.

Ben was special in many ways. He was an excellent scholar, a fine human being, and a generous soul. His life was about scholarship, little else. He had no interest in material things or, for that matter, in things that did not relate to research or public policy. However, his innate *joie de vivre* made him a delightful companion.

Ben had a distinguished career. He taught, variously, at Harvard University, Massachusetts Institute of Technology, McGill University, and the Université de Montréal. He published seminal works in economics and international development and had friends all over the world. He had taught both John F. Kennedy and Robert Kennedy at Harvard (he told me that Robert worked harder than his brother) and was a classmate of Nobel laureate Paul Samuelson and a close friend of John Kenneth Galbraith. He knew Joseph Schumpeter, one of the leading thinkers of the twentieth century.

We had lunch with Paul Samuelson at the MIT faculty club, and I could sense the warm friendship between the two. Samuelson asked about Ben's children and knew them all by name. I recall Samuelson saying that a recent MIT productivity study had revealed that French Canadians from Quebec working in the Waltham area were highly productive in the construction sector when compared with their peers. I quickly corrected him – they were French-speaking Canadians, all right, but they were Acadians, not Québécois. I explained the difference, and he seemed interested by my explanation. I was not about to let the Québécois take credit before a Nobel laureate for something that Acadians had done.

Ben also introduced me to the Canadian-born Harvard economist John Kenneth Galbraith, and we remained in touch until his death in 2006. I wrote to Galbraith after he gave a talk at Mount Allison University in 1986. I had been struck by what he had to say: here was one of the world's leading Liberal thinkers arguing that government bureaucracy had, in recent years, given government a bad reputation. His talk prompted me to start work on my book *The Politics of Public Spending in Canada,* and I wrote to tell him so. He wrote back to encourage me to continue my work on public bureaucracy, insisting that we needed more work in this area. I acknowledge Galbraith's encouragement in the book's preface.

As is well known, John F. Kennedy appointed Galbraith U.S. ambassador to India. When I visited Galbraith at his home in Cambridge, the lady who answered the door was East Indian and I told her that Galbraith had invited me for coffee. She asked me in, and then off she went at a snail's pace to get Galbraith. I couldn't imagine that someone could walk so slowly, so unhurriedly. It was truly amazing. She wouldn't have lasted half a day working for my father. I also recall one of Galbraith's observations that has stayed with me ever since. He commented that signing a letter with "Ph.D." after the name was a sure sign of a "failed academic." That was some years ago, and I have noticed ever since that Galbraith's observation almost invariably holds true.

Galbraith wrote parts of *The Scotch* while listening to speeches during his time in India in the early 1960s. He discovered that while one can't get away with reading a book, because it would be too obvious, it is perfectly possible to write one. I can now admit that I often wrote during meetings of unbearable length in Ottawa, trusting that it looked as if I was dutifully taking notes.

Ben Higgins was a close friend of Pierre Trudeau. They met in Montreal while they were both teaching at the Université de Montréal. Ben wrote some policy papers on economic development for Trudeau when he ran for the leadership of the Liberal Party. They had lunch every summer, often at the McGill faculty club when Ben was at the institute. Ben would always brief Trudeau on how things were going at the institute.

Ben and I decided to honour the French economist François Perroux by sponsoring a conference to review his published work. Perroux, it will be recalled, launched a new fad in public policy when he published his work on the growth pole concept. Perroux had limited confidence in the free market and believed that dynamic capitalist economies required some level of planning and management. He argued that economic activity tends to concentrate around certain focal points and that efforts to strengthen these focal points in slow-growth regions can start a process of self-sustaining economic growth. During the late 1960s and 1970s, there was scarcely a developed or developing country that did not make use of this concept, and Canada was no exception. DREE developed its programs around the growth pole concept when it was first established in 1968. The concept is irrevocably associated with Perroux, a prolific man who remained so right up to his death in 1987 at the age of eighty-three. The well-known American economist Paul Streeten once described him as a "giant figure of Nobel Prize stature."

Through Ben's contacts, we were able to assemble a who's who of economists to participate in the conference. William Alonso came from Harvard, Lloyd Rodwin and Karen Polenske from MIT, John Friedmann from UCLA, and Harry Richardson, who held a dual appointment at the State University of New York and the University of Southern California. François Perroux himself gave a paper, which was to be one of his last. I still have his original paper in my office with his handwritten notes in the margin.

I decided to hold the conference at Grand-Pré in the late spring of 1986. Ironie de l'histoire, the hotel where we held the conference, overlooked the Minas Basin, where the Grand Dérangement had begun some 230 years before. I hoped the ghosts of my ancestors were there to see scholars from the English-speaking world honouring a French economist.

I paid special attention to Perroux, given his advanced age. We had a minor incident when he fell while taking a bath, but he was soon up and about again. He attended the conference but paid attention to the various papers only when he felt like it. He had a hearing aid, and when things got boring, he simply turned it off and had a snooze. At one point, he woke up to turn on his hearing aid precisely at the moment that Fernand Martin, an economist from the Université de Montréal, was raising some concerns about the application of the growth pole concept to Canada. Perroux was outraged. As only a Frenchman can, he showed no mercy as he laid into Martin. Deliberately (I suspect) mispronouncing his name, he said, "Who is this Martin Ferdinand? What stupidity is he here to voice? Who invited this imposter? What has this individual ever published?" We all felt awkward, especially Martin, of course. As he said later, if only Perroux had kept his hearing aid on throughout his presentation, he would have reacted quite differently. At one point, Perroux jumped up and began to walk out of the room. Someone asked where he was going. "I am going to urinate," Perroux shot back, saying that it would be time better spent than listening to "this Martin Ferdinand's" diatribe.

The conference, nevertheless, ended on a high note. After things calmed down, Martin was able to explain his views at some length to Perroux. Ben and I put together the conference papers, which were published by Unwin Hyman of London, England. The book was very well received by critics.

That was the first of many joint publications with Ben Higgins. Ben was a delight to work with, always cheerful and always coming up with new ideas or new projects to explore. We published a number of articles and four books together. I also co-edited a book in his honour. I had the good fortune of visiting

Ben and Jean on their ranch in Australia in 1993 to work on our book *Regional Development Theories and Their Application.*

Ben and Jean had an infectious zest for life combined with a complete lack of pretension. They visited many communities in the Maritime provinces every summer and fell in love with every single place they visited. They invariably came back saying how lovely the people were and with suggestions on how the last community they had visited could turn its economic fortunes around.

Ben had a regular schedule. Although he spent the evening drinking scotch, he was in the office next day by 11 AM. He worked away on an old electric typewriter until past 6 PM. That was his standard routine, and there was no sense trying to alter it. I did try once, and it upset his productivity for a few days. He was an excellent writer, always able to produce a remarkable paper at short notice. He would start the day with a coffee, cough a few times, and then off he would go. All he ever wanted out of life was a supply of scotch, a decent library, an old typewriter, an even older automobile, friends, and Jean. Nothing more.

I have other fond memories of my early years with the institute. I had some correspondence and a few telephone calls from Clément Cormier, founder of the Université de Moncton. His letters were beautifully written. In one, he wrote to congratulate me on the publication of one of my books on regional economic development. He wrote that he was in some ways jealous of my work because that is precisely what he wanted to do. He had gone to Laval, he said, to study and do research, but his religious community had never permitted him to pursue his research interests. Instead, he was continually called on by his religious order to lead a project such as the establishment of the Université de Moncton. Cormier took great satisfaction, however, in having laid the groundwork to enable Acadians to do what he had always wanted to do.

I very recently learned, while going through old files here at the university in gathering material for this book, that Cormier was a key player in promoting my appointment as an officer of the Order of Canada. In his letter to the order's advisory committee, he wrote that I had, through my publications, been able to give the institute a strong academic reputation and had made an important contribution to the development of the Université de Moncton. Cormier, perhaps more that anyone, understood what I set out to accomplish at the institute.

THE PRIME MINISTER CALLS

In the last week of August 1986, Premier Richard Hatfield invited me to lunch in Fredericton. He had just returned from Toronto, where he had met the Ontario provincial minister of industry, who had urged Hatfield to read my book on regional development. Hatfield said over lunch, "When a provincial minister from Ontario recommends that I read a book on regional development in Canada, I worry. What did you say in that book?" He then asked whether I thought that DRIE was doing good work in Atlantic Canada. It will be recalled that in Trudeau's 1982 government reorganization, DREE (Department of Regional Economic Expansion) became DRIE (Department of Regional Industrial Expansion) as part of Ottawa's decision to strengthen central Canada's industrial base and manufacturing sector.

I said, "Absolutely not."

"What should we do then?" he asked.

I argued that the last thing Atlantic Canada needed was more government programs and more government money. We had plenty of both, I said, and we should have them work better, focus on local entrepreneurs, review federal policies and programs that discriminate against Atlantic Canada, assist small businesses with their marketing and their research and development, and have an agency dedicated solely to Atlantic Canada's economic development. Above all, we needed an agency with a "bias for action," rather than top-down bureaucratic programs. I told Hatfield that we needed to be innovative in resolving issues concerning the administrative and bureaucratic structure of the agency.

Hatfield agreed with most of my analysis and asked if I would prepare a "five pager" on the matter. I did and sent it to him within a few days. The following week he gave the prime minister a copy, without so much as changing a comma, when Mulroney made a brief stop in Fredericton on his way to a cabinet committee meeting in St John's. Mulroney returned a few weeks later to meet with the Atlantic premiers, and he informed them that he would be asking me to prepare a report on establishing the Atlantic Canada Opportunities Agency (ACOA) and that I would be consulting with them and other Atlantic Canadians.

I was well aware that DRIE was generally thought to be a failure. Nowhere was this view more widely held than in Atlantic Canada. DRIE was regarded as essentially preoccupied with central Canada, with only limited interest in the economic fortunes of the eastern provinces. Atlantic premiers told Mulroney during that visit in September 1986 that DRIE had become a significant part of the problem in Atlantic Canada. How could it possibly help to alleviate regional disparities, they argued, when it offered more generous financial assistance to firms wishing to locate in southern Ontario than, say, in Nova Scotia? There were several such documented cases. It would be better to disband DRIE completely, the premiers claimed, than to keep it operating. After all, the only thing DRIE was really accomplishing was to exacerbate regional disparities between Atlantic Canada and the rest of the country.

DRIE had other serious problems as well. The Treasury Board discovered that the department was going to overspend its 1986–87 grants and contributions budget by nearly $350 million. In addition, its minister, Michel Côté, was forced to resign over a conflict of interest. In any event, DRIE was Trudeau's creation, not Mulroney's. As every prime minister likes to leave his or her own imprimatur on the machinery of government, DRIE's future was doomed. The point here is that I did not need to spend much time defending the status quo; it was already dead by the time the prime minister asked me to write a report on the way ahead for Atlantic Canada. He suggested that I work closely with his office on the project. Initially, at least, I did so, but in time Dalton Camp became my main point of contact. He had been appointed a senior official in the PCO, but he felt uncomfortable working with career bureaucrats. As I understood it, the feeling was mutual and so, for all practical purposes, Dalton hung his hat in the Prime Minister's Office.

We worked very well together. We either met or talked by telephone at least once a week. Dalton had a visceral dislike of career public servants, so communication between him and them was difficult. As a result, I decided to establish contact with the PCO through Jack (John L.) Manion, associate clerk of the privy council. I had learned while working in the PCO earlier that it was always best to keep the office informed of developments and to avoid surprises if we wanted to promote a file successfully. Manion's advice and support proved extremely valuable, and he and I formed a lasting friendship. In brief, Camp looked after the politicians while I looked after Manion and the senior bureaucrats, and criss-crossed Atlantic Canada to consult with over a hundred public- and private-sector executives.

I worked on the ACOA project from October 1986 to May 1987, virtually full time. I decided not to begin writing the report until I had completed most of the interviews, from which I learned a great deal. I recall asking an entrepreneur from Trepassey, Newfoundland, "How's business?" He answered in a thick Newfoundland accent, "Boy, she's slow; any slower than this, boy, she'd be goin' backwards." Things were tough in Trepassey, and I imagine that they still are.

Camp always had a keen interest in finding out who said what, particularly the provincial premiers and federal cabinet ministers. I reported in general terms but wisely decided not to repeat specific comments, especially any criticism. Camp had an excellent sense of humour and was extremely wise, and I could tell that he knew that I was always holding back on some gossip. He also had a very deep attachment and commitment to Atlantic Canada – it was in his DNA. He had a healthy distrust of Ottawa and central Canada's attitude towards the Maritime provinces. He was convinced that Ottawa could never designate policies and programs tailored to the region's economic circumstances. He never spent much time talking about Acadians, but I didn't detect any animosity towards us. He was a partisan Conservative, but, at least in private, he never hesitated to be critical of Conservative cabinet ministers or even the government when it made what he regarded as bad decisions.

When I met with premiers and federal cabinet ministers, I would walk in, introduce myself, and ask where they wanted me to sit. John Crosbie, then Mulroney's minister of transport, inquired, "Aren't you on a special assignment for the Prime Minister of Canada?"

"Yes," I said.

"Well, then," he said, "if I were you I would sit any f…. place I wanted to."

I exploded in laughter, sat down, and had one of the most informative and useful sessions of the whole consultation process. Crosbie, more than any other politician I met, impressed me not only with his intellect and insight but also with his deep knowledge of Atlantic Canada.

Camp and I had one disagreement. He felt that the new agency should be a crown corporation, operating completely at arm's length from Ottawa's bureaucratic system. I disagreed. I felt (and still do today) that national policies and national programs do not apply well in a country as large and diverse as Canada, and this has been particularly true in the case of Atlantic Canada. A crown corporation operating at arm's length from other federal agencies and departments would, in my view, have no hope of influencing the policies of central agencies or line departments. I urged, however, that the agency be established with a degree of autonomy from some administrative and financial requirements and that it be headed by a deputy minister who would be located in Atlantic Canada. I would not change my report to accommodate Camp's wishes or anyone else's in the PMO. Of course, the prime minister was free to accept or reject any of my recommendations.

Mulroney came up with a name for the new organization – the Atlantic Canada Development Corporation. Camp immediately shot it down, saying, "You know what people in Ottawa are like – they have an acronym for everything. They will call it ACDC, not the image that you want to project." A decision was needed on where in Atlantic Canada to locate the head office. Many suggested Halifax, but I wanted Moncton because it would be easier to attract Acadians to work there. The decision lay entirely with Mulroney, of course, and I made no reference to the agency's possible location in my report. To my delight, however, he decided on Moncton. I want to stress with more than usual emphasis that it was Mulroney's decision alone to locate ACOA's head office in Moncton. I would be happy to claim some of the credit, but I cannot.

We all went to St John's on 6 June 1987 to see Prime Minister Mulroney unveil a new agency for Atlantic Canada – the Atlantic Canada Opportunities Agency. He boldly declared, "We begin with new money, a new mission, and a new opportunity" and then said that "the Agency will succeed where others have failed."[1]

The Mulroney government did adopt many of my recommendations. The agency's headquarters were to be in Atlantic Canada; a deputy minister would head the agency in order to ensure that it had more autonomy than a typical government department while still not being a crown corporation; and its main focus would be the promotion of entrepreneurial development.

The government agreed to give the agency three additional mandates: to play an advocacy role for the region in Ottawa; to coordinate the activities of other federal departments and agencies in Atlantic Canada; and to promote federal-provincial cooperation. I urged the government not to create new cash-grant programs but rather to rely on existing government programs. I argued that there was no shortage of government programs handing out grants. I also recommended that the government limit the size of ACOA to one hundred top-flight officials. Given that the agency would rely on other government programs, I saw no need to create a large bureaucracy. I envisaged an agency that had the capacity to influence other federal departments and agencies to strengthen their role, presence, and activities in Atlantic Canada.

I imagined an agency with some high-profile officials, with a number of them borrowed from the private sector for a period of time who would, in concert with the business community, identify economic opportunities. I concluded that the agency could play a catalyst role, not only to identify opportunities but also to make them happen. I recommended the establishment of a $250 million fund to support this role, but the government decided to give the agency $1 billion of "new money" and also to transfer part of DRIE's old budget to it. I also recommended that Atlantic Canadians be allowed to accumulate capital tax free to start new businesses – a kind of RRSP for entrepreneurs wishing to invest in our region. In the end, the government didn't introduce the tax scheme and decided that the agency should have its own cash-grant programs. As a result, ACOA had a much larger staff that I had pictured. As for the rest, it looked a great deal like what I had proposed in my report.

The agency, especially in its early years, went through some difficult moments, notably with the national media but also with the local media. For the most part, the criticism stemmed from the agency's grants to private firms. Some firms got government cash to set up activities in direct competition with existing firms, while others received extremely generous levels of financial support that caught the attention of the national media; still others went out of business or left town after the government cash had run out.

Setting aside the early years, when there was tremendous pressure on the agency to be visible and to show results, I believe that ACOA has been a remarkable success story. I admit to a certain bias, of course, if only because I have been introduced on many occasions as the "father of ACOA." (I always reply jokingly that if this is so, why have I never met the "mother"?) A journalist coined the phrase, "the father of ACOA" some years ago and it stuck. Of course, as I wrote several years ago, there is only one father of ACOA, and that is Brian Mulroney.

ACOA is the longest-surviving regional economic development model ever conceived in Canada. Think of the Agricultural Rehabilitation and Development Act and the Fund for Rural Economic Development, which existed for several years; DREE, which lasted for thirteen years; and the Ministry of State for Economic and Regional Development and DRIE, mercifully for only a few years. ACOA is responsible for many, many success stories in Atlantic Canada, and it is the one federal agency that concentrates all its efforts in our region. Waiting for federal departments of finance, industry, and energy, and several crown corporations to adjust their programs to correspond to our region's economic circumstances is much like waiting for the Greek calends.

I always marvel – no, actually, I get irritated – at the national media and some of our own regional observers who are all too willing to point an accusatory finger at ACOA for spending public funds to support the region's economic development, but who calmy accept Industry Canada and other federal departments pouring billions into Ontario and Quebec in support of the auto sector, the aerospace industry, the IT sector – and the list goes on and on.

I challenge anyone to compare ACOA's track record with that of any other federal department and agency in the economic development field. ACOA has been a partner to private firms, aspiring entrepreneurs, universities, and provincial governments in numerous projects that would otherwise never have seen the light of day. As is commonly known, ACOA no longer hands out cash grants to private firms, relying instead on repayable assistance. Consider the following: ACOA's cumulative default rate in its repayable assistance to the private sector stands between 5 and 15 percent. Contrast this with Industry Canada's Technology Partnership Canada (TPC) program's default rate – of between 75 and 90 percent, according to departmental officials. I note, however, that the TPC program has recently been overhauled. Critics of ACOA in the region, central Canada, and the national media have never explained why they believe economic development programs are bad for our region, yet never apply the same logic to similar programs in Ontario and Quebec.

Mulroney's announcement about ACOA went down very well throughout the region, even with some Liberals, including Frank McKenna, leader of the Liberal Party of New Brunswick. When I met with Mulroney in St John's, I was ready for any questions that he could possibly raise about Atlantic Canada or my report, but the only question he asked was how Acadians were reacting to his proposed Meech Lake Accord. I was completely unprepared for that question, and I have no doubt that my answer was inadequate. I wanted to talk about Atlantic Canada; he wanted to talk about national unity and Quebec.

Mulroney, as everyone who has ever met him knows, is very charming and has a warm personality. He thanked me profusely for my work and for the report. He knew that I had not been paid as a consultant for the work (only travel expenses were reimbursed), nor did the Université de Moncton get reimbursed for my services. I recall him saying that the government would have to find a way to acknowledge my work and the university's willingness to provide my services.

On my return to the university the next Monday, I went to see our president, Louis-Philippe Blanchard, and told him of my conversation with the prime minister. I said that this would be a good time to establish a research chair at the Université de Moncton, with a mandate close to ACOA's interests. I told him that the agency's head office would be in Moncton and it would be looking for ways to promote research in its sector. I added, however, that the university would have to put some funding into the deal to make it happen. The time had come, I told Blanchard, to honour the founder of our university, Clément Cormier, and we should establish a chair bearing his name. His answer: "Go for it. You have my full support."

I put together a proposal for ACOA. A few weeks later, I met the ACOA minister, Lowell Murray, a true gentleman, a man with integrity. He reacted very well to the proposal and explained that he had known Cormier for some time and had a very high regard for him. He told me that he had first met Cormier when the latter served as a member of the Laurendeau-Dunton Commission on official languages.

Within weeks, we had a research chair at the university, one of the first to be established and endowed on campus. ACOA agreed to share 60 percent of the cost. Blanchard picked me to tell Cormier that we would soon have a chair in economic development in his honour. I met him on a Saturday afternoon at his Moncton apartment. He was seventy-seven years old, and sadly he died shortly after the announcement. When I gave Cormier the news, he simply stared at me for a few minutes without saying a word, and then his eyes filled with tears. Anyone who knew Cormier knew that he was a very modest man. So it came as no surprise to me that the first thing he had to say was how far the Université de Moncton had come since he founded it in 1963. He never made any reference to the chair in his honour. Rather, he spoke of his beloved university – that he was proud of his child that had grown up to the point that it could now house its own endowed research chair.

Blanchard and the university's executive committee asked if I would be the first occupant of the Clément Cormier chair. It was much too early for me. After the ACOA report, I turned my attention once again to the research institute. In addition, Gérard Veilleux had been on the phone more than once, asking when I was planning to return to Ottawa. He asked if I had any interest in being appointed assistant deputy minister in the federal-provincial office at the PCO. I said that my work at the university was not yet done. However, something vitally important to both Linda and me would shortly come to change things.

DIAGNOSING A LEARNING DISABILITY

It was time for our first-born, Julien, to go to school, and we enrolled him in an early French immersion program because he spoke English at home. He developed very well in his early years, and we knew that we had a highly intelligent boy on our hands. I recall his asking me at bedtime when he was four or five years old, "Papa, we are on a spaceship, earth. We don't know where it comes from or where it is going. We do not know who launched it and why he launched it. Do you know why we are here and do you know how it will all end?"

"Son," I said, "that is a very good question but I don't have the answer. I don't think that anyone has the answer. What we need to do is do our best."

We also had many signs that he was creative, highly intense, and determined. He has a good sense of humour. I once said something rather silly and Julien looked up at me and said, "People say that the apple doesn't fall far from the tree. On the day I was born, I wish there had been a slight breeze."

Things, however, were not working well for him at school. To our surprise, he was struggling. We met with his teachers, and they too were puzzled by his performance, given his obvious intelligence. We all agreed that we should request a psychological assessment.

We went to see a highly respected local psychologist, an Acadian. He put Julien through a battery of tests. His verdict – Julien was gifted, with extremely high intelligence, but he had a learning disability. As I remember the discussion, the psychologist said that in one component in a test designed to evaluate intelligence, Julien had scored higher than he had ever seen in his career, and overall the boy had superior intelligence. That was the good news. The bad news was that he had "a language-based learning disability combined with attention problems." The psychologist went on to say that it is much better for someone with a learning disability to be of average intelligence rather than to be gifted. They are much better at dealing with the accompanying frustrations and in coming up with coping skills. He had other bad news – Julien should be taken out of total immersion. Language was at the base of his learning disability, and it would be difficult enough for him to master one language.

We immediately set out to find help. There was none, or very little, in New Brunswick; but we knew that there was some in Ottawa. Frank McKenna, our newly elected premier, asked me at that time if I would go to Fredericton in a senior position to help him deliver on his mandate. I had helped plan his transition to power, and I had (still have, for that matter) a high opinion of

McKenna, but I had to decline and I explained why. I note that McKenna did in time introduce measures to assist students with learning disabilities – I was not the only parent raising concerns with him and his government.

We decided that we would do everything we could to help Julien. Linda, Margaux, I, and, more importantly, Julien himself have become something of experts in dealing with learning disabilities. Though I have doubts about how well I was able to help Julien, I have no doubt that his mother and sister were very understanding and supportive, and very helpful.

I learned a thing or two about learning disabilities that I would like to share with the reader, since it is possible that the reader has or will have a child or grandchild with learning disabilities. First, there is no cure. There are only coping skills. One should never equate learning disability with a lack of intelligence – often the opposite is true. The following people, among many other luminaries, had learning disabilities: Albert Einstein, Nelson D. Rockefeller, Winston Churchill, and Thomas Edison. The key is to appreciate that all people do *not* think and learn the same way.

Consider, for a moment, what it must be like to be at school trying to concentrate but finding that every little sound distracts you. When you try to read, the words don't make sense, and when you try to write, you can't spell the words that are bouncing around in your mind. School, like society, is very competitive, but you cannot compete. You know that you may well be more intelligent or more creative than the student sitting next to you, but you can't keep up with him or her. Your self-esteem takes a big hit. You constantly feel out of place, unable to fit in with your peers. You feel rejected, and the rejection pushes you into anti-social behaviour. You want to strike out at the unfairness of it all, and sometimes you do, which only makes things worse.

You have to accept that there is no known cause to explain learning disabilities, and some teachers don't even believe that learning disabilities exist. They think the student lacks discipline, is lazy, or unwilling, rather than unable to concentrate. Sadly, too many students give up and turn to drugs, alcohol, or, in more recent years, computer hacking, perhaps because it's a solitary activity. Our school system is designed for average students, and above-average students do very well. Students with learning disabilities, particularly those who are gifted, soon develop self-esteem problems, and school becomes a living hell. I recall Julien telling a psychologist in Ottawa to stop saying that he was "gifted." He said, "Whatever you may mean by being 'gifted,' I can tell you that this is no gift!"

Parents have a crucial role to play. There are telling signs that can be spotted fairly early – uncoordinated behaviour, words spelled backwards, and letters reversed. Very often children with a learning disability have excellent hearing and can hear conversations where others are not able to. So if parents or grandparents want to discuss a child's problems, they should go out to a restaurant or for a drive, away from the listening child. They should understand that no one knows for certain what causes learning disabilities, and they should not try to allocate blame, because the child can start blaming himself or herself. Another mystery: learning disabilities are more common among boys than girls.

The key, at the risk of sounding repetitive, is to come to terms with the fact that there is no solution, certainly no single solution. I had great difficulty accepting this. I have always believed that there is a solution to every problem. When it comes to learning disabilities, solutions are really about identifying the best possible coping skills. Such children will grow, will learn to cope, but will never be what they cannot be. They will struggle more than others – but the struggles can make them stronger. A colleague at Georgetown University, a well-known scholar with a learning disability, insists that the struggles in the end bring many benefits. Over the years, he has had many graduate students, including a number of PhD students. The ones to look for, he says, are those who had to struggle, who never found it easy, who had to put in the extra effort. He often hears about them later through their publications or other success stories. He rarely hears of those who were able to sail through graduate programs.

I will never regret doing everything I could, including using my contacts, to help Julien. I was able to open many doors for him, and many of my friends have proved very helpful to him over the years. They know who they are, and so does Julien.

At the time, the family had to make a decision: remain in Moncton and try to find help as best as we could or move to Ottawa where the resources were. The Ottawa educational system has had a capacity to accommodate students with learning disabilities for some time. Shortly after Veilleux was appointed secretary to the Treasury Board, he once again called to see if I was ready to return to Ottawa. I explained the situation with Julien and told him that Linda had done a fair bit of research on the Ottawa school system, as well as on private schools in the area, and we had decided to move back to Ottawa. As I was leaving the university, my assistant Ginette said, "I have a feeling that you will not be back." My response: "Don't bet on it. I will be back."

In retrospect, I can see that our move to Ottawa helped both Julien and Margaux. Ottawa had the resources, both in the public school system and in private schools, to help Julien and give a boost to Margaux. Linda's loving and gentle hand took care of the rest. Julien went on to complete a computer science program at the University of New Brunswick. He made the dean's list and is now working at the Université Sainte-Anne in Nova Scotia. Margaux completed a law degree in French at the Université de Moncton and now practises law in Saint John. We are very proud of both our children, and as is the case for parents the world over, they mean everything to us.

9

Back in Ottawa

I reported to work at the Treasury Board Secretariat as assistant secretary, Policy, Planning and Communications, in September 1987. Within weeks, I realized that I was not cut out to be a happy public servant. There were too many participants at too many meetings that accomplished nothing or very little. Apart from particular matters in which the minister and deputy minister were interested, things only moved by committee, if they moved at all, and it became impossible for me to figure out who was actually responsible for what. The focus was never on the individual, always on the process. Anything new required new resources, and anything dated just kept going and burning up what resources there were. At first, I marvelled at how the system decided who was competent, who should get promoted, and who should not. Competence in bureaucracy, I became convinced, was in the eye of the beholder. It was easy enough, however, to spot the non-performers, but they were simply left hanging. Nothing good or bad ever happened to them; they simply went through the motions, finding things to keep themselves busy. I also saw people working away on projects or initiatives that were never developed or taken up in any way. Some public servants must think that they are being kept busy turning cranks that are not attached to anything.

The morale problem, which has haunted the federal public service for the past twenty years – and which seems to get worse, year after year – has, in my view, everything to do with the fact that individual public servants are unable to "own" their work, to carve out a responsibility, however small, that belongs to them. The collective approach worked all right in the age of deference, but the age of deference is dead or on life support. The poor morale is certainly not the result of pay or social benefits, both of which are extremely generous. Moreover, there are a number of public servants who work extremely hard under difficult circumstances. It is the system, not the individual, that is the problem. However, the system can wear down individual public servants, who eventually give up. They then become part of the problem.

Public servants are well qualified, well intentioned, and initially at least, eager to make a contribution. But it is not easy for a senior bureaucrat to balance departmental interests against the interests of many ministers and other departments. And it is discouraging for them to learn from a front-page article in the *Globe and Mail* that there has been a change in government priorities overnight or to have legions of oversight bodies (for example, the auditor general, the Treasury Board Secretariat, the access-to-information commissioner, the Public Service Commission, the commissioner of official languages, et cetera), always on the lookout to spot a misstep.

I don't mean to paint an entirely negative picture of the federal public service. Without putting too fine a point on it, however, in my view public servants have an image problem because they are unable to deal with non-performers, because they are unwilling to challenge the status quo when it comes to public spending, and because their focus has become overly concerned with Ottawa, its internal processes, and the work of oversight bodies. I have come to the conclusion that the basic problem with government is not that it spends too much on new things but that it spends massively on old things.

But not all was lost in our move to Ottawa. Julien had access to better resources than we had in Moncton, and Margaux was enthusiastic about her new school. Luckily, I inherited staff who knew how to produce what was expected of them, and there were no personality conflicts in the group. I kept my views on central agency and bureaucracy to myself.

There was, however, no sense in pretending that I would become a career public servant. I knew that I would be returning to academe, where I felt I belonged. Given my respect for and friendship with Veilleux, however, I would not leave him without a proper explanation, and I would certainly give him sufficient time to find a replacement. He understood my reasoning, and before long, he too left the public service.

ESTABLISHING THE CANADIAN CENTRE FOR MANAGEMENT DEVELOPMENT (CCMD)

Veilleux asked me to take on a special project – the establishment of a centre for management studies for the federal government. Most industrialized countries already had such teaching centres, but not Canada. In Veilleux's opinion, one was long overdue. This was not the first attempt to establish such a centre. Veilleux had worked in the Treasury Board in the early 1970s when Al Johnson was the secretary, and they had developed a proposal to establish a management training centre. Their efforts were stymied by the clerk of the privy council, Michael Pitfield. The proposal went nowhere because of Pitfield's opposition, but now Veilleux saw his chance to bring it forward, given that Pitfield was no longer in the bureaucratic hierarchy.

I met with all interested parties, looked abroad at what France and the United Kingdom were doing (but did not visit them), and then put pen to paper. I wrote a twenty-three-page document that outlined the purpose of such a centre (there was not nearly enough emphasis placed on the study of public-sector management in Canadian universities), the reason why it should be in-house (the need to promote a unifying and confident corporate culture), and the centre's objective (to develop a strong management training program). The document called for legislation that would establish a quasi-autonomous centre governed by its own board of directors. The initiative, I argued in the document, need not be costly, since the government already owned training facilities in the Ottawa area, on the Quebec side. The existing facility already employed forty-four public servants and had a $4.3 million budget.

When Veilleux and I briefed the Treasury Board president, Don Mazankowski, and his staff, they were not particularly enthusiastic. However, in time and given Veilleux's considerable powers of persuasion, Mazankowski came round. He wrote to the prime minister on 3 November 1987 recommending the establishment of the centre, telling him that "every effort would be made to limit spending to not much more than what is currently available" to the existing facility. The prime minister responded on 15 February 1988 to register his full support and asked Mazankowski to assume "responsibility in establishing the centre."

Mazankowski announced the new centre during a dinner attended by business and community leaders. I sat at a table among strangers. I chatted with everyone, told them all that I was with the government but did not specify that I was with the Treasury Board – nor, of course, did I give away that I knew what Mazankowski was about to announce.

The reaction at my table to the announcement was not positive. One person said, "The government simply doesn't get it. Why does it keep on creating new organizations? That's the last thing we need." I said nothing. I myself had mixed feelings about the centre. I recognized the need for management training courses but was skeptical of the centre's ability to have a viable research program, since this would require a willingness to publish findings that might be controversial or difficult to accept. Having lived through the McGee experience, I had difficulty believing that senior government officials would countenance work that challenged the status quo or was critical of existing government policies and practices. What I feared was that the centre would produce paint-by-numbers research, the kind that plays to the status quo.

The legislation also received a rough welcome in Parliament, not in the Commons but in the Senate. Pitfield, now a Trudeau-appointed senator, had not changed his views. He and the associate clerk of the privy council, J.L. Manion, had a difficult exchange, but in the end the Senate gave its approval.

Jack Manion was appointed the centre's first principal. The problem, however, was that both the prime minister and the current clerk of the privy council, Paul Tellier, were not prepared to see Manion leave his present position for another year. Manion called to ask if I would take the job of acting principal for a twelve-month period. I had by then already decided to return to academe, but both Manion and Veilleux strongly urged me to stay to give them a hand in setting up the centre, given my work in preparing the proposal and accompanying documents. I agreed, on condition that I could also return to my research and publish in the public administration field. I also sought assurances that I could publish what I wanted. In turn, I told them that I would only publish in peer-reviewed journals or with a university press. They agreed.

THE POLITICS OF PUBLIC SPENDING IN CANADA

Pierre Gravelle, the associate secretary to the Treasury Board, was appointed deputy minister at Revenue Canada in 1988. As he was leaving the Treasury Board, Gravelle said that he had a dozen boxes or so of material that he had accumulated over the years and asked if I wanted them, knowing my interest in public administration. He had one condition – if I were to come across anything marked "Secret" or "Confidential," then I could not quote from it. Without any hesitation I said, "We have a deal," and what a deal it was for me!

The boxes were a gold mine of new material on many aspects of Ottawa policy making and on the expenditure budget process. I knew immediately that there was a good book here when combined with interviews with key policy and decision makers, from senior ministers to senior bureaucrats. I consulted them widely to broaden my insight on how government made its spending decisions. The result was *The Politics of Public Spending in Canada*. The book was built around the following theme: Ten people meet for the first time over lunch; they must decide whether they will share one check or ask for ten separate ones; in theory, if they decide on one shared check they will all choose the most expensive items; but if each is paying individually, they will probably choose differently, because nobody will want to miss the best food while paying for someone else to have it. I argued that this is how things work in government because there are no market forces to impose discipline or to sort out winners from losers.

With this analogy, I tackled government's increased spending and our inability to cut back existing programs. I argued that they are rooted in the regional nature of Canada and in the fear that unless we all eat the best at the public banquet we will lose our share of public largesse. I also identified the forces fuelling new government spending and those inhibiting efforts to reduce it.

The book was published in 1990, and the timing could not have been better. It will be recalled that Ottawa's deficit had spiralled out of control. Less than five years later, the *Wall Street Journal* described the Canadian dollar as a "basket case" and ran an editorial called "Bankrupt Canada?" that declared, "Mexico isn't the only U.S. neighbour flirting with the financial abyss." It argued: "If dramatic action isn't taken in the next month's federal budget, it's not inconceivable that Canada could hit the debt wall and have to call in the International Monetary Fund to stabilize its falling currency."

The reviews poured in and they were all positive. Douglas Fisher wrote that the book "should become a classic." Lloyd Brown-John wrote in the *Canadian Journal of Political Science*, "Savoie's book is a masterful contribution to the literature on public policy and public administration in Canada"; and Richard French had this to say: "The curse of the literature on Canadian public policy has been that those who know, don't write and those who write, don't know. Savoie's readers are blessed." Jeffrey Simpson wrote in the *Globe and Mail*, "Donald Savoie has written one of two or three of the most important books in the last decade for those who wish to understand how Ottawa works. Any serious student of the federal government should read it." The book was the inaugural recipient of the Smiley Prize awarded by the Canadian Political Science Association for the best book on the study of government and policies in Canada. Preston Manning, leader of the Reform Party, wrote to me to say that he was "impressed" by *The Politics of Public Spending in Canada*. He quoted from it often in the Commons and elsewhere, which made some Liberals believe that my views had shifted too much to the right, as I mentioned earlier.

What I found all the more remarkable is that no one in government took exception to the book, though it was critical both of some decisions and of the policy-making process. I recalled Harley McGee's reaction to my first book and wondered why I wasn't getting a similar response to this book, especially as I was acting principal of the government's recently established management training centre. Very little was said, and I suspect that it had something to do with the understanding I had reached before accepting the position, and the fact that the book did not point the finger at any individual or, for that matter, at any government department.

It took more than twelve months for Jack Manion to make the transition from the PCO to the new management centre. I waited patiently, trying as best I could to move the centre forward, hiring some staff, organizing courses, and laying the groundwork for a research program. When Manion finally arrived, I stayed on for a few months to ensure a smooth transition. The Canadian Centre for Management Development has since been transformed into the Canada School of Public Service, with an expenditure budget of $136 million (total spending authorities) and a staff of more than nine hundred people. It is important to note that the school has added new responsibilities over the years, including assuming responsibility for second-language training.[1] But even accounting for the cost of second-language training, the centre is a far cry from what was first envisaged.

As I was making plans to leave the centre, PCO officials and others approached me to see if I would have any interest in a senior public service appointment. My decision was firm: I would be returning to academe. I had found my vocation, my labour of love, and was not about to walk away from it. However, because of our children's education, we were not able to return to Moncton. I commuted from Ottawa to Moncton for my teaching (always a light teaching load) and to look after the Canadian Institute for Research on Regional Development (CIRRD). It was in the days of low air fares, made even lower by my travel agent, who had an uncanny ability to find incredible bargains.

Manion invited me to stay on at the management centre as a research fellow. I would be asked to undertake specific projects in return for office space, a telephone, and access to a fax machine. This proved a godsend. I had a *pied-à-terre* in Ottawa, access to what was being said in the corridors of power, and a base from which I could carry out interviews for my research. My work with the Treasury Board Secretariat and the management centre put me in contact with many senior government officials, a good number of whom proved extremely valuable to my research.

I continued to publish, including the book *Thatcher, Reagan, Mulroney: In Search of a New Bureaucracy*, which appeared in 1995. It identified a common reform agenda and its impact on government operations in the United Kingdom, the United States, and Canada. Together with my close friend and colleague B. Guy Peters from the University of Pittsburgh, I led three exercises at the management centre that resulted in three books on public-sector management from an international perspective. I also published widely in the economic development field, including a book on regional economic development theory co-authored with Ben Higgins.

A GUMSHOE IN THE CORRIDORS OF POWER

Ted Hodgetts, the dean of public administration in Canada and a man for whom I have a great deal of admiration, once suggested that I should write about my various experiences. He added, "I have a title for you – 'A Gumshoe in the Corridors of Power.'" When he thinks of me, he said, he pictures me quietly walking around the corridors of power in Ottawa trying to understand how and why they do what they do and then writing about it. Jeffrey Simpson, in his review of my *Governing from the Centre* for the *Globe and Mail*, offered a similar image: "Although a full professor, Savoie darts around Ottawa all the time working his contacts like a seasoned journalist."[2] It is true that I have had, over the years, access to fascinating people from the political, bureaucratic, business, and the arts communities whose observations have helped me greatly in understanding their worlds. I count myself very lucky.

After his re-election to power in 1988, Mulroney appointed Elmer MacKay minister responsible for the Atlantic Canada Opportunities Agency (ACOA). At the same time, Mulroney introduced stringent spending cuts and froze ACOA's expenditure budget to the level of the previous year. This meant that MacKay could manage only existing commitments, since he had little money to launch new initiatives.

MacKay invited me to dinner to discuss ACOA. He was clearly despondent and said, "ACOA without money is like your father throwing you the keys to his Cadillac after high school graduation and saying, 'enjoy the evening.' I jump in the car, all excited, but then I see that the gas tank is empty." Serving us that evening was Spedi Giovanni Comino, an Ottawa legend, who wore his nickname well. Spedi never walked; he ran from table to table. He was nicknamed the Tasmanian Devil because he moved so fast. Having dinner where Spedi worked was like going to a dinner show: not only would he run around like a Tasmanian devil, but from time to time and without any warning, he would start singing, fairly loudly, always smiling, always happy, and always running.[3] MacKay kept looking at Spedi and at one point turned to me and asked, "Do you know where I could find an assistant deputy minister like him?"

Like so many Acadians, I was delighted when Chrétien appointed Roméo LeBlanc governor general. As the reader knows by now, I worked closely with LeBlanc in the early 1980s, and I visited him from time to time when he served in the Senate during the Mulroney years. I recollect his calling me several times, when I was working on the ACOA report, to offer both support and advice, and I always benefited from his advice. I attended his installation and was seated in the gallery next to his son Dominic and daughter Geneviève. I had two tickets that allowed me to attend all of the day's events and to roam freely. Linda suggested that I bring Margaux for the afternoon, saying that it would be a memorable event for our fifteen-year-old daughter.

We sat in the front row in the Senate gallery watching LeBlanc, a former journalist and a highly skilled communicator, deliver an excellent speech. He spoke about his roots, growing up in a small Acadian village, and reminded Canadians that "Acadians have been around for quite some time." He pointed out, "If there is one group of Canadians whose past could have poisoned their future, it is the Acadians. In the middle of the eighteenth century they were wrenched from their homes and deported to distant shores. Some managed to escape this deportation with the aid of friendly Mi'kmaq. But they were refugees in their own country, stripped of their land. But they never gave up. We survived." He added, "Acadians are not bitter and have learned to live in harmony with their English-speaking neighbours." He concluded with an observation that grabbed the media's attention, though sadly for only a day or two: "Give good news a chance."

After the speech, I saw Trudeau standing alone and decided to go over for a chat and to introduce him to Margaux. We talked for awhile and he asked about the Université de Moncton and the CIRRD. Then he began to banter with Margaux and at one point asked her how she spelled her name. Margaux had a copy of the day's program with her, and Trudeau took it and wrote, "Pour Margaux, avec mes meilleurs voeux. P.E. Trudeau." As we walked away, we spotted a man walking up to Trudeau to ask him to sign his program. Trudeau said no, turned around and walked away. Margaux asked, "Why did he do that? That's not very nice." The place was full of New Brunswickers, familiar faces. Among others, we saw Antonine Maillet, with whom we had a pleasant chat. We ran into Harrison McCain, and he and Margaux had an exchange about French fries, automobiles, and when she would be getting her driver's licence.

I told Roméo LeBlanc about Trudeau's gesture, and he decided that he too would write Margaux a message. He wrote, "À Margaux Savoie, qui vivra la grande histoire de notre jeune pays et qui fera elle aussi cette histoire. Tous les succès! Roméo LeBlanc." Later, Chrétien also added to the program, writing, "Pour Margaux. Bonne chance. Jean Chrétien." Margaux still has the program and guards it very carefully.

On our way home, I sought to explain Trudeau's refusal to sign the program of the man who asked him. Margaux had been only three years old when Trudeau left politics. I told her that he had been our prime minister for about fifteen years and that he had given Canada our Charter of Rights and Freedoms, a very important document. He had earned a well-deserved retirement, and he had probably signed more than enough programs during his career. He was there, like us, to see his friend Roméo LeBlanc and to enjoy the day. I tried as best I could to explain to Margaux that Trudeau had earned the right to be left alone, if that is what he wanted. I am not sure that my explanation had much of an impact. I asked her, "Of all the people you met today, which one did you enjoy the most?" With no hesitation, she said "Harrison McCain." Neither Trudeau nor anyone else could make such good French fries!

A few weeks later, Margaux took her program to school for a "show and tell," and one of the teachers explained at some length who Trudeau was and what he had done for Canada. That evening at dinner, Margaux said, "You know that old man we met in

Parliament? He was quite important." "Yes," I said, and explained that Trudeau's Charter of Rights and Freedoms would serve the Acadian community for years and years.

I became a frequent visitor to Rideau Hall. LeBlanc wanted to be kept abreast of developments in l'Acadie, the Université de Moncton, and New Brunswick. More to the point, we both enjoyed a gossip. I often had breakfast or coffee with him, and after we moved back to Moncton I stayed the night (I slept in the Minto room). At first, we sat in the dining room for breakfast, but he soon decided to have it in his office, where we could chat in private. In any event, the dining room was too big and too ostentatious for two Acadians.

For breakfast, I would ask for a bagel, an orange, and a coffee. One morning, LeBlanc said, "Today, we are going to have a full breakfast." A staff member came, a Québécois, to take our order, and I told him, in French of course, that I would have bacon and eggs. He asked how I wanted my eggs done. I wanted scrambled eggs but suddenly simply couldn't remember the term *oeufs brouillés*. So I said, "Fricassés," though I knew that wasn't right. Acadians eat eggs *fricassés*, but Québécois don't. He gave me a puzzled look and said, "Fricassés?" I looked to Roméo, sitting across from me, for help, while the staff member kept his puzzled look focused on me. Roméo gave me a wink and his face broke into a wide smile. The staff member again asked, "Fricassés?" and I said yes. He turned on his heel and off he went. LeBlanc burst into a laugh and said, "I can't wait to see what he's going to come back with." Rather than scrambled eggs, I had two eggs rolled over several times!

LeBlanc appointed me a member of the advisory committee of the Order of Canada. His predecessor Ray Hnatyshyn had received me as an officer of the order several years earlier and there was a vacancy from Atlantic Canada on the committee. I served on the committee for five years, and it required a great deal of work. We met at least twice a year and had to review hundreds of candidates. Harrison McCain had served on the committee previously, and I called him for advice. Never one to waste words, he said, "It means losing three to four weekends for reading the cvs." Then he added, "Two things. First, don't give it to business people if all they have done is make money. That's the easy part. The hard part is whether they have given some of it to help others and their communities. Second, don't give it to people of the cloth. Their reward is in the next life."

I found work on the committee both demanding and exhilarating. We spent hours reviewing the work of successful Canadians who were making a contribution to their sector and their communities. Our job was to celebrate success, and there was never a negative moment – other than the time when we introduced a policy that would make it possible to strip past recipients of the order. It will be recalled that the governor general accepted our recommendation to remove Alan Eagleson from the order after he was convicted of defrauding the hockey players he represented in negotiations with their NHL teams.

In the evening at Rideau Hall, we met the new members, officers, and companions of the order at dinner, and again these were happy occasions with no blemishes. I met the best from the worlds of business, politics, the arts, culture, sports, and academe. One year, Jean Béliveau and Maurice Richard had been honoured. I said to them, "If only my father could be here instead of me!" They were his heroes. I remarked to Béliveau that he had an Acadian name. He said, "Absolutely, my ancestors are from Nova Scotia, and the old family home is still there around Pointe-de-l'Église." I then said, "Richard is also an Acadian name." And he too admitted to Acadian ancestors. They had gone to the Îles de la Madeleine after the Grand Dérangement. I thought, I'm on a roll, so I turned to Béliveau again and said, "You know, Gretzky, that's also an Acadian name." He looked at me, smiled, and said, "Ah! charrie pas!" – roughly translated: "Don't string it."

I also recall an interesting discussion with Peter Gzowski, the well-known CBC Radio personality. He had a regular morning program (*Morningside*) and invited me on occasion to present an Atlantic Canada perspective on a national panel. The day after the Blue Jays won their first World Series, Gzowksi began the program by rattling on about the Blue Jays' victory and telling his listeners that it was "a great day for Canada." He then asked me to open the discussion by speaking about its significance to Canada. I made the point that it meant little to me, since I was a Boston Red Sox fan, as were many Maritimers. There was a pause and then Gzowski moved to much safer ground, asking the Ontario representative on the panel to share his views. I asked Gzowski, when he was at Rideau Hall, if he remembered that moment. "How could I forget! I never expected that answer." He added that "as a result, there were a few seconds of dead silence on the air."

Towards the end of Roméo LeBlanc's mandate as governor general, the Institute of Public Administration of Canada (IPAC) awarded me the Vanier Gold Medal for my publications in the field. The medal is presented by either the governor general or (if he or she is not available) the chief justice. Roméo decided that he would perform the duty at the Citadel, the governor general's residence in Quebec City. Maurice LeBlanc, my friend from high school days who, the reader will recall, later helped me organize Robichaud's funeral, attended the ceremony. Maurice has been a special friend ever since we met in grade nine at the Collège l'Assomption – a gruff, direct man, with one of the most generous hearts that I have ever encountered. He is a very dear friend, though you would never know it by listening to him. He constantly berates me about my clothes, my golf game, my work, or anything else that strikes his fancy. He claims that I have published forty books only because I can never get it right, so I just keep on trying to write a good one. My books, he insists, only make good doorstops.

We both attended a reception the night before at the Château Frontenac. At one point, I had my back to Maurice and overheard him talking away, as is his wont, to a circle of people. He was saying that Acadians were very proud of my work and my contribution to his alma mater, the Université de Moncton. I could hardly believe my ears but said nothing. I didn't even turn around. The next morning, as we walked from the hotel to the Citadel, I told him that I really appreciated his taking the time to be here. I also told him I'd overheard him praising me the night before, that I was deeply moved and wanted him to know it. His response: "Well, I drank too much. I didn't know what I was saying. Whatever I said, don't take it seriously."

At the Citadel we saw old friends from Ottawa and a few Acadians who had moved to the Quebec area. As Roméo LeBlanc began to speak, he said that Rideau Hall had prepared a speech that he could make available, but he would not read it. Rather, he said, he wanted to tallk about Acadians and the immense progress we had made in forty years or so in every field of endeavour. He spoke about the important role which the Université de Moncton had played and was continuing to play in our renaissance. He told the gathering that Acadians were just now starting to appreciate literature and the importance of the written word. In planning his return to l'Acadie, he had hired a local carpenter to repair his residence, including having him build some bookshelves. At one point, he showed the carpenter my books and said, "You know, Savoie is an Acadian like us, and he has published all these books." The carpenter took a good look at the books, pondered the scene for a few moments, and then turned to LeBlanc and said, "Savoie wrote all of those? When does he find time to work?"

When Jean Chrétien in 1990 was elected leader of the Liberal Party and returned to the House of Commons after a by-election, he represented Beauséjour, Roméo LeBlanc's former constituency, which includes Saint-Maurice and Bouctouche. We met on a number of occasions, often when flying back and forth to Ottawa. I confess that I have always liked and respected Chrétien, particularly his political instincts. And we had something in common: both our sons attended Venta, a private school in Ottawa for students with learning disabilities.

In his run for the leadership of his party, Chrétien had asked if I would help him prepare a policy paper on regional economic development. He said that it would be one of only five major policy statements. I was to "hold the pen" while a former New Brunswicker, Rod Bryden, and Senator Mike Kirby and David

Dingwall provided political guidance. I recall Chrétien praising DREE and Ottawa's decision to decentralize a number of units to the regions. I cautioned him on the first: DREE may have been fine on some points, but it was yesterday's solution. I agreed fully with him on the benefits of decentralizing federal government units. Chrétien gave his policy statement in St John's, Newfoundland, and spoke about the need to move more units to the regions, but to my delight he said he would not abolish ACOA and return to the days of DREE. As we had discussed, he also called for new investments in infrastructure, research and development, and tourism.

Later, I was asked to work on the 1993 Red Book that formed the basis of Chrétien's election campaign and guided his government during its first mandate. I want to stress, however, that I wrote nothing in the Red Book, nor did I participate in the debate that shaped the contents. I was simply asked to look at the pages that dealt with regional economic development and to offer advice on the cost of implementing Red Book commitments in this area.

Chrétien was elected with a strong majority in 1993. The first year was spent implementing the Red Book commitments. By 1995 the country's finances were in serious difficulty with, as already noted, the *Wall Street Journal* suggesting that Canada was going to hit the debt wall. The situation called for tough decisions, and Chrétien did not shy away from making them. The 1995 federal budget was to be tough, and nowhere would it be more difficult to sell than in Atlantic Canada, given the region's reliance on transfer payments.

Chrétien decided to come to the region to sell the budget himself. His office called to see if I would organize a breakfast meeting in Moncton and invite business and community leaders to attend. I agreed, and my institute immediately leapt into action, securing Moncton's Hôtel Beauséjour for the breakfast meeting on 9 March 1995. A press release was issued on 3 March to announce the event, and representatives from the Prime Minister's Office, with RCMP officials in tow, came to help with arrangements. Everything was planned to the minute, from 7 to 10 AM. At twenty dollars a ticket, we had the room sold out within days.

On the evening of 8 March – in other words, at the very last minute – someone from the PMO and Doug Young's executive assistant (Young was the cabinet minister from New Brunswick) asked to meet with me: Chrétien would not be able to come. The PMO staffer said that Chrétien had said Savoie would understand why, and also that he felt very badly about the cancellation. The turbot war with Spain had turned sour, and Chrétien felt that he needed to stay in Ottawa to manage the crisis. And, indeed, the very next day the *Cape Roger*, a Department of Fisheries and Ocean boat, fired on a Spanish fishing trawler on the grounds that it had been fishing illegally. The eyes of the world were on Canada's capital, and the rumour spread that Brian Tobin, Newfoundland's minister, who was minister of fisheries, was ready to press the issue, come what may.

In his memoirs, Chrétien gives a full account of the tense moments surrounding the turbot crisis and says that he had no choice but to play a hands-on role. He writes that Tobin was in his office banging the "top of my desk with his fist," pushing him to be more aggressive, while Jocelyne Bourgon, clerk of the privy council, and Jim Bartleman, his senior policy adviser, were urging caution.[4]

I was in no mood to be understanding on the evening of 8 March. There was no time to cancel the breakfast meeting. Some people had already arrived from northern New Brunswick, Nova Scotia, and Prince Edward Island. I reacted much as my father would have had done: I let Ottawa know in no uncertain terms that I was less than pleased. They proposed a replacement – Doug Young. I asked, "Is Doug Young the best you can do? Where is the minister of finance, where is the minister of industry? We are expecting the prime minister, and now you want people to sit there and listen to Young?" I concluded by remarking that there would be a lot of seriously disappointed Maritimers at breakfast the following morning. Young's executive assistant lowered his head and said nothing. There was nothing that he or anyone else could do.

At the breakfast meeting, those who had come to hear the prime minister were dismayed to see Doug Young instead. I sat at the head table with him and some other MPs and provincial politicians. The conversation was civil but certainly not warm. Young's executive assistant had told him about my angry reaction. A few days later, an assistant to Chrétien told me that Young had said, "I'm good enough to be invited to Bay Street and Wall Street to explain the budget (which was true) but not good enough for Savoie." If nothing else, it meant that a Senate appointment would not be in the cards! I note that Young went down to defeat in his Acadie-Bathurst constituency in the following general election.

QUEBEC: HERE WE GO AGAIN

The collapse of the Meech Lake constitutional accord in 1990 sent the country, and especially Quebec, into a soul-searching exercise. Mulroney had initiated the accord in large part because Quebec had refused to accept the repatriation of Canada's constitution in 1982. The province stood alone in refusing to sign on to the new constitution, and Mulroney wanted to bring Quebec into the Canadian family. He had brought all ten provincial premiers to Meech Lake for an intensive bargaining session, at which Quebec Premier Robert Bourassa laid down a number of conditions, including recognizing Quebec as a distinct society. After a marathon bargaining session, the prime minister and the ten premiers had emerged with a deal – the Meech Lake Accord.

Before long, however, strong opposition to the accord was being heard in different parts of the country. Trudeau came out of retirement to denounce it. Some new provincial premiers said that they could not support it unless changes were made. Frank McKenna (though he later signed on) said he could not support it. Manitoba had a minority government, which meant that continued provincial support could not be assured, and Clyde Wells, the newly elected premier of Newfoundland and Labrador, declared that he would put a vote to the legislature to rescind the accord. Time ran out for all the ten provincial governments to sign on to the accord. In Quebec, reaction to the collapse of the Meech

Lake Accord was strong. It prompted Lucien Bouchard, a senior Quebec minister in Mulroney's cabinet, to quit and start a new federal party, the Bloc Québécois, dedicated to taking Quebec out of Confederation.

I became deeply concerned that the Maritime provinces were left on the outside looking in as Canada's future was being played out elsewhere. The West had the Reform Party, Quebec had the Bélanger-Campeau Commission looking into the political and constitutional status of Quebec, and Ontario had its powerful political, economic, and financial infrastructure.

I decided to contact a number of high-profile Maritimers to see if we could put together a group that would bring a Maritime perspective to the national unity debate. I said that I would hold the pen and look after all the logistics. I decided to call the group the Northumberland Group, after the Northumberland Strait which links the three Maritime provinces. The reaction was very positive, though one Prince Edward Islander declined when I said we would be supporting bilingualism, and another worried that membership could be bad for business. But a dozen decided to sign on, representing various sectors of society. From politics came Louis J. Robichaud and Robert L. Stanfield; from the business community, Harrison McCain, Allan Shaw of Shaw Industries, Derek Oland, president of Moosehead Breweries, andRegis Duffy, a well-known businessman from Prince Edward Island; my brother Claude; from the academic community, President Howard Clark of Dalhousie University; and from the arts community, Alex Colville, singer Rita MacNeil from Cape Breton, and lastly, Harvey Webber, founder of Atlantic Canada Plus.

Recently in going through my old files for this book, I was reminded that three people in particular played a very active role in the Northumberland Group. I have a number of letters and notes, some of them hand-written, from Robert Stanfield, Harrison McCain, and Alex Colville. My brother Claude also played an active role, but mainly through face-to-face meetings or telephone calls. McCain pushed hard for the group to endorse an equal and elected senate, but Stanfield was strongly opposed to the idea. In the face of this problem, I sought to strike the middle ground. If I could turn back the clock, knowing what I do now, I would side with McCain. As it was, McCain backed down to a certain extent, and the Northumberland Group called for a "full review and an open debate on the future role of the Senate."

The group insisted that Quebec could find its rightful place in Canada, urged the Mulroney government to eliminate duplication of programs, argued that Maritimers themselves would have to play the key role to shake the region free of its "have not" status, and concluded that the federal government should retain sufficient authority to establish the broad framework to set national goals. The report received wide coverage in the region and in the Quebec and Ontario media. As well Joe Clark, the minister responsible for constitutional affairs, wrote on 18 November 1991 to applaud the work of the Northumberland Group. Although I would not suggest that we were the ones to originate the idea, the federal government did soon attempt to eliminate duplication of programs. I regret to report, however, that the exercise did not accomplish much, if anything.

The national unity debate lost some of its urgency as the country turned its attention to Ottawa's deteriorating financial situation. However, things would not stay quiet for long. Lucien Bouchard was rattling around in the Commons in Ottawa, and Jacques Parizeau, leader of the separatist Parti Québécois, was elected to power in Quebec. In 1995 Parizeau called a referendum on Quebec's future, and we were back in the national unity debate.

I took less interest in the crisis this time. Like many Canadians, I had grown tired of the never-ending national unity debate always focusing on a Quebec perspective. It will be recalled that things were going well for the pro-Canada forces in Quebec until Bouchard decided to play a very active role in the referendum. Public opinion surveys soon pointed to a tight race, with the possibility that the sovereignists could actually win the referendum. Frank McKenna called to say, "Put on your thinking cap. Things are not going well in Quebec. I suggest that we produce a paper on Quebec in Canada." He added, "We need to move fast."

"Fine," I said, "but we need to tell the pro-Canada forces in Ottawa and Quebec."

He agreed and dispatched Georgio Gaudet, his chief of staff, to Ottawa and Quebec to brief the pro-Canada forces while I put pen to paper.

The pro-Canada forces, particularly in Ottawa, expressed reservations about having anyone from outside Ottawa and Quebec involved. I continued to write anyway, and before long I had a draft for McKenna along the lines that we had discussed. As agreed, I contacted the Institute of Intergovernmental Relations at Queen's University to see if it would be interested in publishing the paper. It was.

We soon had a paper, but there were problems. As I understand it, the pro-Canada forces in Quebec were supportive of the paper being made public, but those in Ottawa were not. They were confident that they had matters well in hand and that the paper would only complicate things. The Ottawa people asked McKenna to withdraw the paper, and he agreed. So I informed the institute at Queen's that we would not be publishing it.

In the paper we argued that our federal system was highly flexible and that "status quo federalism" was no longer viable. We suggested that Ottawa was far too involved in provincial affairs, creating a costly problem of overlap and duplication and constant federal-provincial bickering. We reported that "public servants meet over 1,000 times a year to coordinate federal-provincial activity." We called for more responsibility to be given to the provinces, if only because the nearer the level of government is to citizens, the more merciless voters are when they see waste.

Michel Cormier, an Acadian and good friend who was a CBC Radio/Radio-Canada journalist working out of Quebec City, called to say that he knew what was going on. I assumed that he had got wind of the paper from people around Daniel Johnson, the Quebec Liberal leader who was head of the pro-Canada forces in the province. Cormier wanted to run with the story. I urged him – no, I pleaded with him – not to break the story. I explained that I did not know all the ins and outs of the discussions with the pro-Canada forces, but if they had decided that it could be detrimental to Canada if we got into the debate, then they must have valid reasons for thinking so.

Cormier sat on the story, but after the referendum he gave it a lengthy report on Radio-Canada on 7 December 1995. He spoke of the discussions between the pro-Canada forces in Ottawa, Quebec, and New Brunswick, and claimed that three days before the referendum, pro-Canada forces in Ottawa, sensing that things were not going well, had contacted McKenna to ask him to write an open letter to the Québécois. It was too late for such a move, but Cormier suggested that McKenna saw the irony of it all, because six months earlier these same people had asked him not to proceed with a paper on Quebec in Canada.

Word soon spread that McKenna and I did indeed have such a paper, and the media asked for a copy. The *Reader's Digest* called McKenna's office to say that it wanted to publish the paper and pledged not to change a word. McKenna suggested that we should agree and I saw no problem. Although I had never published in a popular magazine such as *Reader's Digest*, we did so, we actually got paid, and the article generated a lot of interest.[5]

GOVERNING FROM THE CENTRE

I started work on yet another book that looked at the role of central agencies in government – hardly the stuff that would excite the folk at Tim Horton's in Bouctouche. However, I had a strong interest in the topic, and I decided to interview senior government officials to gain fresh insights. I had breakfast with a senior Chrétien minister who said, "You academics don't get it, do you? Cabinet is nothing more than a focus group for the prime minister." I have been asked over a hundred times by government officials in Ottawa to reveal the minister's identity. I never did and I never will. One of the reasons I am able to gumshoe around the corridors of power is that I have never betrayed the trust of those who have confided their views and frustrations to me. The fact that so many senior officials in Ottawa have speculated on this minister's identity suggests that the minister's observation has struck a nerve.

Given the minister's comment, I decided to explore the role of the prime minister, the Prime Minister's Office, Privy Council Office, and Department of Finance in shaping policy, programs, and decisions. The verdict: prime ministers, beginning with Trudeau, had gradually but systematically strengthened their position at the expense of everyone else, from Parliament to the cabinet and the senior public service.

Governing from the Centre came out in 1999, and once again I was lucky with the timing. There was a full-blown debate in the media around the changing role of the PMO as the APEC inquiry was holding public hearings. It will be recalled that the RCMP's Public Complaints Commission launched the inquiry because of allegations of political interference from the PMO. It had all begun with about 1,500 protesters opposing the APEC summit on 25 November 1997. The protesters had clashed with RCMP officers and some had been pepper-sprayed. The public hearings began in March 1999 and concluded in June 2000, precisely when the reviews of my book began to appear in newspapers and journals.

Within months of the book's publication, I had been on a dozen talk shows across Canada and given numerous interviews. Journalist André Veniot wrote that I had "become a media darling" and had been read, seen, or heard by well "over one million Canadians in the space of a couple of weeks, heady stuff for an ivory tower academic."[6] The *National Post*, *La Presse*, the *Ottawa Citizen*, *Maclean's*, and *L'Actualité* reported on the book, with Chantal Hébert writing a lengthy review entitled, "Premiers ministres ou empereurs?" The *Hill Times* reviewed the book under the headline "Why Savoie Created a Sensation with *Governing from the Centre*," suggesting that "if there was one book on government that caught the attention of many in the media, government and the general public in 1999, it was *Governing from the Centre*." The *Globe and Mail* gave it front-page coverage, which is rare for an academic book, and labelled me "a Liberal insider," which alone probably annoyed Chrétien and his advisers.[7] *Time* magazine asked me to write a column. It ran the column with the heading "The King of the Commons" and had a caricature of Chrétien sitting on a throne with a crown on his head and a beaver under his right foot.[8] Broadcaster Brian Stewart had a lengthy discussion on the CBC national news. He had Brian Tobin and me on – as guests. Tobin's take on the book was that "it was an interesting academic theory" but wouldn't work in practice. I ran into Tobin at the Halifax airport a few years later, by which time his take on the book was different!

Three Chrétien ministers called to say I was bang-on but all asked not to be quoted. Mel Cappe, clerk of the privy council, sent me a hand-written note to say, "I kid you about the book, but actually found it a useful discourse." The most rewarding review for me came from Gordon Robertson, who had been clerk of the privy council under Pearson and Trudeau and has been described as "the gold standard" for top public servants. He wrote that I was the "first to perceive a change in the governing of Canada that has already had injurious consequences for our country."

Veniot was right, the media attention was indeed "heady stuff for an ivory tower academic," and, to be sure, it had many benefits. It gave me an opportunity to share with many Canadians what I considered and still consider to be an important message. The book became a Canadian bestseller and is now in its sixth printing. I do, however, fault the media on one issue: they gave the impression that Chrétien was the only prime minister to centralize power in his office. *La Presse*, for example, published three articles on the book in which they pointed the finger directly at Chrétien. André Pratte wrote an excellent piece in *La Presse*, but the headline read "Jean Chrétien un peu comme un monarque au temps de Louis XIV."[9] In fact, my book documented the tendency of prime ministers, beginning with Trudeau, to centralize more and more power in their offices, a tendency that continued with Mulroney and Chrétien. Chrétien was not the only or even the main culprit. Indeed, I have always respected Chrétien. He showed excellent political acumen in tackling the government's stubborn deficit

(1995–97), in enacting into law the Clarity Act, and in saying no to the war in Iraq.

Before long, I heard from different sources that the Prime Minister's Office was less than pleased with the book. As is well known, there is a tendency in senior political circles in Ottawa to limit their reading of newspapers to headlines. Only a few months earlier Lawrence McCauley, the minister of ACOA, and his chief of staff Percy Downs (later to be head of the appointment secretariat in the PMO) came with a message from Chrétien: Did I have any interest in heading ACOA? I was grateful that I could say no to them rather than to the prime minister (it is never easy to turn down a prime minister), but I politely declined the invitation. However, *Governing from the Centre* meant that this gumshoe would no longer roam the corridors of Chrétien's PMO. Indeed, I detected a certain coolness, and I learned that two recommendations to appoint me to federal advisery committees or the like were blocked by the PMO. I had no difficulty with this, since I have long believed that politicians have every right to appoint whomever they wish to these committees, and in any event, I had more interesting things to do, including planning another book.

One senior Quebec businessman scolded me for writing *Governing from the Centre*, saying that I would otherwise have been in an excellent position to make a great deal of money in Ottawa as a lobbyist-consultant, given my connections with senior politicians and public servants. But no more. I tried to convince him that I couldn't be happier than doing what I was doing and that I was more than content to leave lobbying to others.

The very last thing I would ever want to be is a lobbyist. Too many lobbyists are on the make, identifying with a party leader or a potential party leader, working on his or her behalf and then serving on "transition teams" should the leader become prime minister or premier. They have a direct hand in deciding who gets appointed to cabinet or to key government positions. They then join a law firm or set up a boutique lobby firm to take full advantage of their new-found political connections. I have seen many businesses line up to sign expensive contracts with these lobbyists, essentially to buy access to the most senior levels in government. I find it amazing to see lobbyists doing extremely well financially when their political horse is in power and then quietly going out of the lobbying business when it loses political power.

It is difficult to imagine lobbyists adding to the economy or to the public interest by selling access. In brief, it amounts to little more than using representative democracy and our political and administrative institutions to make a quick buck by selling access to key politician and government officials. Businesses that can afford it pay handsomely to be able to sell their message to the government officials who matter. Businesses that cannot afford it must stand in line waiting for their turn. This is not how representative democracy was designed to work. The practice also contributes to the general cynicism that has become increasingly evident in recent years towards our political-administrative institutions.

By this time, both Julien and Margaux had finished high school, so my commuting days to Moncton were coming to an end. Both children had done well, and to this day we remain grateful to the Ottawa school system that helped Julien make it through his elementary and secondary years, despite some trying moments for him and his parents. Meanwhile, I had been approached by other Canadian universities and by one in the United States, but I never had any interest in leaving the Université de Moncton. By now, the reader will understand why. Although I was much less certain how Linda, Julien, and Margaux felt about moving back to Moncton, I was looking forward to being home every day, every week, and every weekend.

Home for Good: Up to a Point

I t was good to be home and at the Université de Moncton full time and all the time, or so I thought. An academic colleague in Ottawa bid me farewell with the advice, "You will need to leave Moncton from time to time to acquire fresh thinking and to recharge your batteries and to get new ideas." I resolved to do that, and there would be many opportunities to do so.

CLAUDE

Claude took over my father's business and expanded it into a remarkable success story. We were very close. I dedicated my *Governing from the Centre* to him: "To my biggest fan, my dear friend, my brother." Even when I lived in Ottawa, we had been on the telephone several times a week. I tried to help him in any way I could, as Claude was deeply involved in his community. He was the first Acadian to lead a fundraising campaign for the Université de Moncton. The goal was $10 million, but he raised $18 million. Together with Gilbert Finn, he founded the Acadian Economic Council, later renamed the Conseil économique du Nouveau-

Brunswick. He built a multistory office building on Moncton's Main Street which houses, among other businesses, the regional headquarters of the National Bank. The building sits on the site where Lounsbury's used to be and across the street from Moncton's old City Hall, where Claude led the student delegation to meet Mayor Leonard Jones to demand bilingual services in the city.

The day before the movers arrived at our new home, Claude came to give me a hand with some boxes, and while doing so he lost his balance. Moreover, a few days earlier I had had to finish writing a letter for him because he had difficulty holding his pen. I asked Claude what was wrong and suggested that surely he needed to get medical advice. He believed his high cholesterol was the problem. Not to worry, he said, since he had an appointment at a private medical clinic in Montreal the next day.

The next day at supper time, Claude called from Montreal with bad news – they had found a tumour on his brain. "Is it malignant?" I asked. He didn't know but said they would be looking for more tomorrow. The next day he called to say that tumours had been found on both his lungs. He asked me to fly up to Montreal. I was there the next day. The cancer was highly aggressive. It had spread from one lung to the other and from there to his brain. We were fortunate, however, to be in Montreal with access to top medical expertise.

I went with Claude and his wife Angela to see the specialist, who held out little hope. "Anything is possible," he said, "but things are very bad." He compared the situation to 747s crossing the Atlantic. "We can predict that they will make it across, but from time to time one may crash. Your chances are no better."

"How long do I have?" Claude asked. The doctor was reluctant to play God, but Claude would have none of that and pressed him. The response: "About two months." It was wrenching to walk out of the doctor's office and see Angela and Claude's four children looking at us.

Unwilling to accept such a dire prognosis, Claude's children got on the internet to search out the most modern treatment for lung or brain cancer. And I got on the telephone and called everyone I thought could be helpful. In the end, Claude decided to go to the Dana-Farber Cancer Institute in Boston.

Wanting to do everything I could to help Claude, I spent as much time as I could with him. I visited him in Boston and joined him when he was on holiday in Florida. At one point, he said that he wanted to strike a deal with me: whoever died first should make every effort to send a sign back if there was something on the other side. He also gave me some brotherly advice: "It may be too late for me, but it is not too late for you. From now on, do only what you want to do. Don't feel that you have to do or attend to things because you think that it is expected of you. Your remaining days belong only to you and to no one else."

Knowing that time might be short, Harrison McCain put forward Claude's name for the Order of Canada, even though I was a member of the committee. When his name came forward, I stepped out of the meeting and I was not present when his case was reviewed. He was made an officer of the order. Linda and I were there with him and his family when he was received into the order at Rideau Hall. Jean Chrétien was also there, because one of his friends was being made an officer that evening too. I asked Chrétien if he would have a photograph taken with Claude and his family. He was very gracious and showed all the class in the world. He also spent time chatting with Claude. I thought then that it was probably the people around Chrétien, rather than Chrétien himself, who had had problems with my *Governing from the Centre*. In any event, I have always believed that Chrétien would scarcely have had the time to worry about an academic book. I will always appreciate the kindness he showed Claude not long before my brother died.

In September 1999, La Francophonie held its eighth international summit in Moncton. Some fifty heads of state, our governor general, the secretary general of the United Nations, and other dignitaries attended the summit. Roméo LeBlanc arranged to have two passes sent to me to attend all the events. Linda suggested that I take Claude rather than her, hoping that it would take his mind off the cancer. She was right. Claude and I enjoyed every minute of the festivities. We met Lucien Bouchard, and in an attempt to repeat my luck with Maurice Richard and Jean Béliveau, I tried to convince him that he had Acadian roots. After all, Bouchard is a fairly common Acadian name. But he would have none of it: his ancestors were all Québécois pure laine.

Claude fought hard against the cancer. His will to live was truly inspiring. But the battle was taking its toll. I remember taking him out of hospital to see his new house that had just been completed. On the way back, he asked, "Are you tired of fighting cancer with me?"

"No," I said.

"Will you tell me when you are tired?' he added. "I can tell you right now, Claude, I will never be tired of fighting it with you." In hindsight, I realize that it was Claude who was tired of fighting and this was his way of telling me. He died only a few days later. He had fought the disease for twenty-two months, not two.

The call came around 5 AM to say that it was all over. I was the last one to arrive at the hospital because I wanted to delay the moment as much as possible. Within a few hours, I was back home. As I walked in, I saw a tiny yellow bird sitting on the window ledge outside our kitchen window, looking in. We had never seen it before. For fifteen days straight, that tiny bird simply sat there, staring into the kitchen. Then it disappeared, never to be seen again. Linda believes that it was a pet canary that had escaped its cage. For my part, I will always believe that it was Claude holding to his end of our bargain.

THE INTERNATIONAL SUMMIT AT
LE PAYS DE LA SAGOUINE

It is very unfortunate that English Canada has not been able to appreciate to the full the highly acclaimed Acadian novelist and playwright Antonine Maillet. She is known to some English Canadians as having moderated the leaders' debate in the 1998 general election, and some of her plays have been translated into English.

She has given interviews to the English-language media. But there is more, much more, to Antonine.

Antonine lives in Montreal's Outremont on a street named Antonine Maillet in her honour. On one occasion, she called 911 to report a fire in her house. She gave her name and address but was told that it was impossible. She tried again. They argued some more. Finally, she said, "What difference does it make? We'll settle it later. The fire is spreading."[1] Although short in stature, she is a giant in every other way. As already noted, she won the prestigious Prix Goncourt for her *Pélagie-la-Charrette*, at the time the only non-European to receive it, and her books are well known in all French-speaking countries. The book has been translated into several languages.

Antonine has been chancellor of the Université de Moncton and calls herself "an Acadian plus." She is one of the best orators I have ever heard. She has a will of steel yet a warm personality and a keen intelligence. In l'Acadie, she is best known for her book *La Sagouine*, and Le Pays de la Sagouine, the theme village in Bouctouche, is based on the novel. The book consists of sixteen monologues featuring a poor, uneducated washerwoman (La Sagouine) who is very wise and brings insights into politics and the challenges of everyday life during the Depression.

One day, Antonine called to ask a favour. She said that she had agreed to give the opening address at a government-sponsored conference on La Francophonie in return for a meeting with Sheila Copps, the minister of Canadian Heritage. The conference was to be held within the week and no meeting had yet been arranged. Could I help? I called a senior official in the department to see what had gone wrong. He explained that there had been a "miscommunication" and that a meeting with his minister would be arranged on the same day that Antonine was to speak in Ottawa.

I called Antonine to tell her that she would be meeting Minister Copps at 3 PM on the day of her Ottawa speech.

"That's great," she said. "Now can I ask you another favour? Would you meet me in the lobby of the Delta Hotel at 2 PM?"

When I arrived at the appointed hour, the first thing Antonine said was, "Do you know what is our biggest problem, we Acadians?" I could think of several but asked which one she had in mind.

"We are too modest," she said, to which I replied, "Leaving aside you and me, you have a point."

She told me that people at Le Pays de la Sagouine were planning to submit an application to the government for $250,000 to build a sorely needed parking lot. "I think that we should ask for $750,000," she said.

"Why $750,000?" I asked.

"I want to build a barn."

"Antonine," I said, "you don't need $750,000 to build a barn. My brother's business could build you a barn for a lot less."

"You don't understand," she said. "We need an enclosed theatre – what do you think?"

"Antonine, if you build a barn, you still have a parking lot problem, so why not ask for a million?" I explained that some fifty heads of state would be at Le Pays de la Sagouine for the Francophonie summit, and if the event was being held anywhere else in Canada, one could be certain that the necessary infrastructure would be in place. "Can you imagine," I added, "if the international summit was held in Quebec, Ottawa, or Toronto? Yes, indeed, we are too modest."

"Fine," she said, but went on to tell me that she had yet another problem. "I am a federalist in Quebec," she explained, "and the head of the International Development Agency is a unilingual anglophone. I have a problem with that, and we need to change it."

"Antonine," I cautioned, "that is not a matter for Minister Copps. She has nothing to do with that. You know Chrétien – call him. He appoints deputy ministers. I would strongly urge you not to raise this matter with Copps. Don't mix the two issues." But Antonine is not for turning. "It is a matter of principle," she said.

She had one more favour to ask: Would I go with her to meet the minister? I had never met Sheila Copps, but I had of course heard of her. We were escorted to her office, where Antonine thanked the minister for seeing us and then went straight to the point. She brought up the matter of the unilingual anglophone and said that it was creating problems for federalists in Quebec. Copps handled the issue extremely well, telling Antonine that she knew the head of the agency and was certain that he was bilingual. It turned out that it was the minister's chief of staff who was unilingual English.

Copps then asked Antonine, "What can I do for you?"

"I would like a million dollars to build a barn at Le Pays de la Sagouine in Bouctouche."

Copps then inquired whether there was a business plan, saying that her department would need to ask a lot of questions.

"No problem," responded Antonine. "I brought along an economist." And pointing to me she said, "You can ask him any question you want." The minister turned to me but never asked a question. I decided to speak up nonetheless.

"Madame Copps," I said, "we will be receiving many heads of state in Moncton for the international summit, and the opening ceremony is being held at Le Pays de la Sagouine in Bouctouche. September can be a cool month; we could be having rain, and we have no enclosed building. The event is important for Canada, but it is even more so for Acadians. It is easy to imagine that if we are not successful, the sovereignists in Quebec will say, 'See, the summit should have been held in Quebec.'"

The minister did not respond. Rather, she turned to Antonine and said, "Madame Maillet, you should know that I have been a fan of yours for years. We will help you. My own department, Foreign Affairs, and ACOA will be involved. You may need more than a million dollars."

It was the only time during the meeting that Antonine spoke in English. She stood up and said, "Where have you been all my life!"

Copps then asked if she could see her in private. I stepped outside her office, only to meet an old friend, Suzanne Hurtubise, the department's deputy minister.

"What are you doing here?" she asked.

"I think we are about to spend some of your department's budget," I said and explained what had transpired during the meeting.

Antonine joined me again, and as I walked out of the Centre Block with her, I asked, "What did the minister want?"

"Oh," Antonine said, "she asked me if I would serve on the Canada Council. I told her it will not be possible. I am too busy with Le Pays de la Sagouine."

I went to Le Pays de la Sagouine the following summer, but there was no barn to be seen. There was, however, an impressive infrastructure in place to host the summit's opening ceremony.

"Antonine," I asked, "where is the barn?"

"We will get to the barn later," she replied. "Perhaps Harrison McCain will give us money for the barn and we can call it the McCains' barn, given that he is in the potato business."

I am happy to report that the opening ceremony for the summit was a resounding success, and the weather was warm and very pleasant.

SERVING ABROAD

I have had the good fortune to be invited by the United Nations Development Program (UNDP) and the World Bank to serve abroad on a number of occasions. I resisted at first because it meant being away from home on weekends, which were sacred family time when our children were growing up. Having to commute to Moncton for several years was bad enough, so I made a point of rarely being absent from home on weekends.

As the children gained more and more outside interests, I agreed to accept some foreign assignments. I went to Hungary and Russia to assist in the transition from a one-party state to a multiparty democracy. My task was to explain to state employees the merits of a non-partisan public service. It was not easy. We take many things for granted in countries with Westminster-style parliamentary systems, and one of the most important is a non-partisan public service. I can assure the reader that it was extremely difficult for many officials, having been employed in a one-party state throughout their careers, to appreciate the wisdom of serving whoever wins power in a general election. It was no less difficult for them to understand how to make their new world work. It was like introducing a new religion, a new belief structure. They were uncertain if it could be made to work, and I heard more than one official in Moscow ask, "How can a state employee possibly be non-partisan?" We put together a curriculum and a series of lectures and seminars on the merits and applications of a non-partisan civil service.

In early 1996 I was asked by UNDP to go to Bosnia-Herzegovina to help one of its regions rebuild its war-torn economy. It was an eye-opener. I saw ethnic and linguistic tensions from another perspective. People were displaced, removed from their homes and villages simply because they were Bosnian (Muslims, or Serbs or Croats). It is no exaggeration to say that in the region where I worked, some had undergone similar experiences to those my ancestors had suffered in 1755.

I spent time in Sarajevo and in the Una-Santa Canton. The canton needed to rebuild its public service and its war-ravaged economy, moving from a centrally planned economy to a market economy. Only a few months earlier, Bosnians, Serbs, and Croats had been shooting at one another in the streets. I slept in a makeshift barracks in the canton, and one night I heard gunshots outside my window. The next day, I asked my interpreter-guide what had been going on. "Oh," he said, "don't worry about that. They weren't shooting at you. They were just settling old scores."

Here was the challenge. The unemployment rate was nearly 90 percent, the black market was flourishing, and the civil service had collapsed. Civil servants hadn't been paid for months. There were bullet holes in virtually every government building I entered. The challenge, then, was to establish and re-establish everything. Houses, power plants, roads, all had to be rebuilt or repaired, and new administrative processes had to be put in place.

Added to all this was the need to embrace a free market economy. There was no end to the list of things to do.

The biggest challenge, however, was to manage expectations. The war was barely over, yet the officials I met wanted to develop an IT sector, get tourism up and running, and build up a manufacturing sector. All overnight. They expected international organizations to provide both the necessary funds and the required expertise. It was simply not in the cards. How many tourists would want to visit a war-torn country that had virtually no infrastructure and whose roads were riddled with land mines?

We worked on a plan to set up policy and administrative units, to develop carefully selected sectors, and to encourage some local academics to get involved in their communities. We produced the plan, UNDP provided some funding, and a slow rebuilding process began. Recent developments suggest that things are progressing well: economic growth is healthy if not buoyant, public institutions are in place and working, more than one million refugees have returned to their prewar homes, and the government has administered free and fair elections.

I was also asked, this time by the World Bank, to spend time in Brazil to assist the government strengthen its capacity to plan and manage its expenditure budget. I enjoyed the country, the assignment, and working with Sir Alan Walters. Walters was Margaret Thatcher's chief economic adviser from 1981 to 1984 and again in 1989. He was also one of the world's leading thinkers on monetary policy. The reader may recall that Nigel Lawson, chancellor of the exchequer (Britain's minister of finance), forced Thatcher to choose between himself and Walters. Thatcher sided with Walters, and Lawson resigned from the cabinet, plunging the Thatcher government into a political crisis.

Walters and Thatcher were very close and had similar views on many issues, including letting the British currency float to find its own level, insisting that it could not hurt the market. I found Walters very friendly, obviously very knowledgeable, and willing to share "war stories" from his years with Thatcher. I learned a great deal over lunch and dinner during our stay in Brasilia about No. 10

Downing Street, the workings of the British government, and public policy issues. We worked well together in advising government
officials on managing the expenditure budget process. We spoke
to them about international experience, new approaches to budget
making, and what had worked in Canada and Britain. Heaven
only knows if we had much of an impact.

I twice went to China to offer advice on the establishment of a
regional economic development agency for western China. China
looked to the Atlantic Canada Opportunities Agency as a model
to develop its own agency. As is well known, western China has
not benefited from the country's decision in 1978 to shift from a
command to a market economy. The coastal regions have grown
at breathtaking speed, which has attracted workers from western
China. Out-migration from western regions has exacerbated the
problem, hence the decision to establish an economic development agency. While I was in China I participated in a number of
field trips, seminars, and meetings with government officials to
review the proposed legislation on establishing the agency. The
government subsequently introduced legislation to establish an
economic development agency for western China and to implement a number of measures designed to stimulate economic growth
in the region.

I am scarcely the only Acadian who has gone to China in recent years. Barely a month goes by when there is not a New Brunswick Acadian on his or her way to China to pursue business
opportunities. A good number of joint and new business ventures
have been launched between local entrepreneurs and Chinese
businesses. In 2003 a Moncton entrepreneur in the wood-manu-
facturing sector established a new plant to produce kitchen cabi-
nets in China. I asked him why. His response: "The reason is very
simple. I can ship a tree from Canada to China, produce a finished
product from my plant there, and ship the product back to anywhere in Canada much more cheaply than if I took the same tree
and processed it at my plant in Moncton."

What a difference a generation or two makes! As a student in
Saint-Maurice, I contributed five cents to help the Roman Catholic

Church save souls in China. I recall well the faces of poverty-stricken Chinese infants, whom the church called *les païens*, pasted on *les images* and given to those making a contribution. I was left to wonder what Third World countries were like, and it was beyond my imagination to think that some day anyone from my region, other than a missionary, would ever visit such a far-away land. There are now no faraway lands, and economic space is now greater and more important than political space. How Acadians will fare in the economic space will ultimately decide l'Acadie's fate.

FROM THE TREASURY BOARD TO GOMERY

In 2003 my book *Breaking the Bargain: Public Servants, Ministers, and Parliament* was published, and once again, I was very lucky with the timing. The country was focusing more and more on the sponsorship scandal, which had dominated the media for several years. At the heart of the scandal was the relationship between public servants, ministers, and Parliament, and the media again gave the book considerable coverage. But that was not all. The relationship between Jean Chrétien and Paul Martin had broken down, and Martin often spoke about the need to fix the country's "democratic deficit." He quoted from my *Governing from the Centre* as he took dead aim at the concentration of power in the hands of the prime minister and his office. The only way to get things done in Ottawa at present, he declared, depended on who you knew in the PMO. Things would change, he insisted, under his premiership.

Daniel LeBlanc, a *Globe and Mail* journalist, obtained, through an access-to-information request, material that revealed the government had paid $550,000 to a communications firm, Groupaction Marketing, for a report that did not exist, or at least could not be found. Rumours circulated in Ottawa that this was only the tip of the iceberg. Chrétien responded by asking Auditor General Sheila Fraser to look into the matter. By the time she reported to Parliament, Paul Martin was sitting in the prime minister's chair. Fraser's report was a scathing indictment of what had transpired under the sponsorship program. She employed such words as "scandalous" and "appalling," and accused public servants of "breaking every rule in the book." Martin called for a public inquiry and directed his Treasury Board minister, Reg Alcock, to introduce measures to prevent sponsorship-type scandals from recurring.

Alcock had heard of my *Breaking the Bargain*, and we had met in Ottawa on a few occasions. He and Jim Judd, the Treasury Board secretary, asked if I would give them a hand at defining the new measures. I was in no mood to move back to Ottawa, and I made this very clear. However, the Treasury Board Secretariat has for some time had a visiting fellowship for Canadian academics – the Simon Reisman Fellowship. It enables the government to borrow an academic to work on a special assignment and reimburse his or her salary to the home university. This was offered to me, and once again I found myself commuting from Moncton to Ottawa.

In an interview with me, the magazine *University Affairs* reported that the "media put the spin on it that you were being drafted by the Martin government to reinvigorate the public service and fix Canada's corroding democratic institutions." I responded that there was nobody "this side of heaven who would be up to the task."[2] I now doubt that even someone in heaven would be up to the task. In any event, my assignment was much less ambitious – to assist the Treasury Board review the responsibilities and accountability of ministers and senior public servants, the governance of crown corporations, and the provisions of the Financial Administration Act.

My job was also made simple for other reasons. I took a careful look at how the Treasury Board Secretariat was proposing to reform the governance of crown corporations, and I had no difficulty with it. The only change I suggested was that the board of directors rather than the government appoint the president-CEO. This is the main role of boards of directors in the private sector, and without such a mandate they are invariably left floundering.

Boards cannot and should not manage a firm, but they should select the management and hold it accountable for its performance. The secretariat staff agreed with me; the problem, they pointed out, was at the political level. There was not much that I could do about that, and nothing had yet been done.

I learned that prime ministers will never easily part with their power of appointment. It is an extremely powerful instrument to reward or punish, or to direct the work of a crown corporation. The prime minister is the only person with the power to modify the appointment process, and for this reason I hold little hope that we shall see meaningful change in the near future.

With respect to the responsibilities and accountability of ministers and senior public servants, I came to the conclusion that in fact no one really wanted to alter the status quo in any significant fashion. We had many meetings, and it soon became apparent that the existing state of affairs would continue, come what may. It is in the interest of everyone in government, it seems, to cling to the status quo. Current arrangements allow everyone to say that they are responsible when things go wrong but not to be blamed for it. Trying to pin blame on someone in government is much like trying to grab smoke.

We also had numerous meetings on possible revisions to the Financial Administration Act. The act establishes the rules under which public servants operate, and I was as cautious as anyone about overhauling its requirements. That is where reforms can give rise to their own set of new problems.

While I was at the Treasury Board, Justice John Gomery called to set up a meeting in Montreal. The prime minister had earlier asked Gomery, a Quebec superior court judge, to lead the public inquiry into the sponsorship scandal. I met Justice Gomery for lunch in Montreal, along with several lawyers, including Bernard Roy, the lead counsel. Gomery reported that "someone in Ottawa" had strongly recommended that he read my book *Breaking the Bargain*. He had done so and said that he had learned a great deal from it. He asked if I would be interested in joining the inquiry as director of research for the second phase of its work.

I told the gathering that I felt uncomfortable discussing any possible association with the inquiry, given that I was still the Reisman visiting fellow at the Treasury Board. I would need first to discuss this with Treasury Board officials and, second, I would have to reflect on what role I could play. We nevertheless had an interesting discussion on the role of ministers and public servants. I met with both Reg Alcock and Jim Judd on my return to Ottawa to report on my discussion with Gomery. My term as the Reisman fellow was coming to a close, and both Alcock and Judd encouraged me to accept the invitation, Judd saying that "it could guard against reinventing the wheel."

I met Gomery for breakfast in Ottawa as I was leaving the Treasury Board, and I agreed to head the research side of phase two. Public inquiries have two phases: the first is to investigate what went wrong and who did what; the second is to make recommendations to prevent the problem from recurring. My role was limited to phase two, and that is precisely how I wanted it. I knew some of the players who would be asked to appear before the inquiry during phase one, and I also had and still have a very high opinion of some of them. I would rank them very high in terms of integrity and their desire to serve the public interest.

The lawyers ran the first phase, and I did not participate in their briefing sessions or in their meetings with Gomery. I monitored the testimony from witnesses who appeared before Gomery in both Ottawa and Montreal by reading the transcripts of the various testimonies. I did not, however, attend any of the sessions. But I did produce a paper designed to identify the key issues that flowed out of phase one. The paper was largely descriptive and was never published. I noted that there was both confusion and disagreement among those who appeared on the question of the proper role of ministers and public servants. Witnesses had different interpretations of what was meant by accountability, responsibility, and answerability. Even two clerks of the privy council interpreted the meaning of these words differently: one (Alex

Himelfarb) insisted that had the other (Jocelyne Bourgon) used the term "answerability" or "responsibility" instead of "account-ability," he would have agreed with her. I saw this as a fuzzy zone, a grey area which, I concluded, serves both ministers and deputy ministers well. It enables ministers to accept "answerability" but also to blame public servants when things go wrong. Phase one of the inquiry was, in my view, essentially an exercise in finger point-ing, and there was enough blame around to point the finger every-where and at everyone.

I met Gomery on a number of occasions when planning phase two of the report. Gomery wanted to make certain that it would be "his" report and "his" recommendations. I had no problem with this, given that it was his commission and that he would have to wear the report, its findings, and recommendations down through history.

Early on in my work, he laid out an important challenge for the research program by asking, "Do you know what makes a good judge?" I did not know the answer, as my puzzled look surely re-vealed. He answered his own question: "Two good lawyers in front of the judge representing both sides of the case in a very competent manner." The point was not lost on me: Justice Gomery was prepared to consider any issue, so long as the research pro-gram was able to provide a solid case for both sides. At no point did he indicate a bias on any question; nor did he have any pre-conceived notions or suggest that the research program should consider any issue from a given perspective. I came to the con-clusion that Gomery was a man of integrity, and I have never re-vised this view. He would arrive at a position after carefully considering the various arguments; and once formed, it was very difficult if not impossible to move him off it. This, I was told, is what judges do. That said, I enjoyed working with Gomery and saw him as a man with a sense of *noblesse oblige* and a strong dedication to the public interest and to doing the right thing.

Gomery had had to make the transition from the bench – where deliberations are relatively free of partisan consideration and one works in relative isolation – to a highly charged political environment. To survive in a partisan political environment, one needs sharp political instincts, an ability to go for the jugular at the right moment, and a capacity to sense an opponent's next move. Jean Chrétien was at his best in this environment, and one sensed that he would somehow, sometime get even with Gomery for calling him "small-town cheap" for having his name on government-issued golf balls. Gomery would learn the hard way that politics is a game of survival and that one always needs to walk with elbows out. In short, he was not prepared for this world, and he would pay the price.

I enlisted Ned Franks from Queen's University's Department of Political Science to help with the research program. Ned has published extensively in the area and has strong views on the role of Parliament and accountability. He put in long hours and pursued many issues, including his pet project, the introduction of the "accounting officer concept" to Canada.

I decided that as Gomery tabled his reports, I would not comment publicly on their findings and recommendations. It might have been entertaining for some (I suspect a very small group) to see where I disagreed with Gomery or which recommendations I endorsed, but it would have been wrong. I do want, however, to set the record straight on one issue. A group of notables wrote to Prime Minister Harper to support some of Gomery's recommendations but also to warn him of the dire consequences if his government implemented others. They made this letter public, and it was widely reported in the media.

The notables wrote: "Another part of the Report that causes us serious concern is the recommendation that in future, Deputy Ministers should be chosen by their Ministers. We strongly believe that Canada should retain the current practice in which Deputy Ministers are appointed by the Prime Minister. This practice serves to underline to all concerned that a Deputy's knowledge, loyalty, and engagement must extend beyond a single department to the whole of government." Gomery *never* recommended that the power to appoint deputy ministers be turned over to individual ministers. Here is what he recommended: "Recommendation

12 – The Government of Canada should adopt an open and competitive process for the selection of Deputy Ministers, similar to the model used in Alberta." Gomery explained how an "open and competitive process" should work and then made it clear that under the Alberta model, "the Premier retains a veto power over the appointment."

I also note that lawyers representing Chrétien have gone to court to quash Gomery's findings. The media reported that the lawyers appeared "particularly interested in the opinions of University of Moncton professor Donald Savoie. Savoie has suggested that decision-making power for the sponsorship program was concentrated in the Prime Minister's Office." I do not recall making such a suggestion. In any event, the court decided "that Gomery only consulted Savoie while writing the second part of his report, and not the first, which laid blame for the scandal."[3] The court was right.

In the spring of 2007, New Brunswick Premier Shawn Graham asked if I would lead a review of the province's right-to-information legislation. New Brunswick was only the second jurisdiction in Canada to introduce such legislation, but it hadn't been updated since its introduction in 1978. I agreed to take on the task *pro bono*. I did not want to be paid for the work, partly because I wanted to help my province (my contribution to New Brunswick's efforts at economic self-sufficiency) but also because I felt that there were already too many consultants, often producing shoddy reports and usually charging exorbitant rates. I did not want to be party to this practice. As well, I wanted to be free to call a spade a spade and to speak out on what I consider to be misguided public policies. I have, for instance, criticized the Graham government's decision to do away with the province's early French immersion program, and I have expressed concern over its health-care reform initiative. Part of our role as academics, surely, is to speak truth to power. Yet over the years, I have seen that many consultants and some fellow academics working on government contracts too often write what the government wants to hear.

Working for the government for free has some drawbacks. I only asked that my expenses be reimbursed, but given that my work was *pro bono*, government officials had a most difficult time processing my expense accounts; initially at least, I had to wait nearly three months before being reimbursed. It seems that the government has lost its ability to work with individuals who are prepared to volunteer their time.

We produced the report on schedule at a cost of $19,000 (essentially, translation and publication costs). I hired no consultant to prepare background reports or to work on the review. The report had forty-three recommendations built around the notion that government officials at all levels should not ask, as a matter of course, why citizens should have access to government, but why they should not. The report was well received by the media and, I believe, by the Graham government. I am very proud that this report cost New Brunswick taxpayers only $19,000. Ottawa's Access to Information Review Task Force took eighteen months to complete its work. It generated a number of consultants' reports and cost millions of dollars. And it is still not at all clear how Ottawa plans to update its access-to-information legislation.

Ottawa is hardly alone in throwing taxpayers' money at consultants. The New Brunswick government has in recent years commissioned consultants to produce report after report on virtually every public policy issue under the sun. Between 2007 and 2008, the government hired consultants to review, among many other topics, post-secondary education ($1.2 million), the early French immersion program ($180,000), the work of voluntary groups ($200,000) and to design a new model of public engagement (cost unknown). The report on post-secondary education has been tossed in the garbage and the Croll-Lee Report on early French immersion has been dismissed as particularly bad. Academics from the University of New Brunswick, Mount Allison, and the Université de Moncton, all experts in the field or in research methodology, have to a certain point scorned the report. It has been called "biased," its reasoning "flawed," and its conclusions "misleading." At one point, twenty-one UNB professors signed a letter of complaint to the ombudsman. Even the government acknowledged that it was a bad report, and it now claims that there were other factors at play in its decision to do away with the early immersion program. What other factors? The government has never identified them, leaving New Brunswickers free to speculate of what they may be. This suggests that the government had already made up its mind to kill the early immersion program before it even commissioned the report. Why, then, go through the $180,000 expense? The two consultants have not been heard defending their report, nor has any expert in the field come to their defence.

I read the report. It is a bad report, as bad as everyone says it is. One cannot help but think that the consultants went to the government and asked, "What do you want to hear?" They then delivered the goods.

But there is a larger problem here – accountability. Consultants should be held to account for producing shoddy work, and the government officials who hired them should be held to account for not only accepting but also paying for incompetent work. Taxpayers see this and feel helpless. There was a time when a parsimonious culture permeated every level of the public sector. This culture no longer exists. No wonder the public sector has such a poor reputation and that bureaucrat bashing has become a popular sport in Anglo-American democracies. It also explains, at least in part, the rise of neoconservatism in Western democracies.

BITTER ROOT, SWEET HARVEST

On 5 December 2003 the Government of Canada endorsed a royal proclamation acknowledging the wrong done to Acadians in the Grand Dérangement. A number of Acadians had been pushing for an apology for 1755 from the British monarch, and in the end they were able to secure a royal proclamation acknowledging the expulsion. I was never a promoter of this initiative, thinking that an apology or an acknowledgement of wrong would not solve anything other than recognizing an unfortunate historical event.

Still, when Sheila Copps made the announcement on behalf of the government, many Acadians were pleased. The minister even revealed that she herself had "Acadian roots." As Antonine Maillet once observed, "It is in fashion today for people to claim Acadian roots. Forty years ago, it was not possible to find anyone outside small Acadian villages willing to admit to having Acadian roots." On this basis alone, we have come a long way.

Copps called the royal proclamation an "historic moment" and said that Acadians were "a model of perseverance and determination." She designated 28 July each year as "a day of commemoration of the Great Upheaval." The royal proclamation was handed over to Euclide Chiasson, the president of the Société nationale de l'Acadie. For his part, Chiasson simply said that he was "very pleased with the positive conclusion of this file."[4]

Jean-Claude Villiard, a friend and at the time deputy minister at Industry Canada, was asked to sign the proclamation as Canada's deputy registrar general. His was one of only two signatures on the proclamation (the other was that of Morris Rosenberg, the deputy attorney general of Canada). Villiard decided to bring the document home to sign so that his fourteen-year-old son could witness the solemn event. He sat at the kitchen table with the proclamation at hand and explained to his son what he was about to do. He told his son, "This proclamation is a form of an apology for the Grand Dérangement. Do you know what the Grand Dérangement is?" His son pondered the question for a while and came up with a possible answer: "Is it when the NHL suspended Maurice Richard?"

The *Globe and Mail* invited me to write a piece on the royal proclamation, which they ran under the heading "Bitter Root, Sweet Harvest." I would like to reproduce here part of that column, which speaks to this book's central message. I wrote that my parents and my ancestors taught me how to wear the burden of history. Bitterness, rancour, and vengeance can lead a people only to a dead end. It is the Acadian capacity to put aside bitterness that explains why Acadians did not seek financial compensation or a legal settlement as part of the royal proclamation. The goal was simply to secure a formal recognition of an historical event. I went on to say:

> I learned the lessons of history well. I studied in England, and at no point did I ever feel even a tinge of resentment against the British. Rather, I gained many friends and it was there that I discovered the genius of British political institutions. I have spent the past 20 years writing about them and their application to Canada, singing their praises and warning against moving away from their basic requirements. It is fitting today that these are the very institutions that generated the royal proclamation. I would compare the capacity of British-inspired political institutions to protect minority groups with any others, including French and American. Acadians in New Brunswick, for example, are doing better at retaining their identity and language than our Cajun cousins in Louisiana. The history of the Acadians and the royal proclamation in many ways speak to Canadian values. Canada gives individuals a chance to rebuild communities and broken lives. There is a parallel here with the Acadian expulsion – and perhaps because of this, and the difficult experiences of my ancestors, I am always proud to see my country welcome new Canadians seeking a home to start over again. New Canadians have numerous opportunities, provided they leave their old battles behind, along with any resentment and bitterness. There are many messages contained in the royal proclamation. Two that I would like to retain are that Canada makes collective dignity possible – and that our political institutions work. Both have served us well and we should guard against taking them for granted.[5]

RETURNING TO OXFORD

I took to heart my friend's advice to leave Moncton from time to time to recharge my batteries. My recent stint as a Reisman visiting fellow and my work for the Gomery Commission had kept me abreast of recent developments in public administration. It was no less important for me to remain abreast of the literature and fresh thinking from academic circles. I had the good fortune of being selected senior Fulbright scholar for the 2001–02 academic year and spent the year at Harvard and Duke universities. There, I saw first-hand the advantages of great libraries and well-equipped seminar rooms, and very much enjoyed meeting faculty members at lunch in well-appointed faculty clubs. I benefited greatly from the experience, which allowed me to complete the research for my book *Breaking the Bargain.*

I also completed the research on *Visiting Grandchildren: Economic Development in the Maritimes.* This book would be my last work on regional economic development. Alex Colville agreed to have one of his paintings serve as the cover for the book. He wrote to say that he admired the work I did on behalf of my region but sometimes felt that he was a voice in the wilderness. He added, "Of course, there are also good things in the wilderness and perhaps you and I speak of them in similar voices." It is a handsome book, and I wanted to send Alex a copy with a special dedication – to write something original, not the standard "with best wishes" or "many thanks for this." I finally came up with a dedication that he later told me he truly appreciated. It reads, "This is one book that I hope people will judge by its cover."

But it was to Oxford that I returned time and again. I became a regular visitor at Nuffield College. These frequent visits allowed me to establish contact with practitioners in London and renew my contacts with the Oxford academic community. I visited both Geoffrey Marshall and Nevil Johnson on many occasions, and both claimed that they enjoyed reading my work. Marshall, in particular, said that he saw a great deal of merit in my *Governing from the Centre*. He maintained that my central thesis was increasingly resonating in Britain. He reported that he would be happy to sponsor my candidacy for a Doctor of Letters (D LITT) degree from Oxford. This meant a great deal to me. Forty, thirty, even twenty years ago, it would have been unthinkable for an Acadian to imagine that some day an Oxford don would suggest such an honour. By now, Geoffrey Marshall had been made provost of the Queen's College. He later said that putting my name forward was one of the last official duties he performed as provost.

The Oxford D LITT is awarded by a board that reviews the work of individual scholars who are Oxford graduates. The board is made up of scholars from Oxford and at least one other university. Its role is to judge whether a scholar's work "constitutes an original contribution to the advancement of knowledge of such substance and distinction as to give the candidate an authoritative status in some branch or branches of learning." On 3 March 2000, Oxford contacted me to tell me that the university would be awarding me the degree. On hearing the news, my mind raced back to *mon oncle Calixte* and his difficult battles some seventy years before to get the Province of New Brunswick to agree to French schools for grades 1 to 3.

Being awarded the D LITT prompted me to let my name stand for election as a visiting fellow at All Souls College. The reader will recall my earlier description of All Souls as having no students, just fellows. It is one of Oxford's richest colleges, it houses the great Codrington Library and is the one college where scholars are largely free to concentrate on research. All Souls was founded in 1438 to pray for the souls of those who had fallen during the Hundred Years' War with France.

Visiting fellows are elected by the other fellows on the basis of merit and have access to the college for six years. They come from all corners of the globe. From time to time, a former senior politician or public servant is elected, but that is rare. When Julie Edwards, secretary to the Fellows' Committee, called to tell me of my election, one of nine for that year, I told her that I was honoured but warned her that "I would be praying for the other side." Her response: "The fellows may have to rethink their position and vote again!"

All Souls ranks as one of the best experiences of my life. There I found best table, best wine, and some of the most fascinating conversation one could possibly have. For me, it was like "going to heaven without having to die." At All Souls, you are free to read, think, and write; the college staff worries about everything else. Linda and I had a very attractive two-bedroom flat with all the modern services and conveniences. While at the college, I completed work on *Court Government and the Collapse of Accountability in Canada and the United Kingdom*. The book would not have been possible without All Souls.

There are many things to enjoy at All Souls, and dinner at high table with the fellows is the highlight of the day. Fellows came from various disciplines, from jurisprudence, economics, politics, mathematics, philosophy, and history. I recall one dinner where I listened to a fascinating discussion about recent developments in mathematics. This was a new world for me as I discovered that one could work on a particular problem knowing that it could not be solved in a lifetime. The purpose was to advance knowledge so that the next generation of scholars would have a better chance of solving the problem.

One evening Gary Hart, former U.S. senator and presidential candidate, joined us for dinner. The reader may recall that Hart was the clear front-runner for the Democratic nomination in the 1988 election. However, rumours circulated that he was having an extramarital affair, which he denied. The *Miami Herald* later obtained photographs of Hart with a 29-year-old model, Donna Rice, aboard the yacht *Monkey Business*. Hart decided to withdraw from the presidential campaign. He returned to university, earning a doctorate in politics at Oxford, and he now holds an endowed professorship at the University of Colorado.

I found Hart very engaging and well informed even about Canadian issues. A student whom I had met earlier joined the conversation and asked Hart, "If you had to do it all over again, would you do anything different?" The student – young, bright, and English, with limited knowledge of American politics circa late 1980s – had no knowledge of Hart's difficulties during the election campaign. Hart responded, "That question requires a long and elaborate answer, but the short answer is no." After dinner, I told the student about Hart and Donna Rice and Hart's decision to pull out of the campaign. His face dropped and he said, "I must go and apologize." I urged him not to, arguing that it could make matters worse, for Hart knew intuitively that the young man had absolutely no idea what had transpired on the yacht *Monkey Business*.

I found the All Souls fellows to be gracious and interesting – all except one, to whom I took a dislike. He was pretentious – always had the answer to every question, whether it was in his field or not – attached a great deal of importance to protocol, and was always on the lookout to see who would get which office or which benefit. I soon discovered that none of the other fellows were in a rush to sit next to him at lunch and dinner.

One evening I was invited, along with nine other fellows, to a wine tasting from the college cellar. I warned our host, who was not only responsible for the cellar but was widely respected in the United Kingdom as a wine connoisseur, that I did not know much about wine. "Not to worry," he said. "When it comes to wine, I am sufficiently arrogant to listen only to myself." He added, "Come. You will enjoy the experience."

On arriving at the appointed hour in one of All Souls' best rooms, I spotted a large spittoon sitting on a table surrounded by about thirty bottles. I went to take a closer look and saw that the spittoon was made of solid silver and was dated 1728, thus predating the Grand Dérangement. There were only ten fellows present, including the pretentious one. It was quite a spectacle to watch: each person sniffed the wine, took a sip, tossed the wine back and forth in his mouth, with one cheek puffing for a few seconds and then the other, and after a while went over to the spittoon and spat it out. I thought, if only Acadians in Bouctouche could see this! And what would the two bootleggers in Saint-Maurice think of spitting expensive wine into a spittoon? I told my wine connoisseur friend that the wine tasted fine to me and that, as a matter of principle, I was not going to spit it out. "That's all right," he said, "but just keep an eye on the door jamb as you leave."

The pretentious fellow came over to strike up a conversation. In a plummy accent, he said, "You are from Canada, I understand."

"Yes," I replied.

"What part of Canada?"

"From Bouctouche."

"Bouctouche," he said superciliously, "Oh, yes," implying that he knew where it was. The conversation ended on that note. I imagine that the next morning he went to look up Bouctouche on Google to see where on earth it was.

I feel my roots very strongly, as do many Acadians of my generation. My roots have both defined and motivated me. We have no territory to call our own and no important political institutions that belong to us. We have learned to survive against the odds because people such as Calixte Savoie, Clément Cormier, and Louis J. Robichaud fought to give us the tools not only to survive but also to take our place in society. A number of my generation were driven to succeed because we were the first since pre-1755 days to have the necessary infrastructure and support to do so. In many ways, we did not want to let Robichaud down. In the absence of anything else, our roots became our touchstone and our call to action.

L'Acadie today is not the same as l'Acadie of my generation. The new generation of Acadians has to look to other sources for motivation. Like everyone in society, Acadians are witnessing a shift that favours the individual over the community. This in turn raises questions about the future of l'Acadie and Acadians.

Acadians: Shaped and Reshaped by Experience

If I had to begin all over again, I would of course try to avoid this or that mistake, but I would not change the main course of my life. I was shaped by the experiences of my parents and their parents before them, and so on back through history. My generation, the Louis J. Robichaud generation, has lived in a transition period, from the downtrodden days – when Acadians in Moncton named Brun became Brown, and LeBlanc became White – to today's world, in which we stand tall, a people with strong pride in our roots and our history.

In his study of the Cajuns, of Louisiana, Griffin Smith Jr wrote that there was a time "when Cajun was not a nice word." The same can be said about the word "Acadian." He also wrote, "I never met a Cajun who puts on airs."[1] The same could be said about Acadians. Now, however, it is chic to be Acadian. Distinguished historians from Yale and political scientists from Toronto and elsewhere have decided to visit, to discover l'Acadie, and to write about us. Our struggles throughout history have become a topic of interest to Canada's chattering classes. Today's historians describe us as the original "boat people," whose ancestors were subjected to a form of ethnic cleansing.[2] One hundred and fifty years ago, historians described us as "half savages, illiterate, obstinate and untrustworthy."[3]

In one generation, I saw a people literally transformed. To be sure, Robichaud was the catalyst, but his initiatives unleashed a series of events that sent shockwaves to every corner of l'Acadie, New Brunswick, and the other Maritime provinces. His presence and his political success sent a message to every Acadian – it was now possible to have a place in government, at both the political and the administrative level. Robichaud's initiatives, however, generated a backlash and Leonard Jones became its symbol.

The enemy was now out in the open, no longer operating discreetly in hotel rooms in Fredericton or quietly in the corridors of political power, to which few Acadians were invited (and those who were invited had neither the numbers nor the capacity to challenge the status quo with any chance of success). Now, suddenly, we were exposed to two opposing camps – Robichaud versus Jones – and in the end, Robichaud won. It was the very first time since before the Grand Dérangement that our side had won. And if Robichaud could succeed, so could we.

There have since been a number of remarkable success stories of Acadians from the Robichaud generation. Bernard Cyr is one of many thriving entrepreneurs; Paul LeBlanc won an Oscar; Rhéal Cormier recently completed a long career as a pitcher in the American and National baseball leagues; Raymond Bourque became an all-star defenceman in the National Hockey League; several Acadians have recently participated in both the summer and winter Olympics; more than a few Acadians at the Université de Moncton are increasingly making their presence felt in academic literature; Acadians now occupy senior ranks of the federal and provincial public services; and the list goes on and on. Camille Thériault, an Acadian and one of my former students, became premier of New Brunswick in 1998. We are all Louis Robichaud's children. And while Antonine Maillet is not part of the Robichaud generation, she has become a dominant figure in French literature. All of this from a population base of approximately only 300,000 in the Maritime provinces.

Shaped by shared experiences, the members of Robichaud's generation have many things in common. We came of age with the baby boomers, we were the first generation to have our own university (as opposed to classical colleges), and as noted above, we had a common and highly visible enemy – Leonard Jones and what he stood for. Above all, we were the first generation to leave our small villages *en masse*, small villages that had both a strong community spirit and a deep sense of history. The values of these small communities shaped who we were.

Political power, primarily exemplified by Robichaud but also by Trudeau, gave purpose and energy to my generation. Trudeau sought to strengthen French Canada by promoting francophone communities outside Quebec. His government invested in our institutions and encouraged us to create new associations to develop our capacity to demand more rights and more representation in government circles, to formulate more demands to develop our communities and generate better access to government programs. Suddenly, governments were on our side.

While Trudeau was promoting a pan-Canadian perspective to French Canada, a large number of Québécois were turning inward. In short, Québécois lost interest in looking outside their territorial boundaries, and French Canada as an entity began to lose currency. In the past, French Canada had been defined not by territory but by a common language, a common religion, and similar institutions, from schools and classical colleges to hospitals. However, by the 1970s, there were two French Canadas, one in Quebec and the other outside it. The one in Quebec set out to be master in its own house, while the one outside Quebec had to continue to share its home with the anglophone majority.

We discovered that when Québécois began to proclaim themselves *maîtres chez nous*, they meant Quebec and only Quebec. Acadians, meanwhile, had no territory, only roots. If we were to be "masters in our own house," we had to find other ways of doing so. We had to look to our roots, to a sense of pride in our identity (witness, for example, the Congrès mondial acadien and many other events held over the past twenty years or so to celebrate l'Acadie) and to involvement in business, the arts, sports, and government. We could become *maîtres chez nous* only if we could secure more influence and a larger presence in all sectors. Leaving aside local school boards and health authorities, we had no territory; we only had a shared identity and a desire to take our rightful place in all facets of society.

Acadians were left on the outside as federalist and sovereignist forces duked it out in Quebec. Acadians could relate to Quebec when it sent 75 out of 75 federalist MPs to Ottawa. But they could no longer do so when Lucien Bouchard and his sovereignist party gained a majority of federal seats in the Province of Quebec or when a sovereignist party won power in Quebec City. French Canada was no more, at least in the eyes of many Québécois.

There were other changes, also with far-reaching consequences. Ottawa decided to strengthen francophone communities outside Quebec by turning them into pressure groups, by financing associations pursuing all kinds of endeavours, and by supporting groups representing virtually every segment of Acadian society. Thus began the bureaucratization of the Acadian movement. Volunteerism, for the most part, gave way to paid advocacy. "Have federal funds, will travel" gave rise to parallel bureaucracies at home, staffed by Acadians but funded by Ottawa. A colleague at the Université de Moncton recently observed that the federal government now supports directly or indirectly some three hundred francophone associations or events outside Quebec, though in some cases the funding is very modest.

Acadian associations soon began to exhibit some of the same characteristics as government bureaucracies. Protecting their own turf and their expenditure budgets became important, and they learned that one does not bite the hand that feeds one. They challenged government policies, but only up to a point. They served Trudeau's purpose by becoming more assertive and by demanding better government services in both official languages. But then what? What do you do with advocacy associations after they have served their purpose? Governments are not particularly adroit at stopping things, at challenging the status quo. Government-sponsored organizations all too often go past the "best by" date, searching for a new role.

It is only a slight exaggeration to suggest that paid advocacy groups are now paid to keep quiet. As in other bureaucracies, bold moves have become rare events. The associations' staff long ago began to focus more on federal bureaucrats, such as their counterparts in Canadian Heritage, than on Acadian communities. I do not have a public opinion survey in hand, but I suspect that very few Acadians are aware of the activities of the government-funded Société nationale de l'Acadie (SNA). The SNA is not the only Acadian association receiving government funding, and the others are no more visible. This has given rise to what Maurice Basque has labelled, *Acadien d'État*, or state-sponsored Acadians.

I don't mean to suggest that the SNA or other associations have not had a positive impact. They have, especially in their early years. You can't throw millions of government dollars at associations or causes without having some impact. The point, however, is that Acadians have become overdependent on them: Why worry about language rights, economic development, or an education strategy when there are people paid to do that? It is time to ask the question, Do we need to be paid to be Acadians?

Given my experience, I may well be accused of "golden ageism" – comparing today's society unfavourably with that of a bygone era when people were more self-reliant. Certainly, I look back in awe at the five thousand Acadians who gathered in Memramcook – with no government paying their expenses, let alone a salary – to select national symbols and a national anthem, to identify the means to resist assimilation.

Trudeau gave Canadians the Charter of Rights and Freedoms, which has had a profound effect on Canadian society, and again l'Acadie is no exception. Sections 16–23 outline language and minority-language educational rights. We now have lawyers and the courts doing what Calixte Savoie, Clément Cormier, and Louis Robichaud once did. In some ways, the Charter has replaced political power, and we have discovered that legal rights are particularly important to those who possess little political or economic power. They provide a sense of security for minority-language groups: there is less need to mobilize Acadians for political involvement because the courts will take care of things.

L'ACADIE: WHAT NOW?

I once asked Antonine Maillet, "Will l'Acadie still be here in a hundred years?" She pondered the question before answering, "I don't know and I don't think anyone does. But we are going to put up one heck of a good fight." The goal, as always, is to survive; that is, to resist assimilation and to promote strong vibrant communities. In turn, survival means that Acadian communities need to be strong culturally. L'Acadie will survive culturally only if it prospers economically and becomes increasingly self-reliant. Economic strength transcends time and space and can move political decisions. It is the new frontier for Acadians, and we need role models in business, much as we needed Louis Robichaud some fifty years ago.

Canada's constitution provides a powerful legal instrument for Acadians, an instrument that, apart from the country's English-speaking majority, is not available to other groups. We Acadians may never be stronger politically than we are today. New Canadians are reshaping the political map, and in time they will have a profound effect on the country's political agenda and priorities.

However, Acadians now have new political allies, whom we should learn to cultivate and work with. We saw signs of this in New Brunswick's ill-considered decision to eliminate its early French immersion program. The organization Canadian Parents for French launched a vigorous campaign against the government's decision. In the middle of the debate, I received an email from Rob Hoadley, a twenty-six-year-old English-speaking Monctonian who was seeking advice on how to lobby the government to change its position. He said that his generation had "no memory of Louis Robichaud, nor Leonard Jones" and, for him, bilingualism "was not a dream, but a project." Today, he added, we have "a bridge between anglophones and Acadia, while in the past the bridge was only one way – only Acadians would walk across it." He told me that he had developed a website to support early immersion and within days 5,500 New Brunswickers had registered their support for the program. In many ways, Hoadley is fighting the same battle that Calixte Savoie, Louis Robichaud, and Clément Cormier fought fifty-eight years ago. But he is an English-speaking New Brunswicker, not an Acadian. He is the product of a very different Moncton from the one I moved to in 1959.

We should also remember that it was Mayor Brian Murphy who led his city council to make Moncton officially bilingual, the first city to do so in Canada. We are still waiting for Ottawa, the nation's capital, to do the same. The vote at Moncton City Council was unanimous and the city chambers were filled by community representatives. They gave council a standing ovation. As Leonard Jones was probably turning in his grave, Acadians came to appreciate that they now had allies in their struggle for survival.

It is important to recognize that in an Acadian community that is increasingly urban, detached, and, relatively speaking, economically prosperous, the challenge is to resist assimilation; whereas in a community that is rural, economically vulnerable (as many rural resource-based communities in Canada have become), the challenge is economic survival. In l'Acadie as elsewhere, migration to the cities is on the increase. The Moncton-Dieppe area has attracted large numbers from northern New Brunswick, and Halifax attracts Acadians from all three Maritime provinces.

Residents of Caraquet in northern New Brunswick live in French, and the community's infrastructure operates almost exclusively in French. Many of its residents do not speak English. Caraquet, among other communities on the Acadian peninsula, is certainly not threatened from a linguistic or cultural perspective. No less than, say, Matane in Quebec, it will remain a French-speaking community so long it can survive economically.

Acadians who move to Halifax or Toronto confront a vastly different challenge from when they lived in Bouctouche or Caraquet.

Mixed marriages are now common. At the moment, about 30 percent of all students eligible to attend a French-language school in New Brunswick have one parent who is English-speaking. As well, the Acadian birth rate, which was high into the 1960s, has dropped off significantly as the influence of the Roman Catholic Church has waned.

In many ways, however, all Acadian communities are now urban. For societal values have changed. As elsewhere in Canada, l'Acadie is more secular and less deferential. In his book *Bowling Alone*, Robert Putnam made the case that societal capital has declined substantially in the United States since the 1950s, which undermines the community spirit and civic engagements.[4] His observation applies to Acadians no less than to other Canadians and Americans. As elsewhere, Acadians go to church less often, the rate of divorce is increasing, volunteerism is on the decline, we are less likely to join a political party than in the past, and we watch television more often. Every Acadian home now has its own television set, and community television watching of the kind I experienced in Saint-Maurice is no more.

L'Acadie must now sell itself to new Canadians. I need not remind the reader what new Canadians bring to the country: a new perspective, new ideas, energy, and a desire for a new beginning. In brief, they bring vitality to our communities. L'Acadie has been able to attract some new Canadians, and one needs only to look at the Université de Moncton to appreciate their contribution. But we will need to do more to show that l'Acadie welcomes diversity and, given our history, that we are a tolerant and open community.

IT IS NOW UP TO US AS INDIVIDUALS

Acadians individually will have to decide what the future holds for l'Acadie. Society has shifted towards neoliberalism, and our social relations have shifted from collectivist to individualistic. Urbanization, television, the Internet, and computer games have all had an isolating influence, and large strip malls have replaced the local corner store. Individuals are less likely to keep the same job throughout their working lives, and the search for better economic opportunities will often uproot families.

The rise of market capitalism has reinforced liberal values and the tendency of individuals to act in ways that reduce our ability to make collective choices. The attributes of the individual now matter more than those of the community. Governments have been looking at ways to lessen the dependence of communities on their programs, although with little success. But one senses that a number of federal programs supporting various Acadian associations are surviving on a wing and a prayer. There are signs that the era of state-sponsored Acadians is coming to a close as Ottawa redefines its relationship with minority-language groups. In addition, there is anecdotal evidence to suggest that the idea of state-sponsored Acadians does not appeal to young Acadians. That is what I am hearing from my students.

Globalization has imposed a market discipline on many activities, and there is precious little evidence to suggest that its influence will wane in the coming years. We can, like King Canute, try to hold back the tide, but just as he could not make it obey his command, we cannot make globalization go back where it came from.

The way forward for l'Acadie and Acadians is to embrace both change and competition with enthusiasm. We should view globalization in a positive light, for it holds countless economic opportunities. Globalization values economic success, not space or territory, and economic space has become more important than political space. If political space has lost some of its importance, if responsibility for language and educational rights has been handed over to the courts, and if Acadians now have in place the necessary institutions with which to grow, then the onus is on the individual to ensure that the Acadian community thrives. To come out of its shell, l'Acadie needed Louis Robichaud in 1960. Today, it needs committed individuals in every sector if it is to remain vibrant.

Governments or government-sponsored programs cannot provide the good fight that Antonine Maillet spoke of. We now have the laws and institutions, the skills, the role models, and the confidence to compete. We have a presence on the world stage that may well be the envy of many small states. Japanese scholars have recently published two books on l'Acadie, German scholars four, and on it goes. We now need to exploit the economic potential that accompanies such a presence on the world stage more fully.

I can hardly overstate the case that individuals and their actions will ensure l'Acadie's survival. Only as individuals can we fight the good fight. The government can provide a helping hand, but it can do little more. The reader has no doubt concluded that I see limits to the role that governments can usefully play in society or in promoting a stronger Acadie. There are two reasons. I have seen that all too often government intervention leads to dependence; individuals and even communities become dependent on government spending and lose their ability to become self-reliant and perhaps even their interest in being so.

I have also seen government operations from the inside, and they are all too often riddled with inefficiencies and waste. There is either an inability or an unwillingness to deal with non-performers. No one, it seems, is able to control civil service growth, and governments appear unable to cut activities once they have been in place for a few years. The machinery of government increasingly appears to be organized for a world that no longer exists. The world today is highly competitive, and regional and even national economies have morphed into a global economy. Loyalty to communities, regions, space, and employers is not nearly as strong as it was forty years ago. Acadians need to adjust to this new world to fight the good fight.

Stripped down to its bare meaning, globalization is about political and economic power, particularly the latter. L'Acadie will survive only if individuals and individual businesses want to define themselves as Acadian in this new world. The challenge will be immense because it is no longer clear where either political or economic power is located. But we have everything we need in order to compete in business, the arts, and scholarship, the key to economic growth.

Globalization also means that borders and boundaries are collapsing. Governments are less and less able to operate within defined geographical borders (the nation-state, a province, or a municipality). Borders used to provide the locus of authority, but power is increasingly exercised by the market and transnational institutions. Acadians have never been protected by borders, and they have had to improvise to survive virtually from the very beginning. This should serve us well as everyone seeks to adapt to this new world. In some ways, we have been navigating this kind of world since 1755. Borders, boundaries, and territory have always belonged to others, not to us.

Power has been dispersed as never before – particularly to prime ministers and their courtiers, to multinational firms with activities located on every continent, to the courts, to paid lobbyists, and to the media – and here too the list goes on. Acadians, as individuals, need to grab their share of power, but first we need to have a better sense of where it is located. That will be the topic of my next book.

Notes

INTRODUCTION

1 Michael Bliss, "Bliss on Books – Gratification Now," *Report on Business*, Toronto, June 1990, 31.
2 Calixte F. Savoie, *Mémoires d'un nationaliste acadien* (Moncton: Éditions d'Acadie, 1979), 10. Senator Calixte F. Savoie was my uncle.
3 "Historic Bouctouche Wins a Tourism Boast," www.globeandmail.com, 7 February 2008.
4 Ibid.
5 See Savoie, "Introduction" in *Mémoires d'un nationaliste acadien*.

CHAPTER ONE

1 The best are John Mack Faragher, *A Great and Noble Scheme: The Tragic Story of the Expulsion of the French Acadians from Their American Homeland* (New York: W.W. Norton, 2005), Naomi Griffiths, *From Migrant to Acadian: A North American Border People, 1604–1755* (Montreal & Kingston: McGill-Queen's University Press, 2005), James Laxer, *The Acadians: In Search of a Homeland*

(Scarborough, ON: Doubleday Canada, 2000), and various publications by Maurice Basque over the years. See, among many others, Maurice Basque et al., *L'Acadie de l'Atlantique* (Moncton: Centre d'études acadiennes, 1999), and Nicolas Landry and Nicole Lang, *Histoire de l'Acadie* (Sillery, QC: Septentrion, 2001).

2 It should be noted that some observers insist that the first settlement was St Croix Island.

3 Faragher, *A Great and Noble Scheme*, 3.

4 Ibid., 18.

5 Ibid., 30.

6 Ibid., 40.

7 Naomi Griffiths, "Acadians," in *Encyclopedia of Canada's Peoples*, ed. Paul Robert Magocsi (Toronto: University of Toronto Press, 1999), 114.

8 Note that this is my ancestors' version of the events.

9 Faragher, *A Great and Noble Scheme*, 59.

10 Griffiths, "Acadians," 114.

11 Ibid.

12 Faragher, *A Great and Noble Scheme*, 50.

13 Griffiths, "Acadians," 115.

14 Ibid.

15 Faragher, *A Great and Noble Scheme*, 147.

16 Griffiths, "Acadians," 115.

17 Ibid.

18 Faragher, *A Great and Noble Scheme*, 145.

19 Ibid., 149.

20 The British governor in Nova Scotia and l'Acadie, Richard Philipps, accepted Acadian neutrality.

21 Jean Daigle, "L'Acadie de 1604 à 1763: synthèse historique," in *L'Acadie des Maritimes*, ed. Daigle (Moncton: Chaire d'études acadiennes, Université de Moncton, 1993), 28.

22 Quoted in Faragher, *A Great and Noble Scheme*, 226.

23 Ibid., 262.

24 Griffiths, *From Migrant to Acadian*, 463.

25 Ibid.

26 Quoted in Naomi Griffiths, "The Acadian Deportation: Causes and Development," PhD thesis, London University, 1969, 176.

27 Quoted in Cécile Chevrier, *Acadie: esquisses d'un parcours* (Dieppe: Société nationale de l'Acadie, 1994), 55.

28 Faragher, *A Great and Noble Scheme*, 371.

29 Ibid., 375–6.

30 Quoted in ibid., 410.

31 Ibid., 439.

32 Griffiths, "Acadians," 118.

33 Ibid., 122.

CHAPTER TWO

1 Mike Dunn, "Archie Moore's Most Memorable Triumph," www.eastsideboxing.com, 23 July 2004, and "Moore vs Durelle" and "The Night Sugar Ray Robinson Got Lucky," www.thesweetscience.com.

CHAPTER THREE

1 Calixte F. Savoie, *Mémoires d'un nationaliste acadien* (Moncton: Éditions d'Acadie, 1979), 145.

2 Ibid., 158.

3 Della M.M. Stanley, *Louis Robichaud: A Decade of Power* (Halifax: Nimbus Publishing, 1984), 47–8.

4 Ibid., 48.

5 "Brief submitted to the Deutsch Commission by Saint-Joseph College," in Moncton, New Brunswick, 11 December 1961 (unpaginated). See also *Report of the Royal Commission on Higher Education in New Brunswick* (Fredericton, NB: Queen's Printer, 1962), 34–59.

6 Ibid.

7 Robert A. Young, "The Programme of Equal Opportunity: An Overview," in *The Robichaud Era, 1960–70* (Moncton: Canadian Institute for Research on Regional Development, 2001), 30.

8 "New Brunswick," the *Canadian Encyclopedia Historica*, www.thecanadianencyclopedia.com.

9 Quoted in Stanley, *Louis Robichaud*, 146.

10 Ibid., 151.

11 Ibid., 209.

12 Honorary pallbearers were Yvon Fontaine, Wallace McCain, Viola Léger, Antonia Barry, Hon. Norbert Thériault, Hon. Bernard Jean, Hon. W.W. Meldrum, Hon. Ernest Richard, J.K. Irving, Hon. Henry Irwin, Hon. Bobby Higgins, Hon. Frank McKenna, and Donald J. Savoie.

13 "Special farewell for Louis," *Daily Gleaner*, 11 January 2005.

14 Stockwell Day, "Towards a Modern Confederation: Canada's Renaissance Must Include Quebec." Notes for a speech delivered by Stockwell Day, leader of the Canadian Alliance Party, Quebec City, 18 May 2000, 5.

CHAPTER FOUR

1 Hugh Thorburn, *Politics in New Brunswick* (Toronto: University of Toronto Press, 1961), 68.

2 "Procès-verbal de la réunion du conseil d'administration de l'Université de Moncton," held in Moncton, New Brunswick, on 24 June 1963 (unpaginated).

3 See, for example, Margaret Daly, *The Revolution Game: The Short, Unhappy Life of the Company of Young Canadians* (New York: New Press, 1970).

CHAPTER FIVE

1 Della M.M. Stanley, *Louis Robichaud: A Decade of Power* (Halifax: Nimbus Publishing, 1984), 210.

2 Louis J. Robichaud quoted in ibid., 212.

3 Apart from not being able to see a difference in some colours, I suffer from a form of dyslexia, and perhaps as a result, I have had to struggle over the years to concentrate on the task at hand. This struggle, I am now convinced, explains in large part why I have been prolific in my work.

CHAPTER SIX

1 "Geoffrey Marshall, constitutional theorist, he bridged the gap between law and politics," www.guardian.co.uk, 30 June 2003.

CHAPTER SEVEN

1 Department of Finance, *Federal-Provincial Fiscal Arrangements in the Eighties*. Submission to the Parliamentary Task Force on the Federal-Provincial Fiscal Arrangements, Department of Finance, 23 April 1981, 10–11.

2 Department of Finance, *Economic Development for Canada in the 1980s* (Ottawa, November 1981), 11.

3 See Statistics Canada, "Federal Government Employment, Wages and Salaries in Census Metropolitan Areas for the Month of September," CANSIM II, table 183–0003, compiled by the author.

4 Consultation with B. Guy Peters, University of Pittsburgh, October 2003.

5 *Australian Public Service Statistical Bulletin* (Canberra: Public Service and Merit Protection Commission, 2002–03), 7.

6 "La venue de 2 usines à Bouctouche créera 1,000 emplois dans Kent," *L'Évangéline* (Moncton), 17 July 1981, 3.

CHAPTER EIGHT

1 "PM Launches New Agency for Atlantic Canada," *Sunday Herald*, 7 June 1987, 1.

CHAPTER NINE

1 Canada, *Canada School of Public Service* (Ottawa: Treasury Board of Canada, 2006–07, www.tbs-sct.gc.ca).

2 "All hail the supreme ... prime minister?" *Globe and Mail*, 8 May 1999, D10.

3 "Would That be a Table for Two? The Spedi Giovanni Comino Story," *Capital Style* (Ottawa), undated, 63–6.

4 Jean Chrétien, *My Years as Prime Minister* (Toronto: Knopf Canada, 2007), 108–12.
5 Frank McKenna and Donald J. Savoie, "The Real Choice Facing Canada," *Reader's Digest*, September 1996, 37–42.
6 "Donald Savoie has gained the attention of the Canadian press. His fear? Focussing criticism on centralized government," *Telegraph Journal*, 1 May 1999, E1–7.
7 "Modern PMS growing ever more powerful, Liberal insider holds," *Globe and Mail*, 19 April 1999, A1–2.
8 Donald J. Savoie, "The King of the Commons," *Time*, 3 May 1999, 64.
9 "Jean Chrétien un peu comme un monarque au temps de Louis XIV," *La Presse*, 8 June 1999, A16.

CHAPTER TEN

1 Antonine Maillet," *The Gazette*, Montreal, 19 November 1995, C1–2.
2 Léo Charbonneau, "Our Man in Ottawa," *University Affairs* (Ottawa) May 2004, 16–19.
3 "Federal Court rules against Chrétien's request to see Gomery documents," www.canada.com, 17 June 2006.
4 "Minister Copps announces a Day of Commemoration of the Great Upheaval," News Release Ottawa, Canadian Heritage, 10 December 2003.
5 Donald J. Savoie, "Bitter Root, Sweet Harvest," *Globe and Mail*, 12 May 2003, A19.

CHAPTER ELEVEN

1 Griffin Smith Jr, "Loving Life," *National Geographic*, October 1990, 47 and 53.
2 See John Mack Faragher, *A Great and Noble Scheme* (New York: W.W. Norton, 2005), ch. 16, and James Laxer, *The Acadians: In Search of a Homeland* (Toronto: Doubleday, 2006), part 3.

3 See, among others, James Hannay, *The History of Acadia: From Its First Discovery to Its Surrender to England by the Treaty of Paris* (Saint John, NB: J. & A. McMillan, 1879).

4 Robert Putnam, *Bowling Alone: The Collapse and Revival of American Community* (New York: Simon and Schuster, 2000).

Index

Reform Party, 209
Regional Development Theories and Their Application (Higgins, Savoie), 177
regional economic development: in Atlantic Canada, 158; in China, 227–8; federal government and, 158; Lord and, 83; policy paper for Chrétien, 205–6; Université de Moncton research institute on (*see* Canadian Institute for Research on Regional Development (CIRRD); in western Canada, 158. *See also* DREE (Department of Regional Economic Expansion); DRIE (Department of Regional Industrial Expansion); economic development
Regional Economic Development: Canada's Search for Solutions (Savoie), 172
regions: changing balance of, 155; federal transfer payments to, 160; impact of federal policies and programs on, 160; issues as national vs regional, 156; upper houses and, 156, 157–8
Reynolds, Alan, 71
Rhodes House, 140–1, 144
Rice, Donna, 241
Richard, Maurice, 203, 220
Richards, David Adams, 78
Richardson, Harry, 175
right-to-information legislation, 234–5
Robertson, Gordon, 214
Robichaud, Jacqueline, 15, 76, 78, 79, 83, 84, 87
Robichaud, Louis J., 15; 1960

election and, 64–6; 1967 election and, 73–5; 1970 election and, 75–6, 120–1; and Acadians, 11, 69, 73, 74–5, 76, 243; achievements of, 69; birth in Saint-Antoine, 11; and Beaverbrook, 71–2; and Byrne Commission, 69–71; characteristics of, 64; conference on, 66; death of, 76–7; DJS and, 12, 66–7, 74, 76–8, 79, 84, 89; equal opportunity program, 50, 69–70, 72–3, 75; as first Acadian to be elected premier, 4; Flemming and, 65–6; funeral of, 78, 79–83, 84; Hatfield and, 75–6, 89, 121; and higher education, 67–9; and K.C. Irving, 72, 77, 82; as lawyer in Richibouctou, 51; and McCain brothers, 83; as member of La Patente, 98; and Northumberland Group, 209; and official languages, 75; as partisan Liberal, 90–1; platform of, 64–5; retirement of, 66; as senator, 66; and transformation of Acadians, 245; and Trudeau, 75; and Université de Moncton, 80–1, 90–1, 99, 106
Robichaud, Monique, 80, 83
Robichaud, Norbert, 40, 55, 94
Robichaud, Paul, 80, 83
Robichaud, René, 80, 83
Rodwin, Lloyd, 175
Roman Catholic Church, 3–4; and Acadians, 26, 33, 51–2, 115–16, 251; in Acadie, 19, 24; and Confederation, 32; DJS and, 3–4, 39–40, 52, 227–8; Mi'kmaq and, 19–20, 53; in Moncton, 56; New Englanders

Donald,

Here are some friendly comments:

(1) You have had one hell of a ride. Good on you! (As they say at Oxford)

(2) When "none" is used as the subject, the verb that must be attached to it has to be in the singular. Back to Neville's grammar!

(3) I'd like to have a discussion with you on lobbyists — weren't you one once? My early points would be:

    (1) Don't you think they bring the "outside" in to politicians & bureaucrats — particularly the latter.

    (2) How else can the universe agenda have a sustained presence in Ottawa — cameo appearances are too easily dismissed by a "stuck in neutral" bureaucracy.

    (3) Do you honestly believe that the lobby industry can be removed? If not, then what?

    (4) I would contend at age 71, that looking for the source of power with a preconceived notion that some of its contributors should be extinguished runs the risk of making the searcher more of a preacher than a discoverer.

(4) I'm happy to read your next book will be on the sources of "Power". I have always been intrigued by Power in the context of Government. I have some views from my close to thirty years inside and close to its perceived sources.

(5) The notion of "Policy" also beckons for an updated definition. I sense it is not what some believe it is.

Fred